Endurance
The Rhythm of Faith

Endurance
The Rhythm of Faith

John P. McNamee

Sheed & Ward

Sheed & Ward™ is a service of The National Catholic Reporter
Publishing Company.

Library of Congress Cataloguing-in-Publication Data

McNamee, John P., 1933-
    Endurance : the rhythm of faith / John P. McNamee.
        p.   cm.
    ISBN 1-55612-809-6
    1. McNamee, John P., 1933-   . 2. Catholic Church—
Pennsylvania—Philadelphia—Clergy—Biography. 3. City clergy
—Pennsylvania—Philadelphia—Biography. 4. Catholic Church.
Diocese of Philadelphia (Pa.) 5. Philadelphia (Pa.)—Church
history—20th century. I. Title.
BX4705.M47656A3 1996
    282'.092—dc20   96-6415
    [B]   CIP

Published by: Sheed & Ward
                115 E. Armour Blvd.
                P.O. Box 419492
                Kansas City, MO 64141-6492

To order, call: (800) 333-7373

Cover photograph by Ed Simmons.

Cover design by James F. Brisson.

ENDURANCE

"We overcome not by winning but by endurance."
—John P. McNamee

The huge cross signs a busy corner
where I pass often   fearing
the afternoon shadow falls heavy
          on commuters returning to
the Jewish neighborhood beyond

much as the gold crosses on onion –
domes and steeples were storm
clouds over the pogroms of Europe.

Good signs can suffer bad history:
Constantine reading vague cloud shapes
as a war cry: *in hoc signo vinces.*

We overcome not by winning
          but by endurance.

Good Friday is good:
"Behold the Wood of the Cross"
     our kiss signs our want to
     change pain to patience.

Easter too soon softens
that stark acceptance:
     "Hail Holy Cross"
     is lost in lilies.

Across the year in September
the cross alone:
"In Exaltation of the Holy Cross."
A feast flawed by Crusades: "the
recovery of the Rood from infidels . . . etc."
     cross become sword.

Better the small cross
buckling a string of beads
pressed in hand so hard
that flesh hurts
so fierce the prayer.

Contents

1.

A Primrose Bush

A grand country house   white
against green lawn lined
left and right with trees
holding back thick woods.

At the far end a garden
ah no, just a bean patch
gladiolas   and marigolds
keeping bugs off the tomatoes.

A compost heap   a hose running somewhere for water.
A primrose bush   lackluster
now in daylight.

Toward evening a procession
ah no, only other visitors
inviting me along to join
their vigil for sunset.

Suddenly a primrose tendril
pops. Then thirty,   no
forty flowers open one by
one pale in summer night.

Back on the great porch I
still see them alive as
fireflies. The little moons
mirror moonlight. . .

     –"The Evening Primrose"

. . . In this rage of color
resistance or celebration
I go gladly to return renewed.

     –"To Carol"

"The Miracle of Nature"

Last evening I went with several other residents to sit around a primrose patch to watch these evening or magic primroses blossom before our eyes for their one night of glory which no one usually sees. I guess the purpose of this yellow beauty is to attract nocturnal insects for purposes of pollination.

In a world of ethnic mayhem magic primroses go about their destiny of blossoming at dark once they are sure the fierce summer sun has gone to bed and is not around to burn them up – as that sun will do tomorrow, ending their brief glory.

Simone Weil is right: the universe is a closed system whose meanings are not available within the bubble. Our only passage through or out is the beauty of the world and, according to Simone Weil, suffering as well.

The beauty intimates that something is going on, more than the sum of the parts – "the miracle of nature," as Havel calls it. But ethnic mayhem in the world and even North Philadelphia make one hesitate to say more than that. I know I cannot on my own take it any further without going to the Scriptures where Christ says: "See the lilies of the field. Not even Solomon in all his glory is clothed like one of them. If God takes such care of the grass of the field, how much more you of little faith." Nature as revelation. Father Tom Berry would say that nature is the first revelation – before the Scriptures. Here the Lord seems to be doing the same thing, pointing to nature as intimation that we are in good hands.

All this nature mysticism has been eloquently expressed in the English language tradition by Wordsworth and Hopkins and others. With the industrial grime since then, the blinding out of our decaying cities to watch evening primroses seems Romantic or Victorian. Yet there it is. The miracle of nature suggesting that the mayhem everywhere is not the whole story.

Perhaps the task is not very different from that recommended by Freud. In the welter of human emotion within, he thought the thread of reason could often be discerned and followed to sanity or health. As Simone Weil would say, by paying attention. Or Cardinal Newman searching for full Christian faith in the 19th century by studying the Arian heresy of the 4th century. I imagine him coming to that fullness gradually by turning the pages of many books. The truth of things commends itself by leading us in a certain direction.

So evening primroses or a setting sun do not eclipse the mayhem. They are rather a thin and fragile lifeline. A way out.

Attention is Prayer

The evening primroses are both an access to the mystery and an analogy for the mystery. They only imitate the divine beauty rather than show that beauty to us. Or do they show the beauty after all? Aquinas said that analogous knowledge was true knowledge.

Years ago in my one venture into higher learning, I was required to prepare a paper on the comparison of the analogy of faith in Karl Barth and the analogy of being in Thomas Aquinas. How surprised I was to come upon, in those formidable volumes of Barth, the statement that he regarded the analogy of being of Aquinas as the veritable antichrist and that all other reasons for not being a Catholic were irrelevant.

For Barth, of course, and for the whole Reformation tradition wanting to restore a more pristine biblical faith free of Hellenization, the analogy of being is an affront to the divine transcendence.

Yet Christ himself is some lessening of that Otherness. "Let this mind be in you which was in Christ Jesus, Our Lord, who though he was God did not think his divinity something to cling to."

Christ, like the evening primrose, is sacrament or sign of God which both reveals and conceals the divine glory. That glory was certainly concealed by the crucifixion to the dismay and confusion of the apostles.

Helpful here is the wall image so fond to Simone Weil. She says how the wall between two prison cells is both separation and passage. The wall separates two prisoners and, at the same time, furnishes a medium by which they can communicate by knocking.

Even if the transcendent God, who is also immanent, is within the primrose making the flower open with dusk, still the beauty of the primrose blossoming is only a hint of the divine beauty – hiding more than it reveals.

With Christ whose humanity enabled him to say: "I am the way," his human form more hides than reveals divine glory. As someone said: in Christ the divine mystery becomes not clearer but more mysterious. Yet: "Whoever sees me sees the Father."

So we are helped with the divine mystery, which was such a problem to the ancients that they had to imagine endless and even absurd mythologies to explain things. In Christ the inarticulate and unimaginable does have human form. "Something which has existed since the beginning, that we have heard, and we have seen with our own eyes; that we have watched and touched with our hands: the Word, who is Life – this is our subject, that life was made visible." (I John 1:1-2)

So we watch a primrose unfolding in the night or Christ unfolding in the pages of Scripture or in the lives of the saints or the signs of the Church and know these as access to the divine mystery "in which we live and move and have our being." It is a matter of going where we already are by being there ever more consciously, thus, the meaning of prayer. It is all a matter of paying attention to primroses, say. As Simone Weil says, attention is prayer.

Adoration and Obedience

Quaker meeting here every morning. The silence so welcome. Somehow Catholic worship should take on more silence.

Toward the end of the half-hour, a young person stood up to tell a story about his child. The child prefers science stories to Bible stories, it seems, and wonders what the Bible has to say beyond making people from mud.

The father connected the story with his own – this half-hour effort, to rise through an already humid and heavy summer day to the mystery we call God. In the image of God making him from mud, he said: "I ask God to inhabit every grain of it," meaning his own body and spirit. And I thought of that stained glass of the Agony in the Garden back at Saint Malachy. Sitting across the church from the window, I gaze at it so much that the image is inside me.

And the literal and childlike picture is Jesus, so intense in prayer and intent upon His Father's will, that He has an impossible lean kneeling toward the cup being ministered by an angel: "Father, if possible, let this cup pass from me. Yet not my will but thine be done." Meanwhile the three apostles sleep in the lower window panel.

Thus my image of prayer and asking the Divine "to inhabit every grain." Somehow to rise from the slumber of Peter, James, and John to the adoration and obedience of Christ.

Herbert McCabe, O.P., says that for the Catholic the Eucharist means just that: no other prayer exists but that of Christ. He is, as it were, "sheer prayer," and our task is to awaken and leave our reluctance and half-heartedness and become one with that perfect prayer. Any effort of ours throughout the day is a going to or coming from the Mass where this prayer is constantly being offered. The wonderful reading from Paul that is an Easter Epistle: "You are dead now, and your life is hidden with Christ in God."

Adoration seems to be the first fruit of that awareness which Vaclav Havel wants for "the miracle of Being." Very Platonic. I know my affection for the contemplative life of monks and nuns who seem to do little more than chant praise day and night. Little more, indeed, but what they do so wonderful, so much to the heart of the matter.

"We Are One"

Of course, the Church is also sign or sacrament or wall in that she both reveals and conceals the mystery that we call Christ and God.

So human, so terribly human that whether she is more revealing or concealing depends upon history and geography and culture and how the Church behaves or presents herself both to her own and to the world.

Recently Ivan Illich has been using the old spiritual axiom, *corruptio optimi pessima,* in an extended sense. The meaning I remember is: the downfall of a good person makes for a very bad person. The idea that a good man or woman going sour or worse must go very far to quiet conscience. An example might be Henry VIII, learned in theology and destined for the Church before his brother died and Henry had to be King of England. The residual faith, so nagging in this program of wives and confiscating property and appropriating Church power, that he had to kill a Thomas More and a John Fisher, in whom he heard echoes of his own conscience.

Anyhow. Illich seems to be saying that the mission and work of the Church is so divine and, if you will, so delicate that carelessness or cynicism or pretense or whatever means not only that the work is not furthered but that the work is actually impeded, and a tribal or narrow or intolerant Catholicism can cause crusades or inquisitions.

I recall that flamboyant film, *Brother Sun, Sister Moon,* showing a Pontifical Mass where Francis of Assisi leaves his aristocratic circle of family and friends in the front pews to join the paupers standing in the rear. And I thought: what kind of Mass is that with people separated according to rank. I thought Saint Paul said: "We are one, who eat the one bread and drink the one cup." All the details of this matter should be heeded every time we gather for Mass so that that sign can be a wall that enables rather than hinders.

And history and geography are crucial. Recently a priest, whose work has vast interfaith connections and is himself as devoted to this sacrament of unity as anyone, celebrated a jubilee. His celebration was not the Eucharist because he knew Hindus and Buddhists and whoever would be coming, and he did not want either to exclude them or, I presume, to create a situation in which they might in friendship presume to receive Holy Communion without faith.

Another more tribal Catholicism would say: we are not going to diminish our faith for these outsiders, and the Eucharist is our way of thanksgiving. Let them watch and be edified. I remember precisely that happening when Pope Paul VI wanted Catholics to celebrate the New Year as a day of prayer for world peace. The Quakers in Philadelphia were eager to join in. And the Catholics were glad to have them join in an interfaith service which was attached to the end of a Mass for peace because we were not going "to water down" our faith for anyone.

Of course, the event did not come off well because the observance was too lengthy, was not whole, because, because, because. . . .

Another way the Church can be a wall of separation more than access is by neglect of beauty. From that yearly seminary breakfast pulpit reading of Francis de Sales, I remember something about haste and habit which kill devotion.

Large parishes where Sunday Mass is more or less a hasty performance of poor music and spiritless ritual can actually drive people away from the Lord's Day, which they want to keep by coming at all. As Illich suggests, the mission is more hindered than helped by such carelessness.

Survival or Solutions?

The full text of the July Fourth talk by Vaclav Havel at Independence Hall comes my way.

Throughout he seems to be saying that human life and our problems need more than technical solutions. We live under judgment so that every solution, no matter how effective, is not acceptable. What else can it mean to say: "We are an integral part of higher, mysterious entities against whom it is not advisable to blaspheme."

The coming United Nations' World Population Conference in Cairo, for example. The Catholic Church is going to take a beating for her policies. One matter surfacing more and more – unless I am mistaken – is abortion as population control.

Years ago I had a discussion with an Episcopal priest friend. My opinion was that the idea of the mystery we call God is so connected with the image of life that I find it impossible to believe that the Creator could want us to invoke death as a social method to solve even these very real and terrible problems, such as world hunger.

My friend said that faith might do just that: call us beyond our familiar images of God or right and wrong. He mentioned the Abraham story of Kirkegaard. How God called Abraham in the sacrifice of Isaac to abandon his traditional idea of morality and in blind obedience do what was right because God wanted such, and God wanting such made it right.

Of course, what is going on here is the venerable discussion where the Jewish and Reformation traditions want to say that things are right or wrong because God in Scripture – *Scriptura sola* – says they are right or wrong. Anything else is an affront to the utter sovereignty of God. Blasphemy, if you will.

The Catholic tradition always clings to the natural law idea that the very idea of creation implies some structure rather than another and that once that structure is given, even God must be consistent with it. So the point of the Abraham story is that in the end, God did not allow Abraham to sacrifice Isaac, and the purpose of the story is to prohibit in Israel the human sacrifices of their neighbors.

I wonder what Havel means in the concrete by saying that we live under judgment. One thing seems sure: World governments will do whatever they have to do for survival. Take that ethic which says things are right or wrong by divine decree, secularize it or empty it of theological content, and you have the modern sensibility. There are no absolutes, only real and urgent problems which require solutions, no matter what.

"Help Thou My Unbelief"

Sorry now that I did not travel the few blocks to Independence Hall to hear Vaclav Havel receive the still new Philadelphia Liberty Medal. Reading the excerpts from his acceptance address, I am both surprised and pleased.

Surprised because the Czech playwright-become-President said so much more than I remember reading in his *Letters to Olga* a few years ago. He said that human hope and the political effort will fail as long as the universal respect for human rights "does not derive from the respect of the miracle of Being (the newspaper uses the capital "B"). The miracle of the universe, the miracle of nature, the miracle of our existence."

In *Letters to Olga,* Havel does say that "belief in life can also be understood as a latent belief in immortality. And indeed, all human activity . . . contains deep inside the assumption of immortality – that is, of an 'absolute horizon.'"

Surprised because I do not often notice how people need to believe all that, as I do. My sense is that "man (and woman) come of age" has more the impervious secular sensibility noticed by Dietrich Bonhoeffer in Nazi Germany: that people were learning to live and die and watch parents die and Jewish neighbors arrested and sent off to work camps and read about mass deaths on the Russian front and still go off to an evening concert. In fact, Bonhoeffer seemed to be saying that the evening concert was the only relief available from such a world, and the traditional religious ritual gave man-come-of-age little comfort or meaning anymore. Nor did he need it.

My own experience at several recent deaths is that the milieu of unbelief is so pervasive that even people from strong religious backgrounds seem helpless in the face of the questions which Havel tries to surface and even answer – questions like heaven.

My pleasure comes from seeing Havel put his opinion out there. He expresses himself in images and words which are modest and tentative. That understatement which is so attractive.

I remember years ago a visit to a small and precious Protestant Episcopal cathedral church, an architectural delight, snug in a grove of trees. When leaving, I asked my host, also a Catholic priest, why these modest places seem so attractive. "Our tradition, Mac," he said. "Even if we are Irish, we are Anglicized Irish and have that British love of understatement different from the hyperbole, say, of high Italian baroque which has overwhelmed us." Perhaps understatement is not just British but Celtic as well.

Anyhow. I do feel overwhelmed by the *New Catechism* which spells out in detail over several hundred pages what I must believe. I feel strongly attracted by the words of Havel which invite belief but do so in a way that wants to include all, even those who have a hard time believing anything. The Gospel response of the man whom Jesus cured comes to mind: "Lord, I believe, help thou my unbelief."

Living Deliberately

Saint Catherine of Genoa. Years ago a Quaker student of the mystics asked me whether Catherine of Genoa or Catherine of Siena said: "My God is me." Meaning, of course, that the sense or experience of the divine indwelling (as we called it in my seminary days) was so full. Mystics are often suspected of a kind of pantheism for that kind of talk. They get in trouble with the official Church.

I had no idea which Catherine spoke thus, but since then I have discovered both Catherines through *Enduring Grace* by Carol Lee Flinders.

What is attractive about Catherine of Genoa is that her own life and marriage and troubles were so full that one could hardly expect her to get beyond coping. In a Romeo and Juliet world of the city and century of Christopher Columbus, she is married off to a rambler and a gambler to maneuver peace between her own and another family. Childless herself, she suffers the humiliation of knowing her husband has a mistress and a child by the mistress.

The gambling of her husband brings bankruptcy, and the text of her *Spiritual Dialogue,* which I easily found in the library of the Quaker retreat house, has God saying to her: "You will work for a living."

Such words must have surprised a feudal aristocrat. She and her husband both took jobs tending the sick poor of the vast city hospital.

Eventually, Catherine became director of the hospital, and when the plague came to Genoa in the summer of 1493, the other aristocrats fled to their country villas, while four-fifths of the people remaining in the city died. Catherine requisitioned sails from the shipyards of Genoa and extended her hospital out onto the lawn. Flinders says that 500 years later, the Genovese remember the woman and her summer.

Not only not allowing one's own troubles to create a personal impasse but using those troubles to become stronger and more generous and more believing.

When Catherine discovered that her husband had a child by another woman, she has her husband and herself take on financial responsibility for mother and child. What for most of us would become humiliation and bitterness becomes for Catherine further opening of the heart.

And her marriage must have been miserable. Again "the troubles of life," as the Mass prayer calls them, turn her within so that misery becomes further opportunity for grace.

And not to be detoured by the awful situation of women at such a time in Europe. The energy and assertion coming out of this seeming recluse who spent so much of her nights and days in prayer. Again that voice of God familiar to mystics and unheard by the rest of us: "You will have no friendships, no special family ties. You will love everyone without love, rich and poor, friends and relatives. You are not to make friends, not even spiritual or religious friendships, or go to see anyone out of friendship. It is enough that you go when called, as I told you before. This is the way you are to consort with your fellow creatures on earth."

Some agenda. Therapists could make much of this response to an unhappy marriage and a political family. Yet look where it has her run, while her fellow aristocrats are running off to villas to escape the plague.

The saints push themselves, and that is the human difference between them and the rest of us. The *Dialogue* has some mention about her nausea from foul-smelling sores and lice and running pus. She overcame her horror by eating the lice and "she rubbed her nose with the pus until she freed herself from that revulsion," like Saint Francis of Assisi forcing himself to embrace the leper.

All this sounds crazy, extreme. Yet look at Catherine in the plague, or Francis and his friars, and then look at the rest of us in our world of many plagues: disconnected, apathetic or bitter in our marriages, fearful, paralyzed and feeling powerless with our world and our own small lives. If Catherine and Francis are madness, give me some.

I do not want to reduce Catherine to some neat modern package nor neglect the prayer habits that connected her with the ocean within – within her and us as well. But for purposes of a label which only speaks to our time perhaps, that image of Thoreau who went to the woods "to live deliberately."

The difference between a Catherine and the rest of us is this living deliberately, expressed so strongly in the divine voice: "No friendships, no special family ties. . . . It is enough that you go when called."

Economia. The term economy has a distinguished history – the idea of being with oneself, poised and constantly preparing for the tasks that arise. No energy wasted, no strength dissipated by passing the time. Necessity, as in Simone Weil who said she would not even move something unless she were so moved by grace. Necessity arising out of a bad marriage or having to go to work or the plague coming to Genoa make a Catherine of Genoa. Certainly she did not go looking for these.

And to do all this with a gentleness towards others that conceals the deliberateness with which one is living.

No, conceal is not the right image. We are talking here about the *habitus caritatis.* The habit of charity, so much a habit, that one does it as easily as driving a car.

Faith: Changing the World

A book by the English Benedictine, Sebastian Moore. In the middle of his criticism of the poor understanding our Catholic tradition has of sexuality, he calls: ". . .the Church centered in Rome, the only worldwide and world-old institution that is committed to changing the world."

The compliment which Moore throws toward the Church is at least as important as his criticism. He sees the Catholic Church as having a unique nature and place and opportunity: "The only worldwide and world-old institution that is committed to changing the world."

The Quakers echo that sense; they are self-conscious about being Quaker, but are also aware that the Society of Friends is a very small elite. They know that a Quaker statement, say, on prison reform is predictable and not newsworthy enough to make the morning newspaper in the Quaker city of Philadelphia.

They know, as well, and are in awe of what a similar press release from the local Catholic Church would mean: headlines and probably some response in the labyrinth of politics as well.

A Quaker woman in the work of hospitality for Central American refugees mentioned how continually she had to go to the Archdiocese for help – for families who take in people, for legal assistance, for paperwork, for funds even. A bureaucracy at work handling these foreigners with a familiarity that eluded her because refugees and local Catholics shared a common faith and, hence, parts of a culture as well.

Just tonight at dinner another Quaker, a writer, told me a story of a local couple with a badly disabled child whose hearing and sight impairment made everyone advise the parents to leave the child in an institution lifelong.

The writer went on about how this family of several children found ways to help the child at home, where she even went to daily Mass with the mother and eventually made some manual signs saying that she wanted to make her First Holy Communion as her sisters and brothers had.

So a teaching sister, herself quite deaf, appeared for the task of instruction. Christmas was chosen as the First Communion day, and plans were to have the child receive at one of the many Masses of Christmas at this large parish in a neighborhood of thousands of Catholic families. Word of this accomplishment was out, and attendance at this off-hour Christmas Mass was full. After Communion, the applause was so full that the hearing-impaired child could hear the clapping even with her back to the congregation and could turn and bow to acknowledge the applause.

I do not know whether drawing all this faith and love and family out as a Catholic landscape is accurate. I do know the woman telling the story saw it so – as much as the Quaker woman did the refugee work.

Paying Attention

Hard to enjoy the leisure and comfort of this quiet place of trees and cottages and library without the fret inside about the neighbors back home to whom all this is unknown and unavailable. Summer in the city. They just perspire and cope as they do the other months.

Or perhaps it is just freefloating worry, looking for something to worry about. Reading yesterday the story of Thomas Merton in his hermitage years, I discover that solitude was something he had to work at actively. Merton says: "I am struck and appalled more than ever by the shoddiness, the slackness, the laziness of my response. I am just beginning to awaken and to realize how much more awakening is to come . . . I am so tied up in all this that I don't know where to start getting free."

By all this he means his various literary projects and contacts with many people from his now-many monastic years. He knows himself well enough to know that the desire for solitude was not pure or unequivocal in him. There was that gregarious and curious Merton telling a visitor that this should be their last meeting and then writing that same person a week or month later suggesting another visit.

For me, a difficulty of the aloneness is that living where I work, my life is so full of people that I do not have to deal with solitude, only traffic and exhaustion.

Merton comes through to me, as does Catherine of Genoa hearing the voice telling her: "It is enough that you go when you are called." This withdrawal and leisure can be worthwhile if it helps me to pay attention. Like Merton: "I am appalled by the shoddiness, the slackness, the laziness of my response."

It comes from not really paying attention to the fellow, say, who asks me to help him find a job or detox or a place to live. I make a furtive effort or two and nothing works out because life or this woman's need for housing is complicated, and she and he disappear onto the street again, and I imagine my task is fulfilled by these slack and shoddy and lazy responses of mine.

Paying attention is Catherine paying attention to the suffering and sick of plague-stricken Genoa by begging or stealing sails from the shipyards for her tent hospital.

And all this not as some exercise in personal fulfillment or integration or becoming holy but simply the only way to be with others.

The only way the world will be different is when we are all that way with one another. I cannot imagine a responsible parent helping daughter or son apply to some college, and when that applicancy does not work out letting the matter go for lack of interest.

"The Work of the Cell"

In *The Hermitage Years* which I am reading, John Howard Griffin quotes a phrase from Merton: "the work of the cell" which for Merton meant "paying attention" no less. At first, I was comforted by the idea that "cell work" meant going through this debris of books and notes and reading materials and unanswered letters people have sent me.

Of course, Merton meant something far deeper. By the "work of the cell" he meant rising and sleeping and cutting wood and writing and making coffee, all the while awaking the mind and heart to the "voice of God." His Benedictine rule, unlike more modern religious rules, has no time set aside for formal prayer other than the choral offices, because prayer is what you are supposed to be doing when you are not doing something else. Or more accurately, prayer is the inner state even on a farm tractor. A kind of paying attention that does not make you dangerous behind the wheel of that tractor.

Or in the tradition of the Desert Fathers, says Merton, the best prayer is not to know one is praying. Yet Merton does comment on the "work of the cell" in the more everyday sense: this "awful, automatic, worried routine of piling up books, sorting papers, tearing up some, mailing them out and so forth . . . I wonder how many wastepaper baskets I have filled in the last week."

Paying attention to this tedious wading through one's own clutter. A necessary part of attending to a person with some problem or question, really helping that fellow to find a job means sitting down with that rediscovered business card which just surfaced in the pile (paperclipped to something else) and writing that fellow who wants to help enough to have given you his card. Write and ask him if those jobs are still available because, surely enough, with my carelessness and neglect, the unemployed fellow is still unemployed.

And again all this, not by way of being a neatnik or whatever. Just being as thorough and serious about things as my friends are about the college applications of their children. As Merton says somewhere else, the final goal of our seeking is not proficiency in prayer in some psychological sense; the goal is love, the *habitus caritatis,* which prayer assists.

Surrender

In his hermitage, convert Thomas Merton experienced the Church as wall which separates rather than wall which connects. Barrier rather than sign or sacrament.

The year was 1965, and the danger was that a Vatican II document might give tacit approval of nuclear weapons. He told visitors that "we must do what we can to prevent a disgrace and scandal of such magnitude."

Even the word scandal in Greek and Latin origins means a stumbling block or barrier. So, Church as a barrier or obstacle to faith rather than an avenue. Griffin describes Merton's problem thus: "The monk's one real difficulty with the faith at this time lay in accepting the Church as a redeemed community, not only juridically but so that in fact to follow the mind of the Church meant to be free from the mentality of 'fallen society.' "

Merton saw the bomb mentality as a way of the world, a wicked and sinful solution. For the Church to accept such a conclusion was, well, scandalous. Church as stumbling block, barrier rather than access.

A biography of John Henry Newman was the refectory reading at the time, and Newman was thus a great help to Merton sorting this through. Newman had few illusions about the Church.

The *New York Times* comes here, and yesterday morning an article about the United States' Catholic bishops going to oppose health care reform that would require abortion funding in violation of the conscience of Catholic taxpayers or health workers. Is the Church here opposing the "mentality of 'fallen society,' " as Merton would have her? The position will be unpopular, more unpopular than her opposing nuclear weapons would be.

The same *New York Times* tells the tragic story going on in Haiti. Massacres of boat people fleeing the island. And our government not giving the same refuge to poor Haitians as to others, say, from Eastern Europe. Outrageous, and the reason is race. This liberal administration cannot and will not risk popularity or burden our resources or endanger its political agenda of health care reform and whatever by taking in the Haitians. The idea that some offshore facility become an interrogation center to discern political from economic refugees is a scandal.

So with Merton and Newman and the early Church Father, Origen, whom I am also reading in this incredible luxury so distant from Haitian refugees, I am thrown back on the Church. I so need her to oppose the "mentality of fallen society" which might well be at work in government, both with abortion and turning back Haitian boat people.

The author of the introduction of the Origen book (Rowan Greer) quotes Yeats' "The Second Coming" to describe the decaying, chaotic Roman world into which Origen was born in A.D. 180:

> Things fall apart; the center cannot hold;
> Mere anarchy is loosed upon the world,
> The blood-dimmed tide is loosed, and everywhere
> The ceremony of innocence is drowned;
> The best lack all conviction, while the worst
> Are full of passionate intensity.

Greer goes on to say that Origen saw the Christian Church not as an alternative to the Roman Empire but as something that could rescue and transform what was best in it. Thus Origen's effort to Hellenize the gospel.

Yeats was, of course, describing his and our world, which needs transformation as much as that of Origen. But now the Christian tradition has many conflicting and opposing voices. Some Christian churches support abortion as a form of human liberation even as they criticize the government for turning back the Haitians.

How do we tell who is Church? I guess the question comes down to that of faith. Thomas More refused to go along with the English move to establish a national church apart from the Pope and the universal Church, even though almost all the English bishops were going along.

More, on trial for his life, is asked whether the Roman Church is worth the risk since she shows such flaws, is such a tenuous link with Christ. "Tenuous, indeed," says More, "but the only one we have."

That wall, no less an obstacle for More than for Merton or Newman. Yet in the end, the wall which is barrier is also our precious access.

Hard to live that kind of ambivalence. Perhaps these Quakers here choose not to – no doctrines or clear disciplines.

Archbishop Weakland of Milwaukee said something wonderful about his recent experience of Church as barrier with the papal decision on women priests. He said, in the end, he would obey the Holy Father, and this acceptance would, he knew, deepen his faith. Sometimes that is all we can hope for, although that kind of surrender does not have popular support these days.

But surrender or whatever does not stop me from yearning with More and Merton for a Church that is as clear about nuclear bombs as about abortion. Nor can the idea of surrender be without nuance. Everybody from St. Paul confronting St. Peter to Ignatius of Loyola spelling obedience for Jesuits shows that whatever surrender means, moral or intellectual capitulation is not the picture.

Focused Prayer

Unfortunately, the rooms I occupy have a television, and I have a habit of going to sleep by watching some show or other that makes no demands on me. A habit as harmless, I guess, as that of people who need to read themselves to sleep.

Except that any serious effort at prayer means emptying the mind, diminishing the images that clamor for attention and so fill the mind and heart that silent prayer, already difficult, becomes even more difficult.

I know I am not a cloistered monk whose cloister intends to be a landscape where as little happens as possible so that he will have the quiet within and without which prayer needs.

But the monk is just the rest of us writ large. Someone doing what we all should be doing so explicitly that we who are out and about will not forget the *unum necessarium* – the one thing necessary.

Not that the cloistered sister or monk is doing it to edify us. Something so self-conscious would ruin everything. The best prayer is not to know one is praying. To continue the *unum necessarium* image, Mary at the feet of Jesus, while her sister Martha is busy in the kitchen, is simply choosing "the better part," and the story of her leaning that way is told in the gospel to remind us of the "lean" that we must never quite relinquish, no matter how else we are engaged.

So here I am trying to be about prayer and taking to bed not only all the inevitable images of my waking day but pumping in still more.

Last night a station break announced a special on Haiti at a later hour. Involvement with the local Haitians has me aware of the crisis going on these weeks. I contrast the leisure and luxury of these days here with the tidal wave of poor boat people fleeing for their lives.

If I watch anything, I should watch that since the Haitians gather at our church for Mass monthly and regard me as their local priest.

Yet something in me does not want to watch. That something, I suspect, which has me not seeing recent films like *Schindler's List* or *In the Name of the Father*.

What I suspect is going on is an economy of energy. The sense that my geography and living where I work has me see more than my share of human misery everyday. Some censor or filter inside says: enough. Fierce energy going out of me every hour here without me stimulating more emotions about matters that deserve emotion.

I know I am letting myself off easy here. And on the same evening I might watch a dumb police story.

Once I sat on a porch and asked two Trappists and a religious sister about watching television, whether the habit was incompatible with serious prayer. The sister was quite clear: we have to work at fewer and less distracting images rather than mindlessly adding more.

I notice that Thomas Merton tells his friend, James Laughlin, editor of *New Directions,* not to send him "good experimental writing" of even Lorca or Dylan Thomas. He knows that Laughlin will be dismayed and tries to explain how newspapers and magazines and novels would be a distraction from the focus which is the very point of the hermit's life.

I remember hearing years ago that a Carthusian prior or someone criticized Merton for all these outside interests saying that if he were a true contemplative, he would not know the name of the reigning Pope!

Shepherd the Crowd

Interesting how the Sunday Mass readings become so familiar over the years that a passage can become precious. A passage that might remain casual enough to someone else.

Today, that passage from Saint Mark about the Lord trying to escape from the crowd. He crosses the lake in a boat, and there they are waiting for him as he comes up on shore. It says: "seeing the crowd, he had compassion on them for they were like sheep without a shepherd."

What a relief and help to know that Christ could so experience the world. When I see the slaughter in the world today or even the conditions here in the ruins of North Philadelphia, I am like Job looking heavenward in his personal suffering, saying: "Hey, God, what's going on? What kind of world is this creation of yours?"

And there is Christ who, later or otherwise, knew himself as the Good Shepherd, experiencing the world as a mess without a shepherd. The people follow Christ into the desert and are shepherdless, without food. The Apostles urge him to send the crowd away to find their own food. He tells the Apostles: Feed them yourselves. No shepherd around? You shepherd them.

Simone Weil puts a twist on the parable of the Good Samaritan with a traveller wounded and bleeding by the roadside. She says that given the nature of creation, God is powerless to help the victim and says that fortunately she is not God, and she can help out. Her own position of superiority over God.

But for the moment, my comfort is just to know that Christ could experience creation as such chaos and disorder. And this disorder does not paralyze him or have him deny divine providence or love. It even moves him more and more to take charge, to enter into his mission as Good Shepherd who knows his sheep by name.

Or myself. That time in the public housing projects when the scene in the concrete bunker of an apartment was so desolate that I asked myself: How could this young family have any sense of being loved from on high? The landscape is so forlorn.

The only answer coming back at me was: this is where you come in. Your care, divine love shining on them at this time, in this place.

But I do not want to keep running to the moral conclusion. Today I just want to be reassured that unbelief is not the only answer to my experience of this tumultuous world.

Tolerance

A young British couple visiting here who had lived and worked in the Catholic neighborhoods of Belfast. They show great sympathy for the Catholic cause in the North of Ireland and regard the British government as hypocritical in saying no negotiation until Sein Fein repudiates the insurrectionary violence. Insurrectionary violence has been part of the peace process everywhere else – as recently as South Africa and the Palestine-Israel accords.

The couple are proud of Quaker history in Ireland. How in the terrible years of the famine, the Quakers alone of the Protestants did not include proselytizing in their relief work in the west of Ireland.

They were proud to tell me that Father Desmond Wilson attended their wedding, and they worry about his isolation there in the battered neighborhoods of Belfast.

My own North-of-Ireland connections were of interest to them, and I told them about the Irish trip with longtime friend, Father Michael Doyle. About ten years ago, he was asked by a local newspaper to visit the six counties as an Irishman long-away and write up his impressions.

By way of table conversation here while dining outside, I told the couple about our visit to the home of Irish elder statesman, Sean MacBride, whom, of course, they know as the Irishman of almost mythological stature. His mother was Maud Gonne, the great love of William Butler Yeats. For his work in founding Amnesty International, he was the only person ever to win both the Nobel and Lenin peace prizes.

In the MacBride home, Michael Doyle was eager to take photographs, and I did the interview. Almost brash, I asked immediately what needed to change in Ireland to unite the country. MacBride nodded yes to my questions about divorce and birth control. I pressed him: and abortion? He hesitated, and then in a voice with the hint of a French accent intimating his own extraordinary life story: we must draw the line of civilization somewhere.

His voice and manner of hesitation make those words much softer than they might sound. I know that years later and just before his death, Irish liberals were enraged with Sean MacBride for opposing and probably helping to defeat the divorce referendum. He went on television to say that the Irish Catholic people should come up with some solution to the anguish of unhappy or ruined

marriages other than the consumer solution of the United States or
Great Britain. Again, the words and manner of speaking probably
more gentle than my telling it.

I am not sure why I was telling the British couple the MacBride
visit in such detail unless I am so mindful of the press attention the
abortion issue has now with health-care reform politics.

The response of the young couple across the lunch table was
an almost Quaker silence, respectful that maybe I was spelling out
my own opinion as well as that of Sean MacBride. Finally, the
woman said something about MacBride belonging to an older generation – like deValera.

Here again the conundrum. People so intent upon living
simply, vegetarians and other options so that others may simply
live, do not grasp a Catholic sensibility in this business of abortion.
For them the matter could be simply Quaker tolerance. The tolerance
that made Philadelphia free for Catholics when the other original
colonies restricted their worship. Could my new friends regard the
matter as does our Supreme Court with the privacy concept, or
could they regard abortion as a form of human liberation? Their
Quaker quiet tells me less rather than more. The conundrum remains.

The Seamless Cohesion

The need to question this matter of writing. That scene from
Civilisation, by Kenneth Clark, of the author standing near the
Gutenberg press wondering whether the machine was a fortunate
or unfortunate invention.

So many words. Why add to them? Of course, the very
nature of human society requires that we try to understand, to
connect . . . .

I am encouraged by a letter from Irish poet friend, Michael
Coady, who visited the church in search of the story of his immigrant
great-grandfather. Coady says: "I have some small awareness of
your everyday ministry, John, and don't know how you cope with
its demands. There's the profound ideal, though, of making the
life and the art a single seamless garment."

And while here with the Quakers, I return to an old article
from the *Times Literary Supplement* by George Steiner on Charles
Peguy, whom Steiner greatly admires. He says that the style of

Peguy "defines the seamless cohesion between writing and daily life." Yet Graham Greene, whom I admire, says that the writer has to be more of a curious spectator of life rather than a participant. Someone who watches the parade rather than marching in it. Greene probably acquired the habit from his English schoolboy days and his painful position of being the son of the headmaster and thus unable to be fully one of the boys. Greene suffered terribly from that predicament.

Just yesterday I returned unread to the library that volume of Cistercian Fathers spelling out the growing difference in the Middle Ages between monastic and scholastic theology. The scholastics come more and more to the opinion that they could study and write these matters without allowing them to do their work within. The difference between *lectio,* or reading, and *lectio divina,* which is reading with the heart.

Of course, a problem with writing can be the problem of people from an oppressed tradition like the Irish. Not all the Irish obviously, but there is that history not helped by seminary years of apologizing for having opinion about anything: who does he think he is – The Prince of Wales?

I think the thing that got me writing finally was the rare opportunity of a white guy living where I do. Someone should say it, how abandoned and forsaken the neighborhoods are. How much society and Church need to do.

Yet another reason is simply that business of paying attention. Those meticulous notebooks of Simone Weil handed carefully to a friend as she was leaving France. Her etchings or carving into words everything going on around her and consequently within her in this terrible century.

I shall have to fetch that volume of Cistercian publications from the library again. Look more closely at the wound of separation between *lectio* and *lectio divina.*

Helplessness Hits Home

From my air-conditioned splendor turning on the morning news to see what the weather is out there in the real world.

I always remember the skit from the British comedy, *The Fantasticks,* of proper fellows sitting around the Royal Himalayan Club or some such, discussing an abstract problem. One fellow keeps interrupting saying: "Yes, but you know in real life . . . ." Finally, with exasperation, another responds: "I say, you're rather fond of real life."

The news of the day is that this is the 25th anniversary of the first moon landing. In air-conditioning with windows and doors closed, no street noise and the only sound the rush of cool air through a vent, I always feel as enclosed and detached as someone in a space module.

The other news is beyond imagining. Even with video pictures of refugees in an open field in Zaire, the numbers are beyond absorbing. Thirty-five thousand an hour or a day sound the same. The talk is about a million people gathering in those fields before the week is over. Refugee workers say that providing water for such a mass gathering is impossible.

I cannot comprehend any of it. Not the why of whether this is the longtime fallout of European colonialism in Africa. In 1939 or thereabouts, Simone Weil said that after World War II, when the peoples of Africa entered more visibly into the world scene, she hoped they would not enter by way of nation-states. The world already has too many nation-states whose premise is militarism. Nor do I understand whether tribal hatred could cause this killing without European nationalism stirring the pot. It seems that raw or provoked human nature can be that deadly as now in Bosnia and Serbia as well as Africa.

Nor do I understand how I sustain faith and hope in divine love and providence in the face of such a world and such human suffering. Simone Weil also says that creation is God throwing part of himself or herself into the infinity of space, and human history is our making our way back across that immense distance. It seems we still have so far to travel. Somehow Simone Weil believes this without believing much in the myth of progress. She said that progress rather than religion is the opium of the people.

And finally on this anniversary of the moon landing, I took the English Quaker couple into Philadelphia to see my neighborhood. I notice that I do this with visitors because I am curious to see what response they will have to the appalling conditions to which I never become accustomed. No doubt I want to reassure myself that my perception is not extreme.

Well, they were indeed dismayed at conditions in the Quaker utopia. And like myself dismayed at the extent of the ruins – how they go on and on, looking worse, I think, than East Los Angeles, say, because of the impacted appearance of the tiny row houses across from one another on streets no wider than an alley. Sometimes up and down the street only one or two occupied houses in a block of 30 or 40.

And the British fellow says: impossible that such decay and neglect are allowed to happen in a society which has the ability to mount Desert Storm and the war in Iraq. I add: or on this anniversary of the moon landing pull off such technological achievement 25 years ago. This society does not have the will to take this on. Instead we build interstates so that we can travel wherever without even seeing these "badlands," as the police call them.

We discussed Belfast and Ballymurphy, where the Quaker couple had lived and worked. A difference is that in the north of Ireland, the problems, bad as they are, seem human-size. Something we can get a handle on. Here things seem out of control.

Leaving the neighborhood, we saw little African American children sitting on the step of the only occupied apartment in the brick and concrete courtyard of a public housing project. We waved at them, and they smiled and waved back. The feeling is the same helplessness felt upon seeing the Rwandan children in the encampment on the front-page color newspaper picture this morning of a Rwandan child going through the meager leavings of a corpse.

Fragile Diplomacy

What about Haiti? A question from a Quaker woman starting the Monday meal preparation here in early morning. She knows that the local Haitians gather at Saint Malachy for Mass and wonders what they think about the threatened U.S. invasion. News of that possibility in the newspapers this morning.

Of course, military solutions are as unattractive to Quakers as they have become to me. Militarism is such a scourge in the world: "A crime against the poor in that it robs them of bread," is a recent Catholic teaching.

We talk about alternatives, and I mention my complete cynicism about United States politics concerning Haiti. Father Aristide is so much a hard-liner wanting accountability for past massacres that our administration is hardly going to invade in order to reinstall him. I can only agree with the local Haitian leaders who for months have been saying that our government has only been posturing in wanting to return Aristide.

The Quaker woman told of past anguish for Vietnam expressed to a Vietnamese person here. The refugee told her: we can do nothing for them. They can only do for themselves.

We decided that might be the only solution for Haiti, however unlikely that seems now. Is it reasonable to expect people who are hungry and jobless and terrorized by their government to rise up with some nonviolent resistance that would bring more terror on them?

Yet the idea that this overarmed warship of a United States would go up on the Haitian beaches shooting and bombing as in Baghdad and Desert Storm is so outrageous. Who said we are in charge of the world?

At the noon-day meal I tried all this out on the British couple. The impossible suggestion that the Haitian people might come together in effective protest. The new British friends asked whether this had not already happened with the legitimate and overwhelming election of Aristide.

We talked about South Africa. I asked whether the longtime economic sanctions from without are what brought apartheid down. The newspapers say that the affluent Haitians have learned ways around the blockade. Only the poor suffer still more.

Something very unreal about anguishing over Haiti from this pleasant place. Yet what can we do? I guess the woman preparing lunch was trying to resolve that unreality by quoting her Vietnamese friend.

Of course, my inevitable question to myself: what about the Church? Could the Catholic Church exert any power to relieve the Haitian crisis and perhaps even prevent military action?

The Haitian people are so Catholic. I sit monthly waiting for choir and congregation for the Haitian Mass, asking myself: why am I comfortable with people whose languages I cannot speak and whose country I have never visited? More comfortable, say, than with many, many African Americans in whose neighborhoods I have spent many years.

The answer coming back at me is: Catholic faith. The Haitians and I share a Catholic culture which connects us across so many differences. Even in their support of Father Aristide, they are uneasy with priests in politics, as Catholic tradition suggests we should be. Except that now he is all they have, and Catholic tradition suffers such improvisations. As for the Church, how to justify the whole apparatus of the Vatican as an independent state with diplomats and such unless this paraphernalia can be used to help Haiti? I do not see any such effort, although diplomats say the best diplomacy is invisible. Certainly the last diplomatic gesture of the Vatican in Haiti was visible: the Papal Nuncio was the single only world diplomat to attend the installation of this illegal government. Church as part of the problem rather than help toward solution. Again Illich saying that the mission of the Church is so sublime and even fragile that when she waffles, she not only neglects to do the good she ought, but even does harm.

Hope for the Future

A Quaker leader asked me to have lunch with her. She is a former Catholic and wants to know what the Church will look like and do in the new century soon arriving.

During the hour before our lunch, I notice those two almost opposing currents within me: the immense hope and expectation I bring to the Church and her mission. I am like worker priest, Henri Perrin, in France just after World War II. In a letter or diary he goes on about his dream of a renewed Catholic Mass of people and priest around the altar. A vital and shared worship so nourishing as to renew the face of the earth.

Well, we have a new liturgy, and for a few years Mass was quite alive. Now that the novelty is over, the new seems as humdrum as the old.

And Henri Perrin himself was unable to sustain his fervor and hope when his heroic life and that of the other worker priests were suppressed by the official Church. He sank into inertia and almost despair. He was killed in a motorcycle accident, and they found on his body a two-week-old letter asking for laicization. Apparently, he was able to write the letter but not quite able to mail it.

That other current in me is the later Henri Perrin. Besides the vision and hope of a renewed Church that I want to bring to table to the Catholic-turned-Quaker is that bleak, almost hopeless prospect which is a reasonable response to the present situation.

Someone said that the theological virtue of hope is not human optimism. Hope might even begin where, as Dan Berrigan says,

we touch the outer limits of personal and public despair to recognize
that despair, too, has limits and to go beyond those limits.

On another slant might be that neat phrase that I came up with
all by myself in the spirit of Albert Camus: a benign, reflective
pessimism is not incompatible with a theology of grace. Anyhow.
The Quaker acquaintance brings more visible hope to the Church
scene than I do. From without she has great feeling for the present
Pope and his efforts to speak to a world where, more and more,
anything goes. Our conversation is as abstract as the world economy and as concrete as giving or not giving condoms to ghetto
youth, who, together with suburban youth, are sexually active at
ten or eleven years old.

She says she admires the concern of the Pope for the preser-
vation of the family and has trouble with the anti-family social
mood which can attract Quakers among others so intent upon human
freedom and tolerance. People very wrapped up in family can be
very righteous and near-sighted in their moral passion.

Sympathetic to the concern of the Church for a world of
constraint and firm values, the Quaker went on to say how the
well-being of the family depends so on economics – on people
having work and having a home and good schools and health care
and the rest.

Neither our present government nor small religious traditions
like the Society of Friends seem to have any real response to the
economic problem.

The President of this country imagines that the United States
can prosper by being the leader in new high-tech industries that
will provide employment. Yet in the last world Olympics, pro-
gramming and ticketing were done high-tech in India. Developing
countries can do this work as well and for less.

And my Quaker lunch partner looks almost with awe at her
old Catholic origins, because the tradition has the resources and the
theological and social sophistication to speak to these complex
problems of our most complicated world. I guess she is admiring
the critique that this Pope can bring to "unbridled capitalism" from
his perspective of living most of his life in a socialist state. And I
guess she is talking about the difference that a Church which is
everywhere can make. A different slant but the same tone as the
previous Quaker woman dealing with a houseful of Central American refugees, needing to go to Catholic social services for the
resources and know-how to help the people.

Prayer

Amazing how the intensity of the early Church Father, Origen, comes through across 18 centuries. A volume of his writings in translation in the library here, and I am reading his treatise on prayer.

Despite the regard which John Henry Newman had for the Greek Fathers, I only know them from seminary years in quotation form. Some brief phrase brought up in a doctrinal thesis in the old scholastic theology. *Argumenta e traditione:* proofs from tradition – the faith of the early Church. Fair enough, I guess.

All I knew about Origen was that he had some unorthodox ideas on the Trinity and eschatology and, of course, we knew the fervor of his self-mutilation in the pursuit of Christian perfection.

Overall Origen seems a balanced and sane person living in terrible times and eager to present Christ to his Greek-speaking world so as to transform that brutal world. The Hellenization of Jewish Christianity was, I think, a happy marriage of a rough desert ethical monotheism and Greek mysticism – the best of both worlds. As Aquinas or someone said: to the Jews was given revelation and to the Greeks philosophy. An opinion very distant from the quintessential Protestant Karl Barth, who regarded the natural theology of Aquinas as the only real reason for not being a Catholic.

But I am very attached to natural theology and the world as metaphor for the mystery we call God. Sometimes I wonder whether keeping the biblical text from the people was a real service of the Church. So much awful stuff. The idea of everybody reading it and making up his or her own mind sounds at least undesirable. Back to Origen and his treatise on prayer. He says: " . . . the only way we can accept the command to pray constantly . . . as referring to a real possibility is by saying that the entire life of the saint as a whole is a single great prayer. What is customarily called prayer is, then, a part of this prayer."

He goes on to say how scripture suggests prayer three or four times daily. Earlier in the same chapter he gives *argumenta e traditione* to that wonderful idea in Herbert McCabe, O.P., that the only prayer is Christ who is "sheer prayer," and our only task to attach ourselves to his prayer which we do by the Mass or Eucharist.

Origen says that the person who prays "will partake of the word of God, who stands in the midst even of those who do not know him . . . who is never absent from prayer, and who prays to the Father with the person whose Mediator He is."

With McCabe my own experience of prayer is often so futile that I am tempted to give it up as I often have – for years at a time. Yet when you read the Gospel, the sense coming through is that Jesus prayed more than he did anything else. The Transfiguration and Agony in the Garden, with the apostles sleeping both times rather than joining his prayer.

Sometimes when the twelve woke after sleeping out in the fields, Jesus was not around. Looking for him, they would discover that he had risen much earlier or had prayed all night. When they wanted him to interrupt prayer to eat, he would mention food of his which they knew nothing about. And, of course, he prepared for his ministry by 40 days of fast and prayer.

When Origen says that praying always means "the entire life of the saint as a whole is a single great prayer," he does not mean to let us off the hook about formal prayer. He means that we should never be far from it. So close that part of us is always leaning there.

Thomas Keating says that we should simply do it. Teresa of Avila says that we should continue no matter what difficulties we have, "should your whole world come apart." Dom Chapman or some Englishman said that often the experience would be little more than what appears to be "an idiot state." So then it is an act of faith.

Keating says that we should not evaluate the quality of our prayer by some felt success with the half-hour or whatever. Only how the habit long-term improves our relationship with others.

So we are not far again from Origen saying: "The entire life of the saint as a whole is a single great prayer," and we have Thérèse coming to prayer and falling asleep. She decides that she will put in the time and try not to fall asleep. And if she falls asleep, that will have to do.

Some danger, I know, that prayer can become a narcotic. The preoccupation with methods of prayer or progress in prayer and self-discovery. I will just have to depend upon the grace of God not to let that happen. For now, my sense is that prayer as removal from life is not my problem.

Silent Prayer

Often better to say less rather than more. Or even nothing rather than something. In a preface to a new printing of his *The Triumph of the Therapeutic,* Philip Rieff quotes scripture to that effect: "Whoever spares words is truly wise, and whoever is wary of speech is intelligent. Even a fool who keeps silent is regarded as wise."

The trouble with this advice for the priest or preacher is that weekly (or daily) responsibility to comment on the reading of the scriptures – that going on once called the sermon that has become the homily.

Today I am back at the parish with the responsibility to say something or other by way of extension or comment on the Gospel reading of the Lord feeding the multitude in the desert.

And the Mass prayer goes on about the beauty of the world and the splendor of creation. All this on a Sunday when newspapers and television call the Rwanda refugee crisis the worst of this century.

And the local Catholic paper has a cover color photograph of a Haitian child with an abdomen distended by hunger and malnutrition. Again the newspaper talk about an imminent invasion of Haiti because the blockade is hurting only the poor and not at all successful in bringing down the mighty.

How do I pray about the beauty of creation or read the Gospel of a miraculous feeding of a multitude in such a world of Rwanda and Haiti? Down there in the aisle a basket for the suggested relief collection for Rwanda.

Better say less rather than more. The irony of reading and immediate world should reduce me to some silence.

At least point out the irony. Talk about the danger of invasions and military solutions. Priests and homilies are meant to have answers. So I continue. The Mass which gathers us is a prayer. So at least we can pray for Rwandans and Haitians and our powerlessness in our own neighborhood here. Yesterday a six-year-old girl was caught in crossfire only three blocks away. Today she died.

Not Mass prayer as narcotic excusing us from work. Prayer as petition that we might have whatever enabled Christ to feed the people. That promise of his: "The things I do you shall do, and greater than these, you shall do because I go to the Father." Prayer because government is powerless or immoral. Imagine how welcome the Haitian refugees would be were they white-skinned Europeans fleeing, say, a Soviet Union. Prayer because the same Father of Jesus, who is Father and Mother and more to us, can help somehow.

Tragic Intolerance

A television set here. And despite the desire to give these weeks some monastic tone, still the habit of going off to sleep with television. A habit we call it. And probably a bad habit like needing a cigarette or a drink.

Anyhow. The show is another of the new magazine shows, and the story is about a Jewish policeman here in Philadelphia suing the police department for ethnic discrimination of his civil rights.

An unbelievable story. So outrageous and unbelievable that even alone I am embarrassed. I cringe when I see a Catholic Church very near my own on network New York television because this church is where a police official went to Mass, perhaps even daily, only to come across the street to this special unit and begin telling the Jewish detective that his people "killed Our Lord." What kind of mind or Mass attendance allows such a performance? The Jewish officer in his interview with the television reporter tells how the practice spread to other policemen – calling him "Jew guy" and worse.

He said the drill became impossible. He went to the Department and to the Jewish Police Association. No avail. And now federal court.

Of course, my response is to blame the Church. All that does not get said at Mass and needs saying over the years. Almost all the police officials he accuses have Irish names, most likely Catholic. Such a flawed world, and recently I even saw *The Tablet* of London saying that the human condition is so flawed that the most redemptive act of the Crucifixion could not happen without the undesirable fallout of antisemitism, which is right there in the New Testament. I know friends who have a hard time with the reading of the passion story from the Fourth Gospel in the Good Friday service.

Perhaps I am too hard on the Church. Not aware enough of the opaque and imperious humanity the Church has to work on with ministers who show all the flaws of those whom they instruct: narrowness and prejudice and tribalism.

An issue of *The Tablet* which I brought along for closer reading has a letter to the editors commenting on an earlier report that Jewish people need to reappraise Pope Pius XII. The letter is from a Dublin priest whose life work seems to be gathering comments from Golda Meir, a Chief Rabbi in Rome, and Israeli diplomats and Jewish historians of the Holocaust, all thanking Pius XII for his rescue network operating through diplomatic missions.

No point other than that I focus too much on where the Church does not succeed with this fool of a police official coming from Mass. I neglect to see what is achieved. Most Catholics say easily and clearly that they were never taught to blame the Jewish people.

Of course, I know what happens to police. The same thing that happens to any homogeneous group of men or women who associate mostly with one another. The locker room mentality. Well, this Jewish fellow decided no more, and he is right. Antisemitism and other such hatreds are so virulent that we should resist the slightest beginnings. People say that Catholics are getting their share of ridicule in the media and elsewhere, and that perception might be accurate enough.

Our Own Space

The storm was so wonderful that I had to leave the busy desk work to watch it. This newer house is in the manner of the once-great houses of Ireland and England and has a library looking out on a vast lawn bordered on two sides by large trees. The far side of the lawn is a vegetable and flower garden.

The sound and light show of lightning and thunder, such that I wanted almost to be out there getting as wet as the tree branches bending under the drenching rain. I had to settle for a double doorway opening out onto the stone porch. I pulled a straight-back, straw-seated chair into the open doorway in hope that the rain would come straight down, and I would not have to retreat for getting wet or rain coming in on floor and carpet.

A long time since we have had such summer storms. The lightning would flash and soon the roll of thunder. I knew the traffic was still rolling on the interstate beyond the tall trees in the far garden, but the dull traffic noise was lost in thunder and the soft hush of rain.

Later in the evening an invitation to walk in the dark, still-wet woods. A pathway exists so that strollers and bikers can wander the woods under and over and beside interstate. Great stone and concrete walls blind out the highway. A concession of the highway department to local homeowners to soften their opposition to the highway.

Much space is defined by our senses. The lawn and trees and house create a place for rain and lightning and thunder as though this were the very purpose of these acres. A vast stage for a show not unlike the lights and narration and music of that hillside in Athens looking across at the Acropolis. Anywhere else the presentation would be boring. The importance of space. The importance of architecture. The importance of this defined great lawn containing a display of almost cosmic size – a great summer storm that goes on and on with thunder rolling down the sky and trees coming alive and green in the lightning flashes against the growing evening darkness.

And I define all this. Creating space or stage by seeing lawn or distant Parthenon.

Here in the late evening my companion and I walk a path known in the darkness only the by paving under our feet. The sense is that this modest walkway is the real road rather than the massive highway of bridge and steel and roaring traffic above.

All this because we were there. We were walking and talking and making our way in darkness, and the thunder of trucks and cars overhead, only the background making us speak louder. We are the center of a universe, or at least that is how we experience ourselves.

This lush lawn in a Quaker setting, so quiet and out of the way, seeming reminds me of Mellifont in the Boyne Drive of Ireland. Those lacelike stone ruins are the remains of the first Cistercian monastery brought to Ireland.

And the monks. I wonder what those men were like. Whether they were Irish or Frenchmen whom St. Malachy brought to Ireland to install the Cistercian life there?

In a rural place, were they quiet or rough men coping easily with the lack of amenities, the cold and damp? Were they often ill, and did they persevere, or was there much coming and going? Were they content to wander by that small stream, disappear into the surrounding woods for solitude between bells calling them to Choir? Were they eager to make this place as quiet as possible so that their prayer could be as quiet as possible? I am never far from that Thomas Kinsella translation of a ninth-century Irish monk and recluse telling his very serious purpose:

> And let the place that shelters me
> behind monastic walls
> be a lovely cell, with pillars pure
> and I there all alone.

Of course, the monk of Mellifont or the earlier fellow is myself on the great lawn, watching and even trying to be part of a summer storm. House and lawn even remind me of those great houses of Ireland.

Each of us a universe experienced from within, defining a space. And within that space a self whose appetites and impulses are now pleased and not pleased with the solitude or the rain or the quiet. The struggle the ninth-century monk describes in the same passage:

> With weak, subdued desires
> and denial of the wretched world,
> with innocent, eager thoughts,
> so let us sue to God.

For me as for this monk God is someone and somewhere beyond. Someone to go to beyond the abyss of self and space and clouds covering sky and thunder rolling God knows where.

Some of these mystics I am reading, like Catherine of Genoa, seem able to know or imagine the God within: Catherine said: "The proper center of everyone is God Himself . . . My being is God, not by some simple participation but by a true transformation of my being."

My own habit of imagining God out there beyond is lifelong. Nowhere am I more at home than that prayer space of the cloister where the Eucharist is enthroned in the sunburst monstrance. I can imagine myself sunbathing, and sunbathing does not require words. I know also that I am very visual, and visual contact of monstrance or stained glass window helps my prayer.

What I would want most of all from a Catherine of Genoa or a Teresa of Avila would be a God within that was more than my uncomfortable self. Teresa somewhere complains about that, and what she hears back is that she should think about God and let God worry about Teresa.

The letter of John says that God is greater than our hearts.

Modern Classicism

A review of a new edition of the works of Bernard Lonergan. From seminary days Lonergan has been nothing but a name. I was aware that friends sent off to Rome for studies knew him from the Gregorian University. I only know that his work is theological method. The review describes his "analysis of the transition in Catholic thought from a classicist mentality to historical consciousness."

I wish I did know Lonergan. I feel forever stuck in a classicist outlook. That coherent world of natural law and logic and metaphysics. Most often I am quite unable to be a modern man and am instead *modo minore,* among the last of the Renaissance men. Still familiar with Greek, able enough in Latin so that often the impulse to use a Latin rather than an English phrase from, say, sacred scripture. All the while I know that Latin has no more scholarly value for scripture study than do modern English translations. The critical Greek texts available to contemporary scholars by the new historical tools are probably superior to the texts St. Jerome had to work with in preparing the Latin Vulgate.

I felt very close to Pope John Paul II as he is described by a Fordham Jesuit who says that reading the Pope who taught phenomenology is like "wandering around in phenomenological fog but bumping into scholastic steel."

When I learn that hearings for a new Supreme Court justice want no one with a natural law legal philosophy, I again feel medieval. I know the modern consensus is that we do not want or need theories that presume to understand the nature of things because there is no real understanding. We are interested in working hypotheses, arrangements that help us to manage things.

Even when I want to read classical works on prayer, like that tiny volume of Jacques Maritain, *Prayer and Intelligence,* I read instead Thomas Keating, who maintains that only the psychological explanation of prayer speaks to our times. He talks about getting "out of our heads."

I imagine that Lonergan means something like that with his "conversion" as foundational to theology or the "turn to interiority" that the review describes as essential to his method.

The review continues: "Lonergan saw clearly that this journey demands the complete rethinking of everything. Yet in a manner that preserves a continuity with the genuine achievements of the tradition and that enables one to judge precisely what those genuine achievements are."

A mouthful if ever there was one. How does one place oneself in the breech between classicism and historical consciousness and "judge precisely?" I know that is what scholars like ethicist Charles Curran want to do, insisting all the while that his work is a searching, modest effort.

I suppose that is also the work of, say, Hans Küng, although modest is hardly the word for those promethean-like volumes with their immense titles.

Did Lonergan mean significantly more than Pascal, who is often called the first Modern? The Pascal who was saint as well as scholar and said that the heart has reasons unknown to the mind? Is that what "turn to interiority" as crucial for understanding means?

Perhaps John Henry Newman was Modern in the sense of Lonergan. It seems that Newman was less interested in metaphysics than in history. And his own arrival at full Catholic faith was by patiently turning the pages of the early Church Fathers to discover their truth by way of these truths commending themselves.

No one page or one Father gives a final answer like a scholastic syllogism. Accumulatively they show a direction that can be discerned and followed. The intellectual patience and integrity required for such pursuit seems almost impossible in our time. The unspoken or quite spoken consensus is: how can we know enough about anything to believe all that?

Many just stand off, detached, and think that because they are not overwhelmed by the truth of something, they have no responsibility to the demands of that truth. That friend of mine who is a teacher of theology and who challenges me, saying: how can you pray when we do not know clearly what it means to pray? All I can answer is that if I wait for full understanding, I will never pray. I pray because Christ prayed and told us to pray. After all, praying is an act of faith, and I guess Lonergan with Pascal and Keating would say that praying is as much an affair of the heart as the head.

One very modern image of the method of John Henry Newman and truth commending itself page upon page might be that of Sigmund Freud. His premise, that in the welter of human emotion the thin thread of reason could be discerned and followed.

Well, I do not know if all this is the historical consciousness of Lonergan or not. It took me two years to get around to a second, more careful reading of the 1991 review of what will be 22 volumes of Lonergan. At 61, I have no more patience or intellectual energy than the many friends who do not have even the confidence that the effort would be worthwhile. If I take two years to read the review, I presume I am not going to read much Lonergan.

But I could read some Lonergan. At least find out what the passage from classicism to historical consciousness means.

Teaching Servanthood

The *New York Times* has a front page article on the cost of a fancy college. The fancy college featured is closeby and has Quaker origins and might be the finest small college in the country.

Once I filled in for the Catholic chaplain for Sunday Mass and, as always, I was overwhelmed by the elegance of campus and buildings and wondered whether the students had any idea of the privileges in which they live. All of them seemed courteous and sensitive, and the impression is that the school makes a real effort to educate them so.

The beautiful people in their growing years. Some would say that being beautiful and courteous and sensitive is not difficult when life is so pleasant.

Anyhow. The point of the newspaper article is that the cost of education for a student there is $40,000 yearly. Parents pay $28,000, more or less; the school covers the deficit with an endowment that is over $400 million. Many students even have partial scholarships, and the endowment covers that as well. A $400-million trust for a school of perhaps 1500 students.

The idea is that the excellence such a school can afford turns out a student alive and aware enough to help change things or whatever it is we expect of education.

My fear is that the culture is so absorbing, the affluence and financial security so demanding that however excellent the finished student, he or she is absorbed into the culture. Vacation homes and expensive automobiles and saving a bundle to educate their own children. A project that promises to be more expensive still when that time comes.

Of course, service projects abound. But I am mindful of an African American woman in the neighborhood who, gently enough, called the Service Corps: "just visitors." A ghetto or Third World experience before getting on with their lives, which lives are elaborately defined by the culture of affluence.

I have no answers to all this. Something very inevitable about getting on with life, having a nice home and giving the next generation all the same advantages and then some.

One could argue that the Incarnation suggests other possibilities: "Let this mind be in you that was in Christ Jesus our Lord, though He was God He did not think His divinity something to cling to. Rather He emptied Himself, taking the form of a servant" (Phil. 2:5-7).

I guess that is what the Church had and still has in mind by the religious life as an ideal. I guess that is the idea of celibacy at its best. We know how popular those choices are today. Almost non-existent.

Dorothy Day thought lay people could do as well. Yet not many, for she knew that Catholic Worker community life and marriage did not often mix.

But I am wandering from point to point. The obligation we all have to make the world as gracious a place as the Swarthmore campus is not the responsibility of a few who choose "the better part," while the rest of us go off to dreadful normalcy.

Answers do not come easily. A huge anti-graffiti mural in my neighborhood and near a huge, rough public school has an image of Malcolm X, with a quote about education being the "way out" for African American people.

But Ivan Illich says that education is so structured that the economic benefit comes only from a 16-or-more year immersion unavailable to those who need it most. Few children from my neighborhood schools could do Swarthmore. Almost none, because all the schooling that goes before is inadequate. And the idea neglects the importance of home life for such achievement.

Yet the myth prevails despite Illich. Nowhere have I seen any serious critiques of his ideas. The myth prevails that educating a privileged elite will turn things around or that somehow the disadvantaged can make their way to these places in significant numbers.

Or perhaps the myth is only in my head. Foundations give $10,000 to some service project, and the next decision of the directors is a $100,000 to sensitize private school children about racial issues. When this happens, maybe no one has any illusion that we are doing more than taking care of our own. Helping the beautiful young people to grow into still more beautiful and sensitive grown people.

And when a philanthropist gives $400 million to improve public schools, perhaps most of this going for faculty enhancement – more travel and degrees for teachers – is inevitable. The absolute priority of money in the culture, a priority education enhances by costing so much.

Somehow the Gospel does not want us to see problems so much in terms of money and earning power. Education as a commodity one buys to increase earning power.

2.

Counting December Days Wanting

. . . An exit like the dawn entrance
down the longest night
through the dim sleeve of New Grange
where before words great
stones wove mute advents
counting December days wanting
the light that paves our passage.
                    —"Winter Solstice"

. . . these Advent evenings
when I light wreath candles
against winter darkness
and search holy books
to feel the spirit of this season
that gathers human yearning
into hope. . .
                    —"Christmas 1980"

. . .A kind of incarnation:
endless sky caught in earth hues
as Christmas brings high heaven
across immense space into humble flesh. . .
                    —"Christmas 1992"

A Heavenward Thrust

A Thanksgiving weekend full of weddings and baptisms. This afternoon I was heading home from the second of the weddings and noticed a restlessness or distraction: the desire not to return immediately to the empty rectory. Instead to visit some friend or other, to share a drink and talk. The afternoon was sunny, but the cold has finally come after a warm and wonderful autumn. I know friends who have a fireplace which adds to the warmth of their home.

I hesitated because the flu I have been fighting for several days needs rest. Tomorrow is Sunday, and after that familiar and demanding Sunday morning of Mass and people wanting a piece of me, I have in the early afternoon still another baptism in the far suburbs. I have been out and around and with people all week and why do I want still more company rather than the solitude which I want to believe I both desire and need?

I did delay the urge by stopping for what will be my one real meal today. The diner and early dinner settled me down. I was more or less content to go home and sleep for an hour. I do have to get a handle on this flu before bronchitis sets in and I am down for a week.

After sleeping, I notice that Advent begins tomorrow and that I might say First Vespers of the First Sunday of Advent. Advent would stir us, renew our desire for further or full "coming of the Lord." A few years ago I wrote an Advent poem about not stirring too easily these years. Something about ritual eventually running out like everything else: "leaving us dry as desert wadis." The desert is an Advent image.

Fair enough the dryness. I can at least pull the chair in my room over to the window and watch the last light on the two trees that are part of my daily prayer image. Now bare, the trees are each a thousand fingers reaching into the night sky, and I see them as images of my thousand different yearnings which, in the quiet, I will try to direct heavenwards. That wonderful quote of John of Saint Thomas which I came upon in *Prayer and Intelligence* by Jacques and Raissa Maritain. The quote says how love can help faith find a way in the darkness:

> Faith attains God in obscurity, remaining as it were at a
> certain distance from him in so far as Faith is belief in that
> which is not seen. But Charity attains God immediately
> in Himself, making an intimate union precisely with that

which is concealed in Faith. And thus, although Faith regulates love and union with God in so far as it proposes the object to the will; nevertheless, in virtue of the union by which love adheres immediately to God, the intelligence is moved by the affective experience of the soul to judge of divine things in a higher fashion than belongs to the obscurity of Faith as such, because it *penetrates* the things of Faith and knows that *there is more hidden there* than Faith itself can manifest. It finds more to love and savour in love, and it is precisely by means of this hidden plus-value discovered by love that it judges divine things in a higher manner, under a special influence of the Holy Spirit.

John of the Cross, a contemporary of John of Saint Thomas, would say it differently. John of the Cross would say that Love helps the lover to find the beloved even in a dark room.

No sooner am I at the window than the phone rings, and I notice that I welcome the intrusion. Perhaps a friend who will after all deliver me from this dark searching. Only a wrong number.

I return to the window to consider that the image of my directing my thousand impulses heavenwards like the thousand fingers of the two bare trees is not enough. The center of my being can still be very adrift, and if I do somehow direct that center heavenward, I might be playing rather than praying. I look further down on the trees, the trunk as it were. Does that substantial being of the tree have a heavenward thrust that enables the fingers of branches to reach that way as well?

Living Symbols

An infant baptism in a distant church. A quiet Sunday afternoon with the church open and everything laid out for me: water and oils, candle and baptismal robe and book.

I am aware of how lean the sacramental signs are. Anything I might say after the brief scripture reading to tell the grace or meaning of Baptism seems poor and inadequate. Clothing the child in a generous and full baptismal robe helps: the child "putting on Christ," as Saint Paul says. Or the wedding garment for the nuptial feast, as mentioned in the gospel parable.

"Sister Water . . . useful, humble, precious, chaste," according to St. Francis is, of course, the main sign of Baptism. Wonder that water is, yet it seems a lean sign, especially when Baptism is celebrated in an almost empty church as we did today: no music, no participating community, restless children running through the church aisles.

And yet when Christ had to speak to the woman at the well about himself and divine grace, the only sign at hand was water: "Woman, if you knew who was asking you for a drink, you would ask me for living water."

The truth is that our human words and signs are all we have. The human condition I need learn is that the highly inadequate situation today of empty church and restless children and poor signs is all we have. As Saint Paul says: "We hold this treasure in clay pots." The need then not to be apathetic or flat with the words and the baptismal ritual but regard every word or anointing as crucial and precious. Squeeze every nuance or meaning out to express as well as we can the mystery of divine grace.

Imposing Order on Chaos

Yesterday a morning newspaper caught my eye with photos of Sylvia Plath and Anne Sexton. The accompanying article previews a medical study coming out next year which correlates poetry and all creative writing with mental illness. The physician and author says: "Writing is an effort to impose order on chaos."

Even with a few poems here and there and the book out and around, I can hardly call myself a poet or writer. Graham Greene, speaking about himself, says that a writer is someone more a spectator than a participant in the human parade. At 61 I am definitely a participant. An old man in the neighborhood had no trouble calling me at seven o'clock in the morning on Thanksgiving Day to say he was out of fuel oil and could I do something about that.

Yet I can accept the idea that what writing I do is "an effort to impose order on chaos." Those centenary biographies of Gerard Manley Hopkins suggest that his last years in Dublin were chaotic and out of control. The terrible sonnets seem transparent distillations of that anguish. Verbal tears of his grief. Their beauty seems to redeem that dark human space. I wonder whether there was any comfort in them for him? I suspect there was.

The newspaper article suggests that "the same traumas that leave a painful legacy of mental illness can also give the gift of artistic vision."

For several weeks now I know the need to give verbal expression to that experience of the death of Theresa at 27 leaving two small children behind.

Theresa was a friend from 20 years ago when I was at another parish in a desolate neighborhood not far from here. I remember looking out the rectory window summer and winter to see little Theresa and her brothers and sisters in our schoolyard or just there in the streets day and night. Little birds always in danger of being done in by those terrible streets.

For some reason or other, Theresa died, and the family found me across town, and celebrated the Mass of Christian Burial in the distant church that is now their parish with the recent closing of the parish on their street. In the chaos of neighborhoods and lives, I was surprised that they found their way there. No doubt the funeral director assisted them.

At church that morning a gathering of perhaps 200 people most of whom I have not seen in years. I was dismayed to notice how hard the years have been on them. Beat-up looking because these neighborhoods beat you up.

Some confusion over Mass time. Resident pastor and I waiting at the door of a crowded church to hear that last night the "time was changed."

Later at a nearby cemetery the trees had a lingering October beauty. Look up and there the beauty of the world. Look down and there Theresa in a box over a yawning dark hole with the father of her young children restraining them from too morbid an exploration of casket and grave.

Many of Theresa's brothers and sisters have small children as well. The scene around the grave is chaotic: people crying and people in stunned silence and children running around an unfamiliar landscape curious about the various headstones. The sudden drama of one little fellow pulling a poorly cemented gravestone almost onto himself. The scolding by his father is a poor ending to the graveside solemnity.

And there I am in a loud voice reading the promise of the Fourth Gospel: "Do not worry; have faith in God; have faith in me. . . ."

Do not worry! Who is going to care for Theresa's two children? What is going on here?

Up go my eyes to the trees, which remind me of the promise: "See the lilies of the field . . . you are worth more than these." Down go my eyes to the box and dark grave. Belief and dismay going on in me at the same time. Now the comfort of the promises. Now the desolation of this terrible scene. Not just death, we know we must deal with death. But here, the death of a 27-year-old mother whose children are already deprived enough.

The loneliness of that up and down. So I write it down "to impose order on chaos," as the doctor says. To get a handle on what I am experiencing.

More Than Enough

Curious how a phrase or sentence on a page can leap out at me. An article on my friend, Dan Berrigan, which hardly tells me anything I need to know.

Toward the end of the article, the author says about Dan that "although he is deeply opinionated, he sidesteps questions about the Catholic Church." He quotes Dan as saying: "I am ambiguous about it all. I was never part of the big picture, so it does not affect me . . . I am not saying I have sidestepped or ignored the issues, but I am not wasting time being critical or putting it down or analyzing it all. I have work to do and have people to pray with."

In the quite official role of parish priest, I cannot say so easily as Dan that I am not part of the big picture. Yet his words help because up here in these abandoned neighborhoods I am out of the mainstream. The concerns and interests of the diocese are not mine. Yet the Church provides me with the place and the location where parish school and neighborhood and the torrent of human needs coming in by door and telephone is more than enough "work to do." And I have that eastward-facing window of my room where I can pray or watch for the morning sun. And on Sunday we have a good gathering of good people for a Eucharist, which is an adequate expression of that divine mystery given us.

So. No more than Dan Berrigan need I waste time or energy "being critical or putting down." I have work to do and good people to pray with and that is enough. More than enough.

Christian Anarchism

A letter from a friend lamenting the recent national elections. A clear defeat and setback for policies that would sustain or continue liberal social programs that have been in place for 30 years. Despite a good marriage and a manageable life, he suffers from depression, and his letter grasped the political landscape as something that would somewhat legitimize his bleak spirits. I guess we all do that: free-floating feelings in search of some reason.

The political scene is, of course, quite bleak. As though the people who have succeeded in this society want more and more to unload the burden on the poor. Hard to tell whether elected officials lead or follow, whether they sense the times and speak as they must to be elected, or on the other hand are themselves ideologues pulling the people into this mood.

Living in these neighborhoods makes this abandonment hard to believe: people out there are just going to walk away from this decay and think that running wounds are not going to fester and somehow run clear to the suburbs.

One thing that the recent elections did for me was to deliver me further from messianic expectations of politics. Enough of my friends are so secularized, so disaffected from faith and church that conversation is usually about politics: war and peace and racial and social justice and the relief of the poor are seen as political tasks. They talk about national and local elections as a priest or religious might talk about Advent and the full coming of the Prince of Peace.

Commonweal magazine recently had a special anniversary issue, reprinting a 1949 article by Dorothy Day, who did not vote in national elections and was when she died only considering voting in smaller municipal elections.

In the article, Dorothy talks about the corporal and spiritual works of mercy, how we cannot allow "Holy Mother City taking over, Holy Mother State taking the poor to herself, gathering them to her capacious bosom studded with the jewels of taxation of the rich and the poor alike. . . ." She does not accept political action as a substitute for personal responsibility, those corporal and spiritual works of mercy.

And she is aware that this idea of being "our brother and sister's keeper" can be seen as lining up with "Wall Street and private enterprise, and the rich opponents of state control and taxation." She insists instead that the vision is a Christian anarchism:

"We want to decentralize everything and delegate to smaller bodies and groups what can be done far more humanly and responsibly through mutual aid." Dorothy Day was very fond of E.F. Schumacher and his *Small Is Beautiful.*

Ancient Belief

I am enough a modern to be uneasy and even embarrassed by this feast today of the Immaculate Conception of the Blessed Virgin Mary. What is more, I have Mass this evening, and the Mass will require a homily for the 20 or 30 people still keeping the Holy Day.

And these recent days the disorder of the world so heavy on me that I feel the strain of trying to believe anything. Yesterday two hospital visits: a friend suffering a cruel ordeal with cancer and a young woman losing most of a lung to cystic fibrosis that has been with her since childhood. At her bedside I am more comforted by her than she is by me. She talks gently about how her disease is so degenerative that she must leave her career and do something less physical.

Walking the corridors of both hospitals in Roman collar, I feel useless or helpless against the doctors on the elevators with their charts and stethoscopes and talk among themselves of helping people to make the best of the only obvious life we have. Either my mood or the times suggest that they hardly notice me at all, remnant of another perspective which no one really believes anymore.

Such is the mood from which I have the Mass and homily of the Immaculate Conception of the Blessed Virgin Mary.

Just before Mass I grasp my old standby, *The Church's Year of Grace* by Pius Parsch. I notice the English translation is 1962, and I recall how much Advent and the feasts of the Church meant to me back then.

I can at least tell the congregation and myself how old this feast is. The note about the feast first appearing during the sixth or seventh century in the Greek Church is some comfort to me. The feast was a Holy Day by the tenth or eleventh century.

Nice to know the feast so ancient and Eastern. That venerable theological saying, *lex orandi est lex credendi:* how the Church prayed reveals what the faith of the Church was.

Of course, observing a celebration in honor of the Conception of Saint Anne is one thing, saying that Mary was conceived without sin is quite another. Certainly when that doctrine was defined an older and more literal understanding of original sin was the teaching. Hard even to imagine what the doctrine and feast means with a more metaphorical understanding of original sin.

I continue: we do not know what any of these doctrines mean finally. We understand neither Trinity nor Incarnation. Simone Weil says the mysteries are more to be embraced as true by the heart rather than understood by the head. Thus, the Immaculate Conception means something or other about the fullness of grace in Mary from her earliest beginnings. I go on. Taking a cue from Parsch, who reminds me that "all through the Middle Ages the dogmatic foundation of the mystery was contested." That story of Aquinas wondering how an altogether innocent Mary would still be redeemed by Christ, who redeems us all, including Mary. Dun Scotus came up with the idea that to keep her altogether innocent was to save her eminently.

Thus, the things that scholars talked about in the Age of Faith. Hardly a lively discussion these days. Of course, we always come back to the Church. We believe anything at all, including the scriptures, because the Church presents these to us as needing or deserving belief.

The faith of the Church. Next time I am inclined to think that such unmodern doctrine as the Immaculate Conception is some late Roman innovation, I shall remember that a feast with these doctrinal possibilities started as early as the seventh century and elsewhere than the Western Church.

Uncertainty

Third Sunday of Advent. Our annual healing Mass. What am I doing when I lay hands and rub oil on these old folk? What is it I do when I go over to the neighboring hospital and do the same? Healing? What does it mean to ask God to heal when an earthquake can kill 50,000 people? Thus, my homily for a Mass of healing in Advent followed by a Christmas dinner party for these 50 parishioners. We do not know what it means to reach out in healing or how much healing takes place or how well the world will be healed here or only hereafter. But we do believe in healing. We do have

Advent hope. This hope should give us joy for *Gaudete* Sunday. I show them my blooming cactus (a lovely pink, matching my vestments). I say that if a cactus can blossom so lovely in deserts without good soil or water, we can blossom and rejoice in our dry and sandy and aging and ill lives. Let us have hope – for an end to the arms race and for heaven, too – so that we might have joy for Christmas. Joy for life! Rejoice, Emmanuel shall come to you, O Israel!

I fear that I talk too long at Mass. The Irish penchant for loving the sound of my own voice. Something I should work on in the New Year – shorter homilies. Fewer words, more substance. Not hiding emptiness in profusion.

The Christmas story soon to begin in the readings requires some response from head as well as heart. As Gerard Manley Hopkins told his friend, Bridges: "You do not mean by mystery what a Catholic does. You mean an interesting uncertainty. . . . But a Catholic by mystery means an incomprehensible certainty." Faith was not given to us as a way to escape the human condition. Even Kierkegaard's leap in the dark – a jump into some other condition means a return to the place from which one leaped with all the same problems. William Lynch, S.J., in *Images of Faith* helps me more than Kierkegaard: faith as something we human beings do with the limited human faculty of intellect. So we believe as we love, which is to say unevenly, inconstantly, half-heartedly. Not only does faith not deliver us from the human condition, it suffers from our limits, as does love. So half-heartedly and un-evenly and inconstantly, I believe those infancy narratives about barren women becoming pregnant and Magi, and still I am uncertain about what is true and what is midrash. A painful state, one would want belief to be certain. With all respect to Hopkins, uncertainty is the human condition, and we have to accept it.

Christmas Comfort

Christmas midnight Mass and I hope that my homily was worthy of the music. I hope that I gave all the friends who joined our community bread and not stones for homily. The church is glowing with poinsettias and candles and Magi and shepherds all over. A wonderful lovely, old, festive place in the bleak landscape of North Philadelphia. All of us have such a space within if only we can learn to go there – even the young Puerto Rican fellow who earlier on Christmas Eve was looking for a few dollars to take his girl to a "jam." If Christmas Eve means a "jam" to him rather than church, the reason is that consumerism eclipses any other meaning. Poor as he is, five dollars for a dance is as much of a Christmas celebration as he can manage.

Richard Horseley says in *The Liberation of Christmas* that the mythical infancy narratives embarrass biblical scholars so that they have never really dealt with them. Their focus is away from wise men and virgin birth and a new star (as it is from the Gospel miracles also). Thus the Christmas feast fills up with elves and red-nosed reindeer. Horseley suggests the social context of the infancy narratives. Herod as a client-king of Caesar, who could even get away with the slaughter of the Holy Innocents, as client regimes of the United States in Central America can get away with village genocide. I did not assimilate the book well enough for a Christmas homily. Perhaps the people of the parish need some comfort for Christmas as much as any heavy political rap.

Human Emptiness, Divine Glory

Christmas is a mystery of emptiness. The empty womb of a virgin where the Word becomes flesh. Empty stable where the Christ is born because there is no room in the crowded and noisy inn.

Simone Weil was always looking for some laws of the spirit similar to the laws of the physical universe.

> Grace fills empty spaces, but it can only enter where there is a void to receive it, and it is grace itself which makes this void . . . to accept a void in ourselves is supernatural . . . there must be a tearing out, something desperate has to take place, the void must be created. Void: the dark night (*Gravity and Grace*).

Of course, the phrase "dark night" is a reference to St. John of the Cross. *Doctor de la nada.* The Doctor of nothingness.

Part of the emptying must come from my own effort. I still have that seemingly harmless habit of watching an hour of television before falling asleep. Almost an addiction, I fear, so that I search the channels for something even more mindless than the news. A detective story or whatever. Yet what are these violent and sensuous images doing to the emptiness that need be there if the contemplative habit is to grow? "Contemplation generates contemplation," Benedictine Hubert Van Zeller says.

Contemplation. A big word with the danger of pretense in thinking myself a contemplative when here I am at 11:30 p.m. watching a cop show which is going to delay sleep to an hour which will rob me of some morning. I must learn to go off to sleep with a quiet that will make even sleep part of the "mindfulness" that Buddhist monk Thich Nhat Hanh describes. That is my work: to overcome the natural impulse or need to fill any emptiness or void so that grace can enter me as grace entered the womb of the Virgin or the empty cave of Bethlehem.

Such effort may even be necessary for true faith. John of the Cross says that God is more like nothing than our images of Him or Her. Simone Weil says: "Among those in whom the supernatural has not been awakened, the atheists are right, and the believers are wrong." She even suggests that ordinary tribal belief is dangerous: ". . . that is why mysticism is the only source of virtue for humanity. Because when people do not believe there is infinite Mercy behind the curtain of the world or *when they think this Mercy is in front of the curtain,* they become cruel."

The italics are mine. I sense Simone Weil would thus categorize much self-imagery of the Church here in front of the curtain.

Mysticism. If contemplation can in fact be my effort, mysticism is pure gift – that stripping away more than my effort to detox from television.

In the Christmas story Mary, the mystic, receives the Word into her empty womb, and the darkness becomes even greater than her unknowing: "How shall this be since I do not know man?" The greater darkness of Joseph wanting to divorce her and Mary letting the trouble increase and yet keeping trust that the mystery at work in her will work out.

Difficult trying to be empty by turning the television off or being here in the empty house without needing to go somewhere or be with others. More difficult still is that fragile hold on believing.

Such a tenuous grasp. Yet my honest response is to hold onto faith in creation and Christmas and this Church which Romano Guardini called the "cross on which Christ is crucified." The painful experience of how tenuous that grasp is can be grace by bringing me more to prayer. "Lord, I believe. Help you my unbelief."

Something of that paradox of Paul: when I am weak, then I am strong. Or more amply: "I am well content, for Christ's sake, with weakness . . . for when I am weak, then I am strong."

Holding on and not letting go of belief and dragging myself to prayer in order to continue holding on is my true and honest self. Such need and weakness is itself a grace. And besides, such prayer requires a mental effort which in itself is exhausting.

And yet and yet . . . not all exhaustion. Now at Christmas a joy in going to prayer. The wonderful manner in which the chant accommodates the Jewish scriptures to the Christmas mystery: "A child is born to us, a son is given." Of course, the Creator need come and live here, take our flesh. How else could God ask us to suffer such a world of starving children and wars?

"In the beginning was the Word, and the Word was with God, and the Word was God . . . and the Word was made flesh and dwelt among us . . . and we saw His glory" (John 1:1,14).

So at Christmas something other than the emptiness, a glimpse of divine glory.

Beauty Incarnate

Christmas week was a week of funerals. A friend from seminary days lost a three-year ordeal with cancer, and here at the parish we had two funerals for children. A four-year-old child died in a house fire, and a ten-week-old child died of crib death syndrome.

Neither child was baptized, and both families wanted the Mass of Christian Burial anyhow. In these neighborhoods that concern for infant or child baptism hardly exists. Difficult to contain the experience within any traditional understanding of infant baptism, which probably means that narrow or literal theology should expand. Meanwhile, I improvise by changing the Mass prayers (as I read along) to suit this different situation which is the reality of the larger world out there. Even the Fathers of the Church tried to squeeze the children of the Holy Innocents' infancy narrative into Baptism by saying the Innocents were baptized by their own blood.

The funerals were not the only reason these holidays seem so frantic. A parishioner was stabbed and needed a hospital visit, a disabled child just confirmed by the Cardinal here is in intensive care at a nearby children's hospital. Her young mother so devoted and worried.

All I can do with this at Christmas is to say that the marriage of heaven and earth, which is the Incarnation, does not make life clearer or easier. What Christmas does say is that the mystery we call God is with us in all this: Emmanuel – God-with-us, living our life and dying our death and suffering all that we do.

These weeks I have a tape of the Solesmes monks singing the Christmas Night Office, which they end for the Midnight Mass with a solemn singing of the genealogy of Christ which begins the first Gospel. Years ago, Romano Guardini remarked how that tedious list of names reveals how wonderful and full the Incarnation is: Jesus is so human that He has skeletons in His closet. The names Solomon and Uriah recall the adultery and murder when Solomon got a woman pregnant and then put her soldier-husband in the front line of battle to be killed. And the name Ruth, the Moabite woman is there telling how Jesus in His ancestry was not even pure Jew. He was mixed blood, like these beautiful children in the Latino neighborhood here. So poor, so beautiful.

"Painstaking Care"

Two more funerals quick upon the three during Christmas week. I am very aware that the only feeling is mild exhaustion and worry about getting everything in or staying an hour ahead of the game. Sometimes I go for hospital visits thinking that I can do four hospitals around the city in the few afternoon hours before I need return for the daily evening Mass at five o'clock. By now I should know from experience that four means two, with parking and waiting for elevators and waiting outside a hospital room until a nurse or technician is finished his or her bedside chores. Those ten-minute waits are now precious. An opportunity for a brief return to the mindfulness that is prayer. If I can just stand there and wait and let go of the pace and schedule, those moments can be a "return to the center," as in the centering prayer of every morning. Dom Thomas Keating seems to say that the "letting go" is our part: allowing the emptiness which grace can enter.

Some might call the lack of feeling for still another death "burn out." I just do not worry about that anymore. We feel what we feel or do not feel what we do not feel. How can one summon or experience grief five times in two weeks without some affectation?

I want to believe that the important response is not feeling but attention. Simone Weil says that perfect attention is prayer. While burying those two children last week, my feelings were various: wonder at the frantic emotions going on in church, confusion over the significance (or insignificance) of Baptism, the contrast of the lovely church dressed for Christmas and the sad sight of the little infant dressed in white before me in an open casket.

Once I took a priest friend to task for saying that sometimes he just "goes through the motions." His response was very helpful: "Mac, sometimes going through the motions is as much as we can manage."

So. Five funerals in two weeks can surely mean going through the motions. What I can do is give these tasks as much attention as possible. And with that attention, the awareness that the loss and grief of a family is very real. That these mysteries I handle are holy, that these rites of passage are awesome opportunities of grace for people and deserve infinite care. What the great man said about architecture is also here: God is in the details. That care which poet Thomas Kinsella describes bringing to his own work:

> Another storm coming
> Under that copper light
> My papers seem luminous
> And over them I will take
> Even more painstaking care.

Material "Goods"

A belated Christmas call from an old friend from the street. When I was an assistant at a now-closed Catholic church, Toot was always out there, sitting on the church steps and framed by the rectory windows. There were various jobs we would find for him, the several moves from house to project to wherever during and after his marriage to Lena.

Probably 20 years now since that Saturday when I obtained the only station wagon around to haul his family belongings to that high-rise public housing project on Diamond Street which is now an empty shell. I remember sensing some meaning in my being there with him, the only white face in the rush of black people in and out and up and down the ramshackle elevators of that tower. I remember thinking: there is a poem in this or better, a sign or sacrament. I in my person here on a casual task, white, in a world of Black people this once in my own person closing or healing the awful wound of race so ruinous for this city.

Anyhow. Over the years, Toot has stayed in touch. The habit continues of his needing $20 now and then for needs about which I do not ask. He has married again to a woman more stable than himself: homeowner, father again and regularly employed, a car that runs most of the time. What does sadden me is my cynical response to his telephone greeting:

"Hey, Mac, thought I would call to wish you a Happy New Year."
"Toot, you and I know that is not the bottom line.
The bottom line is bucks. Get to the point; what do you want?"

Sad too that I am so accurate with my cynicism. Sad that over so many years the friendship is always around money. I would insist that we are friends; otherwise, how could I presume to talk to him thus?

Next day he is at the door at nine a.m., as instructed, to catch me before I am out the door. Our exchange is brief. He would want to sit down, talk about the old days on Diamond Street and where the various fellows are. I am the one in a hurry. I am the one distracted by the bottom-line dollars' dimension. And I pass his new neighborhood uptown as often as he passes here, and I do not stop to visit either. Perhaps our friendship is a metaphor for everything in this brave new world. Everything is about money.

Philosophical Questions

I notice my interest in still another book. The last thing I need is another book. Between my purchases and gifts from friends, my rooms swim in books.

This most recent interest is a book in the Oxford University Press catalogue. Something about God and the philosophers. How some modern philosophers maintain religious belief or faith despite the secular and empirical tone of their discipline. I guess I must say that the God question haunts me. Indeed the question should haunt a priest. Especially haunting, I suspect, because throughout those seminary years so long ago, I was far more interested in philosophy and philosophical theology than, say, biblical studies. That might derive from the quality of biblical studies in those years. Catholic thought was only beginning to allow modern biblical scholarship into our classrooms. I can even remember presentations of how the seven-day creation story was compatible with evolutionary eons because of the vague meaning of the word, "day." Even then the discussion sounded absurd.

Scholastic thought, for all its flaws, was another story. I could recognize and admire the intellectual precision of Aristotle or Aquinas.

This morning looking at a sullen winter dawn from my window, I was aware of the indifference of the heavens to this Christmas season. Listening on tape to the wonderful chant Offices of the Solesmes monks, I am aware of how this prayer heart of the Church constantly calls Christmas a marriage of heaven and earth.

Yet nothing in that winter sky intimates that marriage, despite my wanting to find the divine mystery revealed in the beauty of the world. I know the cosmos or creation or whatever it is remains for me a closed system. I experience all that as indifference as much as beauty. Especially this Christmas season with funerals for two children. The indifference rules strongly.

So. I notice that I believe more or less because of Christ rather than the beauty of dawn. Somehow this man promises and reassures: "Do not let your hearts be troubled . . . I am going to prepare a place for you. . . ."

Years ago there was that Death-of-God theology. Almost irreverently: there is no God, but Jesus is His son. The scholars said the method was not acceptable. We cannot use the Christ to avoid the more epistemological and fundamental question of God.

Yet two days after Christmas the feast of the apostle John arrives with that Mass reading from the beginning of the Letter of John: "This is what we proclaim to you . . . what we have seen with our eyes, what we have touched with our hands."

So. Not philosophical theology after all. Rather faith in a person who is Himself a mystery. The older Aquinas wanted to burn his *Summa* because of the divine mystery he was meeting in prayer.

3.

Winter Returns with Nightfall

Winter returns with nightfall as
a raw wind chills our thin huddle
streetlamps and blazing downtown towers
shadow my going on about this New Light
faith signs drowning in these later years

Yet faith ever a lean grasp
we see obscurely as in a dark mirror
the night itself a shade of fiercer times
Patrick on dark Slane with a fire . . .
                    —"Untitled"

a ripe sun
failing from dawn to warm a winter day
reddens with anger   flattens
breaks on the western rim
burns in a thousand windows
like slack from a failing fire

an incendiary evening
ends as orange softens into amber
in light-laced snow-snug houses set
in trees now ink lines on rice paper . . .
                    —"Christmas 1986"

Broken Utopia

Feast of Saint John Neumann. A little man from Bohemia who was fourth bishop of Philadelphia and is buried in the crypt church of our neighboring parish. When I sit by my window waiting for dawn, the sun rises these winter mornings just beside the tall steeple of that church which is in the care of the Redemptorist Fathers and Brothers and was once the German ethnic parish for this neighborhood.

The Redemptorist church is largely Latino, while over here, only six blocks away, no Latinos, all African Americans.

The streets between us are ruinous. From my window I can see abandoned factories, one after another, all the way over to the Port Richmond neighborhood. These streets tell the story of Philadelphia. For a long time this Quaker utopia with the wonderful name was the largest English-speaking city in the world after London.

Then New York City with the Erie Canal or whatever took over, and Philadelphia became somewhat backwater. With ingenuity the Quakers made Philadelphia into a pioneer of the Industrial Revolution in the manner, say, of Belfast.

Thus these neighborhoods which I view eastward from my window: fabric and carpet mills, Stetson Hats, and the huge empty building, to which the sun will return next month rising through a hundred windows, was a leather and chamois factory making the hatbands for Stetson. And each of these factories surrounded by a cluster of those Philadelphia rowhouses called "Father, Son, and Holy Ghost" houses because they were little more than three single rooms one on top of another. The Irish immigrants who were Saint Malachy parish worked those factories. Germans and Eastern Europeans as well, each ethnic group having its own church and school. I imagine life was very hard, and hard drinking was one way of coping with a large family in a three or four-room house. I imagine also that working conditions were terrible in those factories, and the laborers died before their time.

Apparently the little Bohemian bishop was quite connected to all that suffering. They say he tried to learn the various languages, even Irish as spoken by the coal miners in the anthracite regions of his diocese where my mother was born. Recently I saw a letter of his to Rome. He was asking that his diocese of Philadelphia be divided and he retain the poorer, humbler part of the coal mines.

He probably was aware that he lacked an aristocratic appearance
since he was only four-foot-eleven inches and probably spoke broken English. Difficult to figure how he got the job at all with his
size and foreign accent and belonging to a religious congregation
when those jobs in this part of the world went to diocesan priests
of Irish origins. Wanting the job or not, he must have had friends
in high places. He died with his boots on right here in the neighborhood on his way to mail a chalice or something to a church in
the coal regions.

Around here his Philadelphia is still a story of poor, broken
people. No longer Germans and Irish but Latinos and African
Americans. And with the demise of manufacturing in this part of
the world, its removal to Asia or the sunbelt, I cannot on my best
days imagine what the economic future of this city might be. Politicians are eager for riverboat gambling on the Delaware. I can
understand the lure of more taxes, but what a dead-end gambling
has been for Atlantic City.

What they want the taxes for is not encouraging either. They
talk about more police. At a traffic light last month, I noticed a
police car beside me. More closely, I noticed not city police but
housing authority police. I began thinking how many different
police we have: public school police and transit police and university police and so on. What does this say about this society or this
utopian Quaker experiment?

Stirring the Pot

New York City. The occasional pilgrimage to the Big Apple. The
walk up Fifth Avenue with the store windows still dressed for the
Christmas season is exciting. The energy of the streets, people
walking fast and the dizzying contrast of street people and women
elegantly and exquisitely dressed. The cross streets appear, and
from the cold wind you know that both ends open onto rivers.

Fifth Avenue has a rolling slope, and when from the occasional
rise we could see the teeming crowd farther up toward Rockefeller
Center and Saint Patrick Cathedral, I turned to my companion and
said: "Look at this unbelievable crowd. How about our hairs being
numbered and the Divine Mystery loving each of us as though he
or she was the only one here." My friend answered. "How in the
world did we ever come up with an idea like that?" The modern

experience surely stretches our imagination. So much so that many people just put the traditional religious images aside as imponderable.

The New York visit ended in the inevitable Broadway play: *Miss Saigon.* A brutal version of *Madame Butterfly.* Brutal with American marines and Saigon brothels. I expect little or nothing from Broadway or Hollywood which makes me even more uneasy with the incredible expense of the tickets even with the 50% same-day reduction at the Times Square ticket booth.

Yet I was curious at the memories which the Vietnam years stirred in me. Sitting there, I was feeling again all those protests and rallies and draft board raids. How the unofficial Catholic resistance was so heroic against the silence of the official Church. What a baptism or something those years were for me. Certain that the war was wrong and appalled at how the American Catholic Church could ignore the tumult in the streets, I never fully recovered from that disillusionment.

A few years ago I was involved with some younger priests in an important ecumenical social effort. After several years of effort, the heavy hand of authority told us that we must withdraw. I left the meeting half-expecting the decision, more noticing the shaking reaction of the younger priests. Their first experience of the impervious Church, and they were almost unbelieving that it was happening. All I knew was that they were younger and had not been around for the Civil Rights marches or the antiwar years.

I remember the very first New Year's Day Peace Mass which Paul VI required worldwide. It was to be an annual event, but I heard nothing about it this year. Perhaps the ongoing confusion about New Year's Day and the Feast of the Circumcision becoming Octave Day of Christmas and feast of Mary, Mother of God.

Anyhow, that first New Year Peace Mass I was an assistant at the Cathedral and remember the hasty meeting of officials to understand and comply with the papal mandate for a Peace Mass. I believe Vietnam was burning from U.S. napalm, and any Mass for peace was hard to pull off without some seeming criticism of United States policy.

At the Cathedral I had some vague acceptance as a fellow interested in liturgical renewal, and at the meeting I seized at the opportunity to prepare the Intercessions, the still-new prayers for current needs which had been restored to the Mass with the reforms of Vatican II.

My offer to prepare the Intercessions was almost frantic because as the meeting progressed, I saw a disaster in the making. The congregation would be constructed from Catholic War Veterans and such, which meant that a Peace Mass would be celebrated with honor guards in military dress equipped with guns and swords and flags. The idea was that we had to find a congregation somewhere, and these Catholic groups were more interested in war and peace than any others.

My intention was damage control. I would write the intercessory prayers to say: "For an end to the bombing of Cambodia as the Pope requests, let us pray to the Lord."

When I saw later that someone or other further up the line edited out my intercession, papal pronouncement notwithstanding, I was as shaken as were those young priests coming out of that meeting two years ago. I have not shaken that much since. Nor do I have any illusions about the selective way in which papal social teaching is edited.

The ecumenical dimension of that peace service was something of a disaster also. I tried to invoke Vatican II directives saying that if Protestants and others were invited, the guidelines were that the service should not be exclusive. The planners insisted upon the Mass and a peace service attached to the end to accommodate others "without watering down our faith."

The whole evening was such a confused and ambiguous message about the Vietnam war and interfaith relations as well that some participants other than Catholics felt compromised by being there and wanted to have a counter-observance on the Cathedral steps the following morning. Knowing my sympathies, they wanted me to participate. Nothing came of their plans.

Amazing how a Broadway musical about Vietnam can stir the pot.

The Divine Bridegroom

A fancy wedding at a fancy Catholic church. As fancy as any I have seen in my now many years.

The young priest homilist makes what Father Andrew Greeley says is the essential Catholic reference: the analogy of human love and divine love. I completely agree. Catholic teaching and gospel teaching is that human love is a metaphor for divine love. When people asked Jesus why the disciples of John the Baptist fasted, and his disciples did not, Jesus said that they could not fast so long as he the bridegroom was still with them. The Catholic mystics call God or Christ the Divine Bridegroom also. Indeed, John of the Cross never breaks the metaphor. Never once do his poems use the word God. They could easily be Spanish Romantic ballads.

Listening to the homilist and this fancy New Year's Eve black tie wedding, I could only admire his effort at metaphor and analogy. My honest thought was: Well, Father, you and I need to do this. We need to see human love as some ecstatic fragment of the divine love in which we all live like fish in water.

But that attractive young couple seated behind the prie dieu can enjoy but not need that reference. If their love has that transcendent significance, well and good. If not, they can live with that as well. The bride is beautiful enough, the groom wonderful enough, their fleshly love ecstatic enough to them, even if that love means nothing more than itself.

You and I, young Father, have much invested here. Our entire vocations are built on the premise that human love is a fragmentary experience of the divine. Our whole hope is built on this promise and analogy. We need it to be true.

The Personal Connection

Word had come that Blanche was in the hospital, but before I managed a visit she was home.

Home is a neighborhood across town where her parish is now closed. I know Blanche from my six years there more than 15 years ago. Her husband was then living, a handsome man who would frequent a bar close by the church. When I was walking past, he would wave me in to a barstool beside him. The bar was a tough place, and in the image of rough bars from old cowboy movies, this old merchant seaman who had been all over the world would say that our backs were to the wall if any gunfighting started.

Well, merchant seaman husband is deceased, and Blanche is alone in the house, sent home from the hospital to die. Her sister who called me lives on the same street and is with Blanche all day. At night the sister returns to her own house and husband. A hospice service will begin visits, and I arrive cautious and weary, yet pleased that across 15 years and 30 city blocks they remember me and want me to be part of the illness and care.

I am cautious and weary because I know they are probably adrift with their parish closing. Their new parish is a considerable distance, another neighborhood and fairly inaccessible except by public transportation. Blanche does not have the strength to stand up, much less step up onto a bus and then wait on some cold corner for still another bus.

My questions to myself as I drive across to her neighborhood: should I call their new pastor and drop the matter in his lap? He must be still overwhelmed by this new extended parish of his. Besides, I have the personal connection. An old friend who once came to her home every Christmas morning for a festive breakfast, which was a family tradition and included the sister down the street and her family.

The personal connection is a consideration that is important. How can you discover the final illness of an old friend and refer her to someone else?

Yet the step of taking on still another person needing care seems almost madness. I am thinking of a week of five funerals and people to see in four different hospitals spread around the city. Blanche was a hospital visit that I never made, and here she is at home dying, and her sister has to call me a second time.

I am also cautious and weary because I do not know until I arrive what they want from me. Getting people with modest incomes into nursing homes is almost impossible. And no, I do not know anybody who is available to care for the patient every day.

During my visit and return, I am quite ashamed at my caution and hesitation. They were so happy to see me, so grateful for my concern, so proud that "their priest" came with the sacraments of the sick. I am glad that I brought along the holy oils and the Blessed Sacrament. That was all they wanted from me, with the assurance that I would come soon again. The liturgy for the sick in Catholic worship is lovely. I am glad that we have these signs and words and that I need do little more than bring them and administer them without hurry or routine.

Wondering whether they were going to ask me the impossible tasks of finding caregivers and nursing homes is an occupational hazard. Perhaps those requests will come yet as Blanche becomes more ill.

Coheirs

The Solemnity of the Epiphany and the Sunday this year for my annual begging trip to our suburban parish. Easier the begging by letter than this eye-to-eye. I try to soften the directness by being faithful to the liturgy. Reading the Gospel at all the Masses, I shall do a homily which is first and foremost some extension of the Gospel. The begging or money will have to take care of itself, which in fact happens. These folks are very generous year-round. And Christmas and Epiphany are expressions of divine generosity: "God so loved the world . . . ."

Driving into the parish property, I notice that one of the Magi in the outdoor creche is, of course, the black man. Something for a starter. The black wise man is almost universal in Christian art from the beginning. The Europeans saying with Paul in the reading for the feast that the plan is no less than this: "In Christ Jesus the Gentiles are now coheirs with the Jews, members of the same body and sharers of the promise." A mouthful for Paul who called himself "a Jew of the Jews."

An image of our tradition so precious to me. How delighted I was years ago to read that Henri de Lubac called the Catholic Church the final home and destiny of all humanity. He called the human soul "connaturally Catholic." What might sound imperious is the only Catholicism that attracts me.

I perk up when I see that image anywhere. Jewish literary critic, Richard Gilman, noticed that Catholic sensibility years ago after his conversion. In his *Faith, Sex, Mystery: A Memoir* he describes how the women who have a Catholic bookstore in New York City received the news:

> . . . their responses were all low key: quiet smiles, their heads nodding mildly because it was exemplary of the way things ought to be. I was to come upon this attitude again and again: if everything was as it should be in the human world, such Catholics seemed to imply, then everyone would belong to the Church: Protestants, Jews, pagans, infidels and the dreamers of humanism. But of course they knew as I did that everything wasn't right, most certainly Catholics themselves (138-9).

Or the young California couple who in the 60s came to Philadelphia looking for all the world like flower children. They attended daily Mass at the church near the University of Pennsylvania where I was working.

The young woman said the Church was like the Shakespearean comedy, *The Taming of the Shrew,* farcical on one level and serious on a deeper level. The Church was a divine comedy in the then recent visit of Pope Paul VI to the United Nations. Those famous words of his: "Let the weapons fall from your hands . . . no more war, war never again" to hard-nosed political leaders completely attached to their nationalism or ideology. Who else has the station to speak the truth of human brotherhood and sisterhood of the reading: "In Christ Jesus the Gentiles are now coheirs with the Jews, members of the same body?" A truth which makes nationalism almost unimportant.

Or Eva, the strong black woman of that same neighborhood who gradually had her whole family in church and parish school. I asked a friend: "Do you think Eva has thought much about all this Catholic doctrine?" He answered: "Isn't her reason for joining the only sensible one – that she finds the parish an island of grace and good sense and courtesy in the otherwise tumultuous and even dangerous city? Isn't all the doctrine, however true, reflection after the fact?"

I did not go on as I can about Kenneth Clark and his *Civilisation* and his going on about the grace and courtesy of small Italian Renaissance enclaves, which he regarded as the outcome of the Catholic faith.

I did mention how the Catholic Church joining the flight from the city and the sale of churches to evangelicals might be a letting go of that de Lubac image of Catholic Church as human destiny for all peoples.

I mentioned also my experience of my own limitations to preach in a Martin Luther King, Jr. manner desirable to many African Americans.

But there is the school: 220 children and only 20 Catholic. An opportunity to create an enclave of grace and courtesy in the tumultuous city, not unlike the city state of Urbino so dear to Kenneth Clark. Necessary to keep the tuition low, however, absorb more than a thousand-dollar deficit per student by way of the parish. I thanked the people of the sister parish for making this possible, helping us to stay in the midst of that public housing all around us.

And in the spirit of the Epiphany not to have a higher tuition for those not Catholic. The message of the feast is that Jews and

Gentiles, blacks and whites "are coheirs," members of the same body, all equally welcome as the black wise man with the others. There in suburbia I was even able to read from *Soul on Ice,* a famous 60s book by Black Panther Eldridge Cleaver. He said that once in a California prison which required chapel attendance, he became a Catholic: "I chose the Catholic Church because all the Negroes and Mexicans went there."

The Habit of Prayer

This seashore house has a room which reminds me of an Edward Hopper painting or a Richard Neutra space. The walls are white, very little furniture, full-length sliding glass doors and bubble roof openings so that the daylight is always coming in. An abstract impression so that the eyes turn easily toward ocean, inlet and bay which are visible on three sides.

The beach is only an hour from the city, but such a different world, especially in winter. The divine mystery is not unlike this ocean, so close to us and always there, working at the beach even when we are not aware of that constant presence.

And prayer. The effort to become aware, more or less habitually, that we live in that presence. The old and learned word for virtue is *habitus* or habit. The habit of prayer. That our sense of God would be as close to us, say, as the skill of driving a car. Someone whom our senses go to easily and often.

And so life becomes not so much effortful strivings to be good or devout as living close to the Source so that the divine goodness is never far, always flowing into us because of closeness or intimacy.

Teresa of Avila said somewhere that complaining to "His Excellency" about her faults, she heard back the advice: "Teresa, you think about me; let me worry about Teresa."

Simone Weil had the same insight. We do not strive for virtue and thus make our lives good. Rather we live close to the truth that is beautiful and that closeness will overflow into goodness. A method just the opposite of striving. The indirect method. Not unlike going to that sister parish and talking about the privilege and beauty of doing the Catholic tradition in the midst of public housing projects. If I tell it well, the matter of money does not need a mention. It takes care of itself.

Distance

Tired of my canned soups and pasta here at the seashore house, I walk the half-mile to the local bar restaurant. Last night I had a hamburger at the bar. Tonight after a few beers I will ask whether they have pasta.

The place is almost hillbilly, although only an hour out of Philadelphia. Half of the autos parked in the lot are not cars but pickup trucks. At the bar I am comfortable keeping my watchcap on because half the fellows there have on baseball caps. The women all look as though they could be country singers if their voices could match their boots and bluejeans and sweatshirts. At the bar beer is the popular drink, I notice.

Four televisions – or five – are placed so that a screen is visible from anywhere at the horseshoe bar. Amazing how many people are here at six o'clock in the evening, since these streets and beaches seem so empty during the day hours. The inn is as lighted as a lighthouse, and I guess this bar is a watering hole for the year-rounders. Most of the people at the bar are young people.

Three or four different things happening on the television screens. A pool game going on under a lamp that reads: "Budweiser Light." Young guys come and flirt with the waitresses. The balding bartender seems to know everybody. I feel like the only outsider here.

An electronic screen advertises that gadgets are available at the fireplace to play some video game on two of the screens. People seem to know their way around this high-tech world, fetch these modules, extend an aerial and play the quiz shows available on the two screens. The other two screens have evening news and some cable program that promises to become more exciting later in the evening.

People watch the screens and have conversation with their bar partner at the same time.

The problems of the city or Bosnia or Haiti seems so distant. People are more or less into themselves. The news on the screen is whether rain or snow or neither will arrive tomorrow and when the tides are high or low. I imagine this scene is repeated a million times around the country from this place to Rhode Island to bars and watering holes near Houston and Los Angeles. I am even beyond wondering how some serious social or racial or religious message can penetrate this world. I order my beer, then a second

33

beer, then the pasta alfredo. I tip bartender and waitress and walk back in a cold January evening, with the Atlantic City casinos throwing their lights into the low clouds of a clear winter night which apparently allows some clouds over Atlantic City five miles up ocean.

Daily Bread

A woman once a regular at the door disappeared for some years and now surfaces again. Not a clue concerning where she has been. Perhaps in jail, perhaps working some other church or social agency where she is no longer welcome. Yesterday afternoon after her morning visit here, I saw her at a fancy new automobile dealer closer to downtown. I was driving past, and she was at the door talking to a salesman who was listening, if not allowing her entrance.

Other workers here in the house are put off by her assertive manner. Yesterday she would not leave the small entrance foyer. She insisted on waiting for my return or availability or whatever. The foyer has an amber translucent but not quite transparent window looking into the church sacristy, which is connected to the house.

Anyhow. There she is in the foyer, and there I pass into the sacristy with repairmen and boilermen and a maintenance worker. She begins knocking on the window commanding my attention to her. Last time she was here, she murmured something in my ear about needing money for AZT, thus telling me that she is HIV-infected and needs dollars, not food from the pantry or clothes or even carfare.

Well, of course, the AZT need could be as much a hustle as any other. Given the realities of the neighborhood, I should know the protocol of how the medicine is available. I even have a doctor friend at the nearby hospital whose job is dealing with HIV people right off the street.

But time is always the problem, time to learn the procedures, time to deal with this difficult woman who probably does not want to be helped beyond the immediate dollars, time to connect with the doctor friend about how to deal with the woman at the door again after some years.

And time to deal with her in the midst of my concern about boilers and leaking return pipes and thermostats so that we do not inconvenience the parents of 220 school children because the school is cold and we must send the children home.

One could make a whole life out of these chores: boilers and meetings, schoolyard paving and Lenten devotions. Tedious enough, but perhaps easier than dealing with that woman at the door whose assertive manner is such a put-off. Hey, given the miserable conditions of her life, whether HIV or not, how else can she survive except by this aggressive hustle?

Well, all of this by way of noticing how easy for me to turn a deaf ear to the woman pounding on the window for my attention and be about maintenance concerns. Not that I have a clue how to assist someone who wants dollars and nothing further for now. If I give her the dollars, even for the purpose of getting her out of the way, the money will have her back tomorrow. How fortunate to have these clear tasks of maintenance to avoid such an impossible one as responding to the woman. I should have more sympathy for government and Church authority: the scheduled meeting beginning on time with a clear agenda. And after that meeting still another. Years ago a friend noticed how talking about problems and doing something about them soon blend: talking is doing.

Dorothy Day was aware of that tendency. She always claimed that the *Catholic Worker* newsletter or civil disobedience or social vision was not the primary task, rather the spiritual and corporal works of mercy, the daily bread line and soup kitchen.

A Way Unfolding

The feast of Hilary of Poitiers reminds me of John Henry Newman because Hilary was very involved in the Arian controversy. Newman made his way into the Catholic Church by his study of the Arian struggle.

I always imagine Newman in some dark Victorian library, turning the folios of Migne, discovering a way "commending itself." No sudden or dramatic illumination for Newman, only a way unfolding as the pages turn, a way requiring fidelity.

One does not have to see the way clearly, only the next step as the next step is shown, or the way being followed is affirmed by still another page. The first disciples coming to Christ with the question: "Rabbi, where do you live?" The response so lean or spare: "Come and see."

The card reminding folks of the contemplative prayer meeting here tomorrow has some words of St. John of the Cross: "Whoever wishes to be sure of the road he walks must close his/her eyes and walk in the dark." Whenever I read something or other from John of the Cross, I have a strong sense that this medieval man had a modern sensibility. As though he experienced within that emptiness that we experience both within and around us: that absence of God so strong in contemporary literature or film. John seems to say that the Divine Mystery is more present by absence, more like nothing than any of our images. John wanted to walk more by following the Absent One than looking into images that would eventually fail.

Thomas Keating says we must be willing to process all this in the language of psychology more than philosophy. Thus, the image and confidence Freud had for psychoanalysis might be helpful. Freud said that in the welter of human emotion the thin and fragile thread of reason could be discerned and followed to health.

So faith. The way is never completely clear, and we would want greater certainty. The image then of faith is that we proceed very much like a patient going daily for analysis. We hope that our faithfulness, to a way "commending itself" but never grasped completely, will see us through. And the intellectual integrity required to be faithful to every small turn, when those turns can be so costly.

The responsory psalm antiphon at Mass yesterday was: "If today you hear His voice, harden not your hearts." This verse from a psalm which is the invitatory psalm every morning in monasteries. The idea, I guess, that the task every blessed day is to be faithful to all that is given us. A way unfolding daily, "commending itself." Simone Weil says much about this choosing truth rather than Christ, with confidence that the choice would lead her to Christ anyhow. Also her images of attention and will: "to draw back before the object we are pursuing, only an indirect method is effective. We do nothing if we have not first drawn back. By pulling at the bunch, we make all the grapes fall to the ground."

Eternal Procession

These weeks of January until the Feast of the Presentation are still Christmas for us. Christmas is too precious and warm in winter to let go. We keep the tree and creche in church and sing one less Christmas hymn each week.

Listening to the Gregorian Chant recording for Christmas from Solesmes, I notice how wonderful and elegant the sense of Christmas is in the prayer heart of the Church.

For example, the commentaries say that the traditional three Masses of Christmas express the three births of Christ: His birth from all eternity *in sino Patris,* "in the bosom of the Father." What a lovely image. The second and third Mass of Christmas remember His birth in time from Mary and His birth in us by grace.

That midnight Christmas Mass sung by the monks cannot sing enough that mysterious preexisting Word proceeding *ab eterno* from the Father. The Midnight Mass begins: "You are my son; this day I have begotten you, in the beginning, in the day of your power, from the womb before the morning star, I begot you." That "eternal procession," as the old theology called the Mystery, echoes down the Midnight Mass into darkness and silence again.

A mention somewhere about old Walker Percy, the novelist and Catholic convert who was aware of the deconstructionist sensibility of our age. How he told friend, Robert Coles, about a Christmas Mass in 1986: "The Mass was going on . . . the homily standard . . . a not so good choir . . . it hit me: what if it should be the case that the entire cosmos had a Creator and what if he decided for reasons of his own to show up as a little baby, conceived and born under suspicious circumstances? Well, Bob, you can lay it to Alzheimer's or hangover or whatever but – it hit me – I had to pretend I had an allergy attack so I could take out my handkerchief."

The Mystery is not the scale of the cosmos, rather the particular, the smallness and modesty of the Incarnation: "I thank you, Father, what you have hidden from the learned and wise, you have revealed to merest children" (Matthew 11:25).

The Mystery we call God had to come and know this human experience in the flesh. Life can be such a mess – that friend who went to the Orient to adopt a child and said the orphanages so chaotic, so crowded that women do not even ask admission for their child but leave the infant at the door.

Life can be such a mess that we all could be Job shaking our fist at heaven crying: You don't know what it's like down here, what bedlam and suffering!

Aquinas and the calmer theologians were wrong and Duns Scotus was right: the Incarnation had to happen simply, not from some theology of redemption but simply. God had to come here and know the situation, mysteriously even "grow in wisdom and grace" (Luke 2:52).

These weeks I cannot get enough of the monks' chant about Christmas being this marriage of heaven with earth. The Mystery we call God could not make such an earth and then not come here. And the fact that the Incarnation did happen and God came – the difference that makes all the difference. Now I do not have to understand the impenetrable despite that chronic need to try. All I need do is live the mystery because Christ lived it.

Imagination

Martin Luther King, Jr. weekend and the Sunday Gospel is the Marriage Feast of Cana. Jesus turning water into wine.

Years ago a friend gave me her hand-lettered card with a quote from James Joyce about a writer being a priest of the imagination, transforming the ordinary stuff of life by making that stuff radiant. A reference to this gospel story and, of course, the Eucharist of Joyce's Catholic years which he was leaving behind. He would make a religion out of language. No one would succeed more than Joyce.

At Mass I wondered out loud: could we not turn the turn-around of Joyce around again? Can not faith be an act of the imagination more powerful even than literature? William Lynch, S.J., called faith a way of imagining the world, a way of being in the world.

With faith we can transform the ordinary stuff of work or trouble or love or getting old or illness or even dying into a radiant going home to God or knowing here in the love of a spouse the divine love in which we live. Again that quotation of Catherine of Siena which Dorothy Day loved: "All the way to heaven is heaven." Faith can transform even illness and suffering into the "making up in my own body what is wanting in the sufferings of Christ," whatever Saint Paul meant by that.

Martin Luther King, Jr. did that. This very human and apparently flawed preacher took the earthy and gritty stuff of civil rights and by faith and preaching transformed violence-prone injustice into a biblical freedom movement as holy as the Jews coming out of slavery in Egypt. So powerful that film footage of King leading marchers through police dogs and barricades and beatings and firehosings, and then gathering the marchers into those tiny rural Southern churches at night telling them they must return pardon for injury. A miracle like that of Cana. A ministry like that of transforming ordinary stuff like bread and wine into Christ.

Stirring Flames in the Postmodern Soul

New York, New York. Three visits in a month. Another time I would not get there once in three years. I love the town. The energy of the streets. The people all walking so fast.

This time to accompany friend and artist, Bob McGovern and family to an exhibition at the Metropolitan Museum of Art – *Florentine Illuminations.*

Passing from painting to painting, I cannot but notice the postmodernist or deconstructionist sensibility within me as much as anyone else. I do not want to give it a grandiose name, yet neither do I know what else to call it.

Standing beside another viewer, I am as curious about how he is viewing the tempera on panel or parchment as I am interested in the painting itself.

The illuminations are beautiful, and the progression from contemporaries of Giotto to Fra Angelico breathtaking. Toward the end we could see where we had started, and the New York artist friend who had invited us pointed back to the earlier works and noted the development. He remarked how DaVinci or Michelangelo said that in heaven people would look like these creations of Fra Angelico. "Look at the skin," artist Tom McAnulty kept saying, "Look at the skin. How did he achieve that?"

Many other illuminations were by Camaldolese monks in Florence, and across seven centuries the illuminations of the Nativity and Epiphany and the Bible stories were like mirrors reflecting the soul of these monks. I know the Camaldolese life. The order has a monastery in Big Sur, California, which I have visited. The monks are hermits who live in seclusion. Each monk has his own cottage and garden in a circle of cottages around a chapel where they gather for daily Mass.

Otherwise the monk is alone in his cell. The idea being to withdraw, leave behind all concerns that would prevent direct and immediate conversation with God. Knowing this, I see the illuminations more clearly: a sharing in miniature form of the images that filled mind and heart of these men of faith – *solus cum solo* indeed. The illumination becomes almost the image in the back of the eye. The holy image in the deepest soul of the monk artist projected as it were onto a screen of parchment.

Of course, those scenes are from another age: literal renditions of biblical stories and legends. One has Saint Paul with his skin removed in torture and tied around his neck. His spirit hovering over his decapitated body is returning to a woman a veil she lent him to cover his eyes while he was being beheaded. All this torture in images so wondrous in cerulean blue and gold leaf. That beauty overcomes or transcends the gore.

And so my wondering what the viewer beside me thinks of all this. Is he, like me, someone trying to contain all this old wine in the new wine skins of a sensibility afflicted with all the skepticism of modernity?

I recall the same curiosity in me about Kenneth Clark and his *Civilisation:* almost envy that he could survey all this medieval beauty and appreciate it without needing to believe anything about it. But then I saw in the obituaries for Clark brief references to his becoming a Catholic toward the end. Again the curiosity that had me purchase an early biography to explore the matter. The reference was so slight. An Irish priest spoke at the memorial service in London, and someone explained this by saying that Clark had wanted to be received into the Church for a long time and had finally done so. I guess the mirror image of faith in Florentine miniatures can stir flames in postmodern souls. Yet this stirring does not tell me much about the possibly postmodern museum-goer beside me in the Metropolitan. Nor does it define clearly the stew of faith and culture and nostalgia and modernity stirring in my own insides.

Grateful for Reality

Nine o'clock in the evening and I am just sitting down to put pencil to paper for these entries.

The doorbell rings. The A.A. group is in that meeting room off the entrance foyer. Perhaps one of the members delegated to pay the rent the A.A. insists on paying. Self-reliance or paying your way is part of the program.

Or perhaps they are ringing to signal they are leaving. No, from the second-floor window beside this desk, I would see them walking away, down the narrow path between church and small garden.

All signs are that the caller is a street fellow, someone seeing the light on in the meeting room and finding the front door open into the foyer. He will avoid the turn into the meeting room; the A.A. people have little patience with fellows on the make.

I go down and open the door. Dangerous, no doubt. Last spring two parish women admitted a fellow in broad daylight. He wanted to use the phone and ended up grabbing the purse of one and hitting the other across the face with the phone when she went to call for help.

Wisely or otherwise, I open the door, and the face in the shadows is familiar. He has been here before in these off hours. He is expecting some scold or other, and I tell him that I recognize him. He intercepts any scold by being very direct: "Hey, man, I just got out from being arrested, and I am trying to get a few bucks."

Well, I am just in from New York City where I saw *Florentine Illuminations* at the Metropolitan, and here is this fellow walking the cold streets at nine o'clock at night drawn here because the lights are on, because it is a church, because we are supposed to be concerned about needs like his, because he got help here before, because . . . .

I have enough sense not to open my wallet in his sight. Several twenties still there not spent in New York. I close the door and extract the three dollar bills there beside the twenties. I open the door and say: "Here, man, after hours here we need a break . . . ." Whatever scold was forthcoming got lost in my throat. He was grateful for the few miserable dollars given so miserably. I climbed the stairs, annoyed more with myself than with him. If I am going to do the dollars, why not do it graciously? Why the annoyance that starts with a remark and finishes at least in body language?

Down deep I am grateful for this crazy life of mine. In a world filling up with fellows like this, in a neighborhood near what police call "the badlands" and "the ruins," I am glad that I cannot sit down to pursue the life of the mind or the literary life or whatever these musings are without the intrusion of the real world. My early desire to be a worker-priest in the tradition of the French worker-priests during and after World War II. Perhaps this geography and availability is as close as I can come to that in this thoroughly middle-class United States Church which I inhabit. I am glad that woman from the mom and pop store over by the Catholic Worker House called me about the old bachelor living over the bar who died. She and the neighbors are collecting dollars house to house to bury him. I am glad they want my dollars, glad they want my clout (!) in obtaining a free grave from the Catholic cemeteries' office. I will be glad if they want me to say some prayers at the funeral home and accompany him and a few neighbors to the cemetery, where the soil beside the grave will not have the imitation grass carpet hiding the cold earth from mourners because there are no family mourners, and this is an economy job. I am grateful for all this because it is real. Just as I am glad for the intrusion into my writing by that fellow at the door tonight.

Silence

The death toll of the earthquake in Japan is presently 3,000 and thousands more are injured.

Last year I read the novel, *Silence,* by Japanese Catholic writer, Shusaku Endo. His whole presentation of the drama of the terrible persecutions of Christians in 17th-century Japan is expressed in that title, *Silence.* The awful silence of God in the face of human suffering. In the novel you can see the more modern or tentative faith of Endo, just as you can see the mirror image of early Renaissance faith in Florentine miniatures. Simone Weil talks about the terrible scourge of slavery in the Roman Empire and how slaves had to endure their inhuman lives without the slightest help of knowing the Passion of Christ.

So I wonder about Japan and the terrible loss and suffering coming across the television screen. I wonder whether Buddhism helps them to absorb this grief as Christianity might intend. Or whether modern Japan is so postmodern that Buddhism has little influence on lives. I once heard that Christian mission effort in Japan is unsuccessful over centuries because by culture Japanese people need not ask the huge questions which seem the premise for Western religious faith. Questions like what is the meaning of this suffering or what is the meaning of life. If so, then the earthquake does not present the yearning questions which that tragedy presents to me. For them, earthquakes happen. Endo apparently has the stature in Japan that Graham Greene has here, and he is the same tormented believer. Endo once said his Catholic faith was like his Western business suit. Not so comfortable as his kimono but something he wears nevertheless.

Church vs. State

A headline in the morning newspaper reads: "Dismissed Bishop takes part in protest." The location is France, and an activist bishop removed by the Vatican uses his new freedom to do civil disobedience with homeless people at a Paris welfare office..

I know nothing of the larger picture, but the story is not unlike the recent story of Chiapas in Mexico, where rumor is that the Catholic Church wants to remove an activist bishop who sides with the oppressed indigenous people in their sometimes-violent protest. And another news item is that official pressure stopped a lecture of a Peruvian priest at the Gregorian University in Rome. In a letter to the London *Tablet,* a woman expresses her dismay: "I was invited to Peru . . . we were fortunate to meet Fr. Gutierrez. His humility, simplicity and commitment to the poor was profound and inspiring."

The Mexican bishop under threat of removal was nominated for the Nobel Peace Prize. Reading these matters, my mind presumes to see the larger picture.

The Church has just been restored to official status in Mexico after almost 60 years of exile. Diego Rivera has those fierce murals of prelates stuffing their money bags with the pesos of the poor. Of course, there was holiness and even martyrs like Jesuit Miguel Pro. From childhood I remember the story of his crying: "Long live Christ the King" as a firing squad cut him down. A pamphlet I have actually has a picture of Miguel Pro before that firing squad in lay dress because he was secretly a priest. The pamphlet calls him "priest of the workingman."

Well, all of that seems over, and the Church in Mexico even has a papal nuncio or official representative to the Mexican government. What I imagine is that the Mexican government complains to the nuncio about this activist bishop "stirring up the masses" and wants him out. The Church in Rome is anxious to maintain the restoration and not risk whatever privileges might return, privileges which have a long history in Catholic countries, privileges which the Church deems necessary for its mission, privileges like running schools with some government financing.

The case in France might be very different. Yet the image of a bishop doing civil disobedience is so unhistorical that the Church is embarrassed by this confrontation with government. That older European image persists: Church and state arm-in-arm maintaining Christendom. Even a theology might be invoked: that messianic passage from Isaiah about the Anointed One who "proclaims justice" but "whose voice is not heard in the streets." The image of churchman as more or less a public official, someone who upholds public order, who works out of a portfolio.

Crusty old John McKenzie, the awesome biblical scholar questioned this marriage of Church and state in his final book, *The Civilization of Christianity:* "There is a deadly and irreconcilable opposition between Western civilization and Christianity and one of them must destroy the other." McKenzie would probably remind us that Jesus was arrested for inciting a riot and executed as an enemy of the state. The same McKenzie anticipates that some will wonder why he stays in a Church so wedded to Western society. He claims in the preface to this book that the Catholic Church "is the only game in town."

In fairness to another view, Michael Novak says that unlike Protestantism the Catholic Church has an attraction to the possibility of a Christian culture in the mode of the Incarnation. A civilization so enfleshed in Gospel values that goodness is nourished by cultural milieu.

And again Catholic Worker founder, Peter Maurin, wanted "a society in which it would be easier for people to be good." Or Simone Weil. She thought that the utter separation of Church and state is a great tragedy. I am sure that she does not mean that what presently happens in a courtroom should happen with a cross behind the bench blessing injustice often enough.

Brotherly Love

Friday and the workweek can finish in a frenzy. And living and working in the same house is neither easy nor healthy. Kitchen and dining room and foyer and meeting room today were frantic. We have a funeral tomorrow, and the poor elderly widower is looking to us for a "repast" after the burial. Sister Catherine had generous women who help her cooking up a storm.

About three o'clock Dave Hagan stopped by to borrow some-thing, and I asked him to drop me off across town where an older woman is dying. She has been in my mind all week, and I thought I would stop to see her every day. That might be more than I can handle. I was there Wednesday, and I can ask Dave to drop me there, and I can have a good long walk home after bringing her Holy Communion. Thank God for the ritual of the Catholic Church. Prayers and words and signs when you have little or nothing to say yourself. *Ecclesia supplet.* The faith of the Church filling up my poverty. I know ritual can be misused, used as a barrier between me and a person who needs among other things my person, however inadequate. Well, I can try to use the Visitation of the Sick and Holy Communion without hiding behind the rite.

The walk home was a good stretch. Thirty-second Street to Eleventh Street east and another six blocks south. The winter day is very mild, and I notice the dark does not descend until after five o'clock.

The first blocks are some desolate streets, and the old city seems so soiled, so down-at-the-heels that I wonder what recovery can ever be possible. Abandoned houses everywhere, vacant lots full of ruined cars and trucks, paving torn up and huge holes in streets that have not been repaired or even cleaned in years.

Over the tops of the boxlike rowhouses, I can see the down-town towers, lights coming on in the growing darkness. This is very like what we once called a Third World country. The "greene countrie towne" of William Penn and his utopia is surely in trouble.

When I consider the history of Philadelphia as once the second largest English-speaking city in the world until New York took over. We seem too close to New York and Washington to become a regional center like Boston or Seattle or Atlanta. Eclipsed by New York, the Quakers had the ingenuity to make this a manufacturing center, in the manner of Belfast, with carpets and yarns. With the removal of manufacturing from this part of the world, I cannot imagine what economic future this city might have.

Farther on, I walk through the shopping strip so hard hit in 1968 by the riots following the death of Martin Luther King, Jr. I am not wearing a Roman collar, but here and there a wave of recognition. More than 20 years on these streets, I almost presume people looking out from the bars and shops know me. Most do not. Five or six different neighborhoods I am covering. Friday night coming down fast here as well as back at the rectory: people in stores and bars and even the dreary old laundromats.

I cannot absorb all this: the grime of the streets, the children playing in trash, the old toothless men presiding over a corner.

Beyond Nuance

A young couple visit to ask my participation in their marriage next autumn. The wedding will be out-of-state yet not a great distance away. That whole world out there of friends whose care helps this old place to continue. So many of them and so generous. I have been around a long time, and the friendships abound. Sometimes I believe that all that could be a full-time work without the parish. But, of course, there is the parish. Very much the parish. Tomorrow is Sunday, and I have the nine o'clock Mass here and a 10:30 at Sacred Heart in Camden filling for Irishman, Michael Doyle. The more Camden fills up with disposal plants and waste, the more Michael is determined to make lilies grow in the compost. After Camden, back here for an after-Sunday-Mass meeting and then, at 5:30 in the evening the monthly Mass for the Haitian people from around the city.

The young couple wanting assistance with marriage plans reminds me how few marriages I have here. If we measure how much or little Catholic presence is required in these neighborhoods by familiar sacramental needs, very little presence is required. Yet sacramental presence should not be the measure. Even Saint Paul said that he was needed for reasons other than Baptism.

For years I have been uncomfortable with the tasks of marriage preparation beyond gathering the necessary documents and planning the Nuptial Mass with the couple. Ever since that retreat at a small monastery years ago, when a married fellow courteously interrupted the retreat talk of a priest to say that marriage was largely "a matter of nuance," and the unmarried priest did not know what he was talking about. I know there are moral and theological issues beyond nuance, and I do what is required. Yet that memory has me say less rather than more.

Once at a fancy wedding reception, an intoxicated woman came up to me and quite publicly began complaining how her fancy Catholic convent school education had ruined her for sexual intimacy and the rest. When she finished, I told her that I certainly could not defend any religious instruction which she found harmful but that I thought what the Catholic Church was saying beneath all that excess was that sex does not work outside of marriage and that my experience over the years and especially in my neighborhoods is that this is true. I let it go at that.

Catholic Culture

Haitian people from around the city are arriving for their monthly Sunday Mass. A cold evening, and each time the church door opens a draught of Arctic air spins up the aisle to where I sit in the sanctuary waiting and knowing that at some moment Jean Baptiste and Jocelyn will decide that we can begin. Choir and drummer are already in place.

Why am I so comfortable with people whose country I have never visited and whose languages are so unfamiliar, despite my effort to say Mass with them in my schoolboy French?

The only answer coming back at me is Catholic culture. Across race and geography and tongue we share so much, not that my Irish American inheritance is identical with their vibrant Caribbean heritage of drums and dancing.

But deeper than the differences so much in common. That sacramental sense that we are to express our belief and hope by these signs handed down from apostolic times. That the important thing is not what I will say by way of homily after the Gospel. The important matter is the Eucharist which is words, of course, but more than words. The important thing is having newborns brought for Baptism, the grace given by the pouring of water flowing out of what they and I can only call the treasury of the Church. The important thing is bringing a couple to the priest for marriage or the blessing of some merely civil marriage that happened between here and whatever stops in their journey and story from Haiti. Important to have the Church and the Father bless the union. The obscure or subtle awareness that these human loves are fragments of a greater love and that connection must be made or expressed.

Catholic culture has them understand the priesthood as a symbolic office rather than a preaching ministry. They have the Catholic ambivalence about mixing those symbols of faith and politics which is accepted in the religious traditions of African North Americans. Yet they can be resilient and provisional and accept the political role of a priest-president in Haiti because it happened and is best for now, even if not the rule or a permanent situation. And so the Haitians are sad to hear that Church authorities will not allow the exception and insist that the President, whose present term is ending, resign from the priesthood altogether. But they are patient with these quarrels of clerics. It does not interfere with their gathering and wanting the ministry of the Church. Except tonight perhaps, the crowd is very small. The cold might be a reason.

On the other hand, I cannot understand the neglect of these immigrants by the local Church. They have such special religious needs, and so little is done to serve them. The drift to evangelical and pentecostal churches seems considerable. I passed by one such place last evening, and from the number of cars, the crowd seemed large, far larger than the crowd assembled here tonight.

I suspect that the situation of the President is a reason for this official distance. Haitian priests in the United States might be too political about Haiti. A more official local Haitian Catholic Church might develop a strong opinion about all that and even express publicly a support that the official Church in Haiti or in Rome is withholding. All this is, of course, my surmise. Whatever the reason, the pastoral neglect of these immigrants is quite real, and I believe enough in the basic richness of their and my Catholic culture to think that their needs would be better served by their Catholic heritage than by the evangelicals.

Yet the Latinos are also not being adequately served by the local Church, and they too are Catholic in origin. Perhaps poor Latinos and Haitians are just not important in this society which attaches such importance to affluence. Perhaps the Church simply does not have the resources these days to care for the new peoples of these teeming cities of the poor. Certainly these new peoples are not being tended as were the earlier immigrants from Ireland or Germany or Poland. I heard one Church official talk about the needs of "our constituency." As he spoke, his meaning became clearer: constituency meant older Irish and German and Polish people who, in their day, were generous in their support of the Church. Now that they are old and need nursing homes and senior services or whatever, only appropriate that the Church return the care.

I do not begrudge these folks, whom by age I am quickly joining, whatever they need. I suspect that soon the Church will hardly be able to tend them either. In any case, those priorities should not prevent the Church from her essential mission to the poor.

Monday

Monday morning coming down and coming down with a vengeance. I have neglected the routine of disappearing to the seashore late on Sunday afternoon. Only an hour away and the opportunity to sleep in on Monday morning, but I have to plan the break, be resolute, keep the day open weeks in advance before the calendar crowds up. Sometimes a funeral or a meeting necessary for Monday because of the schedules of others. And when I stay around as I have today, the week begins all over again without a respite, because the weekend around here is hardly a respite.

Today I did little more than standby duty in the house basement because when I awoke, the house was suspiciously cold, colder even than I keep my room for sleeping. The boiler was down, and the morning temperature outside below freezing.

At least the cold is not in the school next door, requiring the great inconvenience to working parents of being called at whatever number we have for them to fetch the children from a school too cold to keep them.

A repairman from the gas company arrived at the house and realized the boilers are larger than he handles. After an hour or two he called a supervisor who also appeared.

Nice to think that I could just leave the two workmen there and get on with my work. The dying woman I plan to visit everyday, well almost everyday, lives across town, and the drive over takes time with traffic lights and finding parking on these tiny and crowded Philadelphia streets. And the need to avoid a rush visit to someone who needs more than a rush.

Even leaving the workmen and going upstairs to call the several people who need calls this Monday morning does not work. The men want to know where and how many the thermostats, and who will take responsibility for the cost of an expensive part.

So I more or less stay there with them, surfacing from the basement to take the Monday phone calls. I try to be grateful for this taste of reality. *De profundis clamavi ad te Domine.* "Out of the depths I cry to you, O Lord." Out of a cellar and boiler room. Not that I am praying in any formal sense, just trying to be aware

of where I am and what is going on by listening to the repairman
tell me how things work. Sharing this place and time and concerns
of workingmen who spend their days in cellars worse than this one.

A cure for any dilettantism. Yesterday three times I gave off
from the pulpit about how to do life. Today I do it myself here in
a cellar, trying to let go of other concerns and pay attention to the
man from the gas works telling me how the boiler works. Simone
Weil says that attention is prayer. She thought that the concentration required of studies, especially mathematics, was the same thing
as prayer. I think she who so wanted to be a lowly farm or factory
worker would have encouraged the attention and presence I was
trying to give to boilers rather than being upstairs doing more lofty
things. At least good for me and my growth, if not for the sick
woman wanting Holy Communion and a visit.

And besides Simone Weil, St. Benedict as well. He wanted
the monks to work with their hands as well as their heads. Besides
lectio and the *opus Dei* of choral prayer, *labora:* out there in the
fields cutting grain.

Burying the Dead

Rising this morning, I was mindful enough to put on my Sunday
suit for Anthony Paul Senage, whom we bury today. Senage was a
man in his mid-60s who lived over a bar in the Latino neighborhood
just beyond here. When the bar changed hands, Anthony, as second-floor roomer, was part of the deal.

No family in sight, so the neighbors collected among themselves $800 for funeral expenses, and I have a deed dated 1872 to
a lot in an old Catholic cemetery not far away. Old clothes and
cemetery deeds come this way. The lot still has three spaces, since
the family has moved away to the suburbs and purchased space in
the newer Catholic cemeteries. With a letter from me certifying
need, the Catholic cemeteries' office will provide a free grave
opening, which kindness makes the neighborhood collection go
much further toward expenses.

As I make my way to the funeral home for a brief service, I
notice the downtown towers over the tiny row houses that surround
the abandoned factories. Philadelphia has a new skyline since the
waiving of the gentleman's agreement about building no tower
higher than the hat of William Penn on City Hall. The glass towers

blaze in the morning sun. One imagines the other energy at work there: buying and selling, wheeling and dealing. And here I am off to still another funeral. This must be the tenth in this still-new year. Someone once told me that the French or Germans call the priest "the undertaker's assistant."

But the tradition and Dorothy Day call burying the dead a Corporal Work of Mercy, so the time is well-spent, even if repetitive right now. Who says that the downtown buying and selling is more important than this?

About 20 neighbors gather at the Latino funeral home, and I regret not bringing a Spanish ritual. Again I am mindful of my not being more able in Spanish, just as I am not able enough with the Creole and French of the Haitians. I think of my friend, Father Brian Karvelis, in that teeming Latino neighborhood of Brooklyn, and his learning in the spirit of Charles de Foucauld to speak the languages of his people without the trace of an accent. I excuse myself from that effort because of age or want of opportunity to speak those tongues regularly.

In the casket with Anthony an old army picture of him to show how he looked in better days. World War II vintage, the framed and fading color photograph has the look of an old Jimmy Stewart movie: formal military hat slightly to the side, face looking at you straight on.

After some prayers I read the Gospel of Jesus thanking His Father for revealing "to merest children what is hidden from the wise and clever," and I tell Anthony's friends how important their care of the deceased is, their collection, their coming here, this Corporal Work of Mercy. I apologize for not knowing "Hammer," his nickname on the program which also has that old army photograph.

Just now I am reading the biography or obituary the neighbors assembled for "Hammer." On the spread page of the program this improvised funeral has no "order of services," since the neighbors had no idea how I was going to proceed.

I tell how our faith is "the victory that overcomes the world," as the New Testament letter of John says, when we take care of one another as they are doing now for their neighbor.

The program says how "those forty years the bar was sold many times over, and 'Hammer' was always part of the deal. Anthony came with the bar or no deal. To that respect he was known by everyone in the community and was loved by all." The program was profuse in thanking me and Saint Malachy for "our help."

After the brief service, about six cars left for the cemetery where the Archdiocese gave this borrowed grave all the courtesies of a paid interment. The mound of soil removed to make room for "Hammer" was covered with an imitation grass cover to soften the severe reality of what we were about on a cold, wintry day.

Nothing is Impossible

Feast of the Conversion of Saint Paul. I recall that this is the last day of something called the Church Unity Octave. In my seminary days the week was a big deal with the celebration of a Mass in some Eastern Rite tradition to remind us that other Christian traditions were out there besides our Roman Rite.

Later, after the Vatican II document on Ecumenicism in 1964, the Church Unity Octave was even a bigger deal. The vindication of early ecumenists like the French Dominican, Yves Congar who at 90 and in a Paris hospital for a decade was just made a Cardinal. In 1954, he was forbidden to teach. Probably because his ecumenism was considered a compromise of "the one true Church" image.

An article on Congar by an American Dominican was in a recent issue of the dignified Catholic periodical from London, *The Tablet.* The American tells how he was living in the same Paris residence as Congar in the 70s and asked the great man (Richard McBrien calls Congar "perhaps the most distinguished ecclesiologist of all time") about his origins in Sedan, northeast of Paris and whether any monument existed there remembering where the Franco-Prussian War ended.

Congar told the American that Bismarck planted a memorial tree there which Congar once urinated on, as he also did on the wall of the Holy Office in Rome. And now a Cardinal!

Anyhow. My sense is that the Church Unity Octave gets very little attention in recent years. Here in the United States the Octave is eclipsed by the anniversary of *Roe versus Wade,* and the Cathedral event is not a Mass or service for Christian Unity "that all may be one so that the world might believe" but, as the diocesan newspaper states, the "Annual Crusade for Life Mass" sponsored by the Knights of Columbus.

Abortion is as unacceptable to me as to anyone, yet I draw back from this use of the sacrament of unity as a battle rally. The image that someone must win and someone must lose this struggle. I believe I am consistent in my sacramental theology here. During the Vietnam years I could not share a "protest Mass" at the Pentagon or wherever.

A recent issue of *Commonweal* magazine was much about the Eucharist and had a helpful quotation about the Mass from liturgist Aidan Kavanagh, OSB: "The liturgy becomes perceived by many as less an obedient standing in the alarming presence of the living God in Christ than a tiresome dialectical effort at raising the consciousness of middle-class groups concerning ideologically approved ends and means."

Years ago an older fellow from my parish was entering the seminary with me. Older means that he had been more around than I: Catholic college, United States Navy, Catholic Worker, and various lay groups in the days of Catholic Action.

I noticed in the man an interest in matters unawakened in me: Jewish concerns, conscientious objection, the social gospel, ecumenism. I asked: "What is this, how come?"

The answer back was a mild and subtle philosophical or theological reflection that only convergence, not capitulation or somebody winning and somebody else losing, only convergence was a humane image of human discourse and interaction. Thus that short story of Flannery O'Connor with a title borrowed, I think, from Teilhard de Chardin: "Everything That Rises Must Converge." Rather than a Mass to win the abortion struggle, the Christian Unity Octave. Mass or prayer service should continue as *sacramentum unitatis,* the hope that prayer and a common faith in Christ will take us to heights where the impossible becomes possible, *coincidentia oppositorum.* The coming together of opposites, a unity impossible on the human level becomes possible through Christ. That beloved phrase of the mystics, *coincidentia oppositorum,* means what the angel said to Mary responding to her Annunciation question: "How can this happen? I do not know man." Answer: "Nothing is impossible with God" (Luke 1:34, 37).

Often enough in history the Holy Eucharist has been a poor sign, a countersign. Ivan Illich uses the saying: *corruptio optimi pessima* to say that the mission of the Church is so awesome and fragile that when that work is manhandled, harm can be done rather than the good intended. Church as countersign.

As when in the Cathedral years ago, starched and scrubbed matching seminarians were sent out for that wonderful Holy Thursday of the *mandatum* or washing of the feet. So antiseptic that the sign says nothing or even the wrong thing. The poor people of the Cathedral neighborhood should have their feet washed.

I remember the Mass in the Francis of Assisi film, *Brother Son, Sister Moon.* Zeffirelli has Francis up front with the aristocrats, looking with longing at the beggars and cripples standing in the rear. If the Zeffirelli scene is an accurate portrayal of those days in church, what kind of Eucharist was that? Reinforcing the existing order rather than celebrating a faith which, according to Saint Paul, wants "to overthrow the existing order."

Courtesy

Years ago, either Frenchman Henri Daniel Rops or Frenchman Jean Guitton said respectfully that the word "apostolate" should be retired, or at least the term should be reserved for the mission of the immediate disciples of the Lord, the apostles. My notice is that the wish seems to have come true, the word apostolate, so common in my seminary days, is hardly ever mentioned.

With due respect for the papal documents and even the biblical origins, I would want the same retirement for the word "evangelization."

All this came with my recent television watching of the catastrophic earthquake in Japan last week. The death toll is immense, and besides the injured, a quarter-million people are homeless.

Yet violence and plundering seem absent from the Japanese landscape. The violence and stealing that happens here in the wake of any disaster.

On television two vignettes: the Mayor of Kobe, so courteous to newspeople, asking them to pardon any inconvenience the earthquake is bringing to their visit, hoping that they have "a nice day" after leaving him surrounded by the shambles of his city.

An old woman selling flashlights which are in great demand with the power outages everywhere. A newsperson asks the woman whether she is charging more for the equipment with the shortage and need. Her response is: "No, that would be wrong, taking advantage of such crisis and need."

Not a full picture to be sure. But Saint Paul says somewhere that the grace of God is courtesy, and the virtue does show profound respect for the mystery of another person.

Just the sense that the term evangelization seems pretentious. The presumption that I am better off than, say, the Japanese when signs are that other peoples might not need all that we want to give them by way of the Gospel and that much of what we want to give them in the name of the Gospel can be harmful.

Perhaps words fail me here. I think of that Christmas article in the *National Catholic Reporter* by the Maryknoller, Bob McCahill, whose articles are wonderful. He lives in a bamboo hut with an earthen floor in Muslim Bangladesh. He wears native clothes and eats the local food: "I go in search of persons who need a brother to care about their broken health. I do not wait in my hut for people to look me up. This outreach aspect requires physical labor, bicycling in particular, the kind of effort that highly educated people in this culture are not expected to exert."

There are people needing brothers like McCahill in every culture, and he can be present there in Bangladesh, just as the Word was made flesh and lived among us. He can tend the sick and leave the rest in the hands of, well, McCahill would say, Allah. To call that work or mission evangelization would give it a pretense that might embarrass McCahill.

Concerning the Japanese and what this Western faith might bring them, I need not know. I can, with McCahill in Bangladesh or the Japanese and Catholic novelist Shusaku Endo, presume that the Christ has something to say to those worlds, probably by a shaping that those cultures might give to the Incarnation.

A Dark Journey

A religious sister friend will have her family come to Sunday Mass in which we shall remember her brother, who was a priest in Puerto Rico for many years before his death back before Thanksgiving.

Last winter I passed through Puerto Rico briefly. A chance to visit the brother at his parish in a barrio outside San Juan. A poor place on a noisy road and next door to an automobile tire garage. My memory of my stay is the constant sound of an air wrench taking tire lugs off car wheels.

My other memory is the big, gentle, shy priest showing off his beloved island, especially the beaches. Finally we stopped at a beach where I remember a long straight row of royal palm trees lining the beach and marking where sand ends and parking surface begins. The royal palms went on for perhaps a half-mile, shaping the beach into an oval. And the water, that turquoise or aquamarine of the Caribbean so different from the gray black ocean here.

We stopped for a swim, and the water so warm that I plunged in, without the hesitation of surf bathing here, when you hit those cold breakers, cold even in the height of summer.

Out beyond the breakers I looked back. Terrence was wading in slowly. He stopped here for a swim often, and I concluded that his calm pace was his habit. His almost daily relaxation away from the noisy road and the air wrench. Easy does it.

No intimation then that he would be gone in a year. He was having some eye problems, but no sign of the cancer that would finish him within six weeks of discovery.

My memory of him is my being out beyond the small breakers and Terrence moving his large self deeper into the aquamarine sea. I wonder if dying can be like that. He was, of course, already moving into death. Faith would have us also moving thus into God. I know that toward the end he was often sick. Yet I wonder whether someone with faith senses more deeply than this distress, a moving into God not unlike Terrence wading into the warm Caribbean. I hope faith can give that comfort. Yet again perhaps not. Faith is faith, a dark journey.

Silent Solitude

A long lonely ride home from Ocean City, Maryland where I was part of a religious education weekend. Most of the drive was just beside the sea, long desolate stretches of Delaware beaches. The sand dunes break every hundred yards or so, and the clouds over the eastern sea still held the glow of the western sunset which I could not see because of the stands of bare winter trees. Hardly another car and few street lights. An occasional crossing with some stores and even a traffic light. Here and there back in trees, a home snug and bright against the winter night.

The gathering I left was an overnight of words, my own more than those of anyone else.

As I started out, dark was falling, I was aware of the quiet of this ocean vacation town almost deserted in these winter months. The huge hotels and apartment buildings on the beach dark and empty with the night coming on.

Driving off, I sensed that after all the words, the silence of the car hum would be wonderful. No need for soft music or the French language tapes of the Gospel which I play to improve my French for the monthly Haitian Mass.

The quiet farther up, out of Ocean City and Maryland into Delaware grew deeper. I could not even fetch the rosary from my pocket and pray the beads. Enough this silence, this desolate sea, the flash of a light snow in the headlights of the car, the distant lights. A rare treat this solitude, the beauty of this winter night along empty ocean.

Human Beauty

The *Cello Concerto in B Minor* by Dvořák by the New York Philharmonic with YoYo Ma on public television. Sometimes on Sunday afternoon after the Masses and what follows, I darken the room with the wonderful slatted shutters of this old house and watch public television. Today the cello concerto, preceded by figure ice skating. I fell asleep during the skating and woke up as the Dvořák concerto was being introduced.

The sheer genius and emotion which the virtuoso brought to the piece drew me from my sleep. Stunning. Tears running down the face of YoYo Ma and his drawing the bow across those strings so that not only his emotion comes through but the emotion of Dvořák, the composer, who wrote the concerto for his Beatrice, the woman who rejected him for another so that Dvořák married her sister.

The cellist seemed almost in ecstasy as his notes blended into the accompanying cellos, the French horns, and the whole orchestra.

That word they use too often now in Ireland comes to mind – riveting. Simone Weil said that a mark of genius was that the creation or work transcends the persona of the artist. Genius at work here, composer and performer. What comes through in sound and even the shades and hues of color television on the face of the cellist is intense emotion: the love and joy and sorrow carried to us across the century since Dvořák and even across the electronic distance of television and whatever night this concert happened at Lincoln Center.

"What a piece of work is man!" as Shakespeare exclaims. Even the figure skating and dancing pushing the human body to exquisite grace. Elegance that becomes more than body. The music is able to be out there by itself, creating in cellist and in us the emotion that his Beatrice created in Dvořák a century ago.

Humanity seems able to transcend itself. The achievement is more than the sum of the parts. We are here in the mysterious realm of Plato and Simone Weil and her "beauty of the world" or Dostoyevski saying that in the end it is beauty that will save us. That mysterious truth the scholastics glimpsed when they said that beauty, truth, and goodness are the "transcendental qualities of being." Wherever there is any one of these, there also are the others.

In the Midst of War

A fierce knocking at the back door of the rectory in the early morning. The back door was once the front door until the construction of the Section Eight homes that border the parish complex even more closely than the public housing highrise. With the Section Eight homes, Warnock Street became a cul-de-sac just at our door. Now the area is a dumpster site. Not a pleasant sight out my window and often enough not a pleasant noise in the early hours when the waste collectors come with a truck that lifts the dumpsters up and over and empty into the grinding truck container.

Anyhow. The noise this morning is the loud thumping of a maintenance man from the Section Eight complex. He notices that a car parked in the cul-de-sac by the two dumpsters has been vandalized, and he wonders whether the car belongs to someone here.

An hour later the car owner is out there in robe and house slippers exploring the damage and cleaning the litter of a broken car window. He blames himself for not putting on the flashing alarm that deters vandals. He did have the club on the steering wheel but somehow forgot the electronic alarm. Nothing much missing, but the expense and bother of a new window, which will cost at least $50 with deductible insurance. I offer the more secure parking of our fenced and locked school yard, which he declines courteously enough.

Amazing how outsiders or political types regard these neighborhoods as areas needing improvement or new housing or more police. We do not see these streets for what they are: places where people live and go off to work and park their cars and send children to school. This old man suffers this expense and inconvenience as part of life, something he must endure with patience and casual acceptance. He has been around a long time, and he does not expect trouble like this to go away.

Albert Camus had that problem with both Marxism and Christianity. He thought both accepted the human scene only with the promise of future improvement, which makes the present tolerable: the workers' paradise or salvation.

Instead this old man gets up this morning, discovers his car window broken and accepts the inconvenience and expense as his story for today. He will deal with it without dissertations on the drug situation or police neglect or social theory. Of course, the neighborhood has countless, often strident meetings on the disgrace of the area, but the protest is absorbed in the larger reality of people going from house to house collecting dollars for the funeral of a neighbor.

It can be a war zone around here. Yet the main fact is not the war but the community and patience and family life my heroic neighbors maintain in the midst of war.

4.

Here in Early February/
The Electric Blue

Here in early February
the electric blue of a small box is
almost enough to undo winter

Outside
there are no colors
only white snow on ash earth

Today
after a heavy gray sky and endless rain
sunset brought some relief the
breakthrough of orange shafts in a western
clearing

Now it is night
and we are inside I
shall content myself with
the shimmer of a small blue box.
                    —"Untitled"

Immense and Infinite Goodness

The beginning of still another cold which will completely distract me with my fear of bronchitis.

The eastern sky is full with fluffy cloud patches moltenlike with the morning sun, which they catch high up before I see that sun breaking onto the horizon.

A different kind of sky – then I remember that the heavens are different every blessed morning. A psalm of the morning prayer of the Church for today proclaims: "Your love reaches to the heavens and your truth to the skies." I recall a Catholic philosopher – either Englishman Brian Wicker or Canadian Leslie Dewart – who thought that the Greek static concept of God as Being was inadequate. God is Becoming so that the *bonum est diffusivum sui.* Good is diffusive of self. The usual understanding of that mystery is the Trinity and also creation.

This morning that deep red sky so afire in the clouds, that I seem to be looking into glowing coals, suggests somehow that every morning the Divine Goodness is even greater by reason of self-diffusion and the beauty of the heavens, some sign of that immense goodness.

The more traditional image is that the immense and infinite Goodness is all there and always there, and sometimes we see more clearly or more fully. As the psalm this morning says: "Your love reaches to the heavens."

Incarnation

The morning newspaper has photographs of children of migrant farm families brought in from a rural county for dental work. One picture has a Latino woman lying in the dental chair with her three-year-old daughter atop her in the chair. The child looks content enough under siege so long as the mother is there embracing her. The caption says that these children often have cavities and abscesses from "baby bottle syndrome," a result of falling asleep with bottles of milk in their mouths. No doubt these children are often alone while mother joins father out in the fields.

Why on an ordinary winter morning does such a scenario absorb me so? First of all, today is not an ordinary winter morning. The Feast of the Presentation of the Child Jesus in the Temple, and the prayer of the Church is filled with psalm phrases like "Here I am, Lord, I come to do your will." All creation fulfilled as He, of whom the Jewish temple is a symbol, comes to begin his mission.

My image of the Incarnation is that Christ would be out there in that rural county living in a trailer, sharing the life of those migrants, working the fields with them, getting them to a dentist. That is the image of him that rises from the Gospel – connecting with the lepers living in caves outside of town, walking through Samaria and meeting the woman at the well when the apostles wanted to walk around Samaria. That vision of him grasped by Francis of Assisi taking in the poor, embracing the leper finally, the vision of the worker-priests sharing the factory life of the workers. Maryknoller Bob McCahill living in a Bangladesh shack, watching the two wives of his Muslim neighbor dig a new latrine. Or the 80-year-old Salesian priest from Holland who has been 40 years in Haiti, mostly in the Port-au-Prince refuse heap called Cité Soleil. He is recovering from prostate and colon cancer and has glaucoma. He has brought other Salesians into his work of overseeing 180 schools and feeding 25,000 students their only daily meal. Despite illness and age, he cannot leave: "I'm going to stay here . . . a normal person doesn't want to do what I do. You have to be a little crazy."

Of course, the local Church is there in that rural county where the migrant farm children need dental work. In all fairness, I must say that some Latino settlement house exists near the fields or in the fields. But the local Church is not there with the migrants as we are there in the parishes and schools of people like ourselves: white and homeowners and college-bound.

The image of a subterranean world. Beneath high schools serving the likes of ourselves, the dentist offices and health plans, the expressways that bring us to work and theater, that vast subterranean world of farm workers and urban blacks which apparently Christ sought out. A sister friend in a rural diocese enraged the local bishop by asking whether in the distribution of priests, two farm workers could count for at least one ordinary parishioner.

If I were younger (and stronger and braver), I would hope that I would jump into that world glimpsed in the morning paper even more than I inhabit such a world already, despite the relative elegance of this rectory. Live in a trailor, eat rice and beans, learn to speak Spanish without the trace of an accent, as does Brian Karvelis in Brooklyn in his house full of refugees.

On this feast of the Presentation my sense is that this is what the Incarnation is about, as though the Mystery called God had to respond to the complaint of Job: "Hey, God, what is going on? You don't know what life is like down here!"

As though God in response to that complaint had to come down, take a look at the leper caves, actually learn something. The Gospel says that Christ "grew in wisdom."

Karvelis, McCahill, the Dutch Salesian in Haiti, all a kind of Incarnation.

Chaos

Saturday now. After Friday midnight a big snowstorm that brings the city to a standstill. Difficult for many people who need to get out, Saturday or not. And the impossible streets and stranded cars prevent nurses from getting to bedridden old people in these tiny row houses that are this city.

A large part of me welcomes the slowdown. I was even hoping that the snow would prevent the few people who come to Saturday morning Mass, so I can have some space and relief from the press of this place. Of course, the phone will ring, and parish school students not knowing where else to call will be calling here to ask about our school basketball game wherever. I do not even know about the game. The only sensible response that I can give is the surmise: no game.

Later I will have to consider snow removal: the almost full city block of sidewalk around the property, the schoolyard and the several cars, the church steps. Some will show up tomorrow for Sunday Mass, and I cannot have old people stepping around snow drifts.

A blessing on my Haitian comrade, Jean Baptiste! When I go downstairs, he is already at the snow, a trade he never learned in Haiti. A young friend of Dave Hagan calls to offer help. During the week I gave him some dollars for helping to dismantle the Christmas decorations in church, and he wonders whether with the snow I will need him again today. Later the maintenance people from the local hospital will plow the schoolyard as promised earlier this week.

And two people do arrive for the Saturday morning Mass. I try to be patient with all the concerns of snow and phone and the arrival of two visitors who must like the experience of an early morning walk through the deserted streets in falling snow.

So I make the coffee, prepare the altar and vest for Mass. I always vest, the sense of putting on the Gospel wedding garment for the wedding feast: "Where two or three gather in my name, there am I in their midst." The Eucharist. The mystery of faith has nothing to do with numbers.

By distraction or routine or hardness of heart I can be as deaf to Mass readings as anyone. Yet this morning the Gospel reading of the Mass that almost never happened was such a grace.

A reading about Jesus and apostles trying to flee the crowd who were "coming and going in such numbers that even eating became impossible."

Well, sometimes I cannot hide because I live here, and people want to attend Mass or do not know who else to call about that basketball game. So I let go of my own leisure or plans and make that coffee and be pleasant on the phone and welcome the Mass goers in from the cold streets.

I turn that inside edge over so that the hospitality is not grudging or minimal but generous and gracious. And if street people come to the door who are working the snow for sympathy, my response to them should be gracious as well, even if not generous, since the emergency food bin is bare for now.

This morning I never got to the vacant stare out the eastward window which I call prayer. Distracted by the early phone call cancelling the funeral of a friend and the other phone call about the basketball game, I shall try to make up that omission later today; but, that letting go of my own space and schedule this morning is not very far from prayer.

Another grace from that morning Gospel: "Getting out of the boat, Jesus saw a vast crowd. He pitied them, for they were like sheep without a shepherd." The Gospel profiles of Jesus so often stylized. Only rarely that quick glimpse at his insides. I am glad that he experienced this tempestuous world as a kind of chaos. So often my experience is a world without beginning or end or sense, and that chaos drains me of any familiar faith.

Narrow Straits

An arctic cold with fierce winds coming after the snow almost shuts the city down. The air blowing across the frozen snow seems to pick up greater cold. Church will be quite empty this Sunday morning. Many people will not venture out.

Curious how weather can stop us in our tracks. Our concerns become so immediate: snow removal, a parking space amid the snow banks of the plowed streets, concern that the heating pipes in the old school do not freeze.

I have similar thoughts when I visit a nursing home for the elderly where life gets down to having someone taking medicine or finishing dinner as though whatever human life is about, it is not about our plans or schemes. Simone Weil thought that progress was a secular religion and an illusion at that. She even blamed the Bible for the linear view that history is going somewhere.

For Simone Weil the Greek cyclical view was more accurate. Human history is a matter of our facing again and again the experiences and joys and ordeals which are the stuff of Greek stories. Only the stage changes, and human growth or development or success is our passing through these adventures like Achilles. Faith overcomes the world not by Christendom or some triumph of the Church but by our making our way safely through narrow straits, our eyes closed to the world. Even the Gospel speaks of the narrow way which is difficult to enter or pass through.

All this because the snow storm stops us in our tracks. The Mystery we call God commenting on our towers of Babel.

Cold Awakening

After midnight the phone rings. The occasional call from the security service telling me that the school alarm is activated, and the police have been notified. The procedure is then to call me and have me go out into the street to await the patrol car and admit the police officers for a walk through the 103-year-old school building. Now with computers in the school, the electronic surveillance is necessary and seems to stop the wreckage and disorder of break-ins.

So out I go from warm bed into the frigid winter night. The downtown towers still blaze, and a crescent moon is like a piece of ice in the winter night sky. The wind tunneling into the fifteen-yard corridor between church and convent and ending at school entrance is unbearable. I fumble to open the gate, and the padlock is cold enough to hurt my bare hands.

I stood waiting for the police who were not coming. The security company operator said that the motion alarm was probably activated by the high wind blowing through the old school and that they have many alarms tonight.

Five or ten minutes of waiting was all I could endure. With the operator, I was sure the wind was the cause. No prowlers out on a night like this. I will not wait for the police who might never come if they have many alarms tonight.

Another padlock, a second lock, the key pad of the alarm and then some lights. The operator said something about "first floor," so I did not look farther. I did check the thermostat. A worry more than break-ins is that the high wind entering the boiler room vents will blow out the gas pilot or jets, and the furnace and boilers will shut down. Then tomorrow would be the chaos of burst pipes and sending 220 children home after calling a contact person for each of them.

The thermostat reads 60 degrees. I again put the alarm on, extinguish the lights and lock doors and gates. Before sleep I call the security company to ask that the police call be cancelled. Otherwise, I could be just back in bed and the police at the door. Sleep comes easily enough.

Wonder

Even in black and white the photograph is beautiful. The space shuttle, Discovery, seen from a Russian space station. The shuttle in dark space, but a white planet Earth curves a border to the picture. The beauty of the world, as Simone Weil would say, or rather the beauty of the universe.

Often enough I wonder what we are doing out there at such expense when so many needs and hungers here need attention. Yet I cannot ignore that awesome beauty which speaks of a wonder greater than ourselves.

And that wonder appears in the newspaper text. The Russian space station commander is ecstatic: his opportunity, "the greatest profession God could give anyone; a fairy tale almost too good to be true." One cosmonaut has been out there 394 days. One would think even the wonder would wane. Aquinas said *consuetudo non fit passio.* The extraordinary gets ordinary.

Surprise to find the Russian commander speak of God. That would not have happened just a few years ago in the Soviet regime. I just presume that these hard-nosed scientists or engineers are content with the task and challenge without having to ponder the wonder or be in awe of the mystery.

Often as priest I feel as though I am the curator of a museum, that sense that Philip Larkin catches in his poem, "Church Going":

A shape less recognizable each week, a purpose more obscure. I wonder who will be the last, the very last, to seek this place for what it was . . .

Yet if there is the Wonder that we call God, as cosmonaut and I both believe, then that mystery deserves all the worship and attention that I want to give, that I even want others to recognize. I am always sending books or articles on prayer to interested and even uninterested friends. But my own prayer is such a desert, and even the great mystics like John of the Cross and Teresa describe the plateaus as dark nights. The little Thérèse described prayer at the end of her life as a closed sky.

Yet the attention which the Mystery requires does not mean that we should neglect other realities. Much religion is boring, and there is a saying that even God must be interested in matters other than religion. Some years ago a conversation in our kitchen with a priest from India, a sociologist doing research at the nearby university and living here some months.

I mentioned my hope that an insight of Marxism not get lost in the collapse of the Soviet Union, the insight that religion can alienate us from our world. "Oh, Marx meant more than that," said the priest, "he meant that religion can alienate us not only from our world but from our deeper selves."

After-School Energy

A visitor wants to walk our city streets. In late afternoon we start out as our school is being dismissed and arrive five blocks east as a local public school is dismissing. Sometimes principals negotiate different dismissal times to avoid street encounters between children of the different schools.

Our random walk takes us to a city playground beside the public school. A young community activist uses the city playground building as center for his neighborhood association, and an after-school tutorial session is beginning for the children just dismissed from the public school. Today the volunteer tutor is president of the Parents' Association.

Farther on we stop at the windowless, once-abandoned garage reconditioned by the Catholic Worker people for their after-school effort.

In both places the children are excited, either a surge of after-school energy or just the tumult of these streets. They seem excited with one another, vying for games or books, not excited about more instruction after five hours of classroom.

These warm rooms out of the snow are someplace to go after school. I would not want the task of controlling the situation. The energy level is almost frantic.

And the young activist at the recreation center or the woman from the Parents' Association or the young Catholic Worker people, do they know how much the odds are against them? Looking out the door of both centers, how can they believe that this chaotic hour with these children can make any difference?

So wonderful that these tutors do not allow themselves to be paralyzed by the impossibility of the task. These children are here, and both children and parents are our neighbors, and this is what we do for one another. A care not unlike the house-to-house collection to bury "Hammer" last week. The corporal works of mercy: burying the dead, instructing the ignorant.

Well, the afternoon walking the neighborhood with a friend kept me from a corporal work of mercy of my own: visiting those two elderly people in downtown hospitals. Mañana, tomorrow.

Afternoon Walk

Tomorrow arrives and the visitation of the sick still needs doing. I maneuver a ride to one downtown hospital with the intention of walking from there to the second hospital and from the second hospital, a longer walk home. The tomorrow that is now today comes too late for the first visit. The elderly woman is transferred to a rehabilitation center. She will need another tomorrow. The second visit is a success. Another older woman so pleased to see me. People expect so little of us priests. My problem is not their expectations but so many with expectations.

The walk home is 18 city blocks through center city and then through the public housing projects between us and downtown. A very bright day, brighter still for the sun reflected off the frozen snow and ice. Part of the way I walk in the street, somewhat wary of the cars coming up behind me on this one-way street. I am bundled beyond recognition: woolen watchcap and coat hood up over the hat with drawstrings pulled around the neck, warm woolen gloves and good winter shoes.

As I walk, I wonder why an equal stretch along the ocean would seem more a prayer. Perhaps city streets have too many distractions. I am trying to fit this walk into an afternoon prayer time by remembering that Buddhists have a walking that is praying. The sky is as available here as on the beach. Gerard Manly Hopkins would wander the Welsh hills, writing down what images cloud shapes resembled.

Whatever. The walk is good exercise and even a relief from the demands back at the house. Demands that would be completely absorbing and even stressful were I there. Towards the end I notice that I have not decided whether these 40 minutes can count for that afternoon quiet which I call prayer.

"Life Goes On"

Ten minutes through dusk and frozen streets and I am in Ballymore in County Tyrone, Northern Ireland.

A Brian Friel play at a small theater downtown. The wonder of city living, the wonder of theater. Ten minutes away and I am on a hill in summer with two young Irish lovers who are expecting a child and will marry in three weeks after their school examinations.

As they spin through the ecstasy of young love and the shame of the pregnancy and the worry of the coming school exams, they imagine and plan and discuss their future, within of course, the narrow limits of Irish town life. Almost off stage an older Irish woman and man tell and even sing the story from another perspective: in a burst of summer joy the young lovers will run down the hill hand in hand to borrow a boat moored at the lough and both will drown before the afternoon is over.

With some pretense I claim a kindred sensibility with Friel. My father came from the same part of Tyrone as the playwright. After several of his plays I presume to know what he is about.

What he is about is not easy to tell. A strange brooding spirit who hides this brood behind a lovely large smile, Friel can spell out the love story with humor and elegance and a keen ear for the joy and desperation that can pass between two people in only a few moments.

And then they are gone. And the audience leaves the theater wondering what it means to say that life in Ballymore, County Tyrone "went on," that even the two families, so different yet so fragile, learn to "go on." And the young unmarried lovers, whose dreams had occupied our keen attention for an hour and a half on stage, remain only as names on tombstones in separate family plots in the parish cemetery.

A Most Unfinished Man

For a few weeks I feel more or less in control, and the premise surfaces: well, with age and experience things are coming together. Then something small enough happens, and the illusion is revealed.

Last night two friends, one new, the other lifelong, stayed for dinner after coming by for daily Mass at five o'clock. At table the conversation came around to the greater hope and appreciation I should have concerning the Church: why not visit the seminary, talk to people there about conditions in these neighborhoods and the need for the Church? Look around, the visitors chided, see the good work being done by many church people out there.

Such a torrent of anger and cynicism surged out of me that by the end of dinner, I was certain that I did not want to have another such conversation for another 10 years. Too draining. Too exhausting. More than enough to drain me here already. Years ago I had learned to regard the Church as more or less benign landlord providing the real estate enabling us to be here. Nothing more. I have learned to live without any hopes or expectations, and I am fairly indifferent to all the concerns that occupy the institution.

My table friends challenged me with the certainty that God acts in world and Church, and the need to hold on to that truth that God is acting even when things seem otherwise. My response was fierce. I wanted none of that language that lets us off easy, that somehow the bereft people in the neighborhoods would be tended even if we did not do it because "God acts." I love that passage from Simone Weil in the *New York Notebook:* Creation is a divine abdication, and our opportunity to assist the starving neighbor is our "one point of superiority over God."

Part of my anger is disappointment with the Church, that Church of Henri de Lubac and French worker-priests and the liturgical renewal which was still only an impossible dream in those years when I absorbed their image of the Church. De Lubac called the Catholic Church the natural destiny and final home of all humanity, and he called the human soul "connaturally Catholic."

That image and vision is the only Church that interests me. I have no interest in just another religion of ritual and rules. The Eucharist is so much more than ritual. "We, though many, are one," says Saint Paul, "who eat the one bread and drink the one cup." Properly comprehended, an end to all separation. So a Church which leaves inner city and sells churches to other traditions more connected to the newer (and poorer) residents angers me. Stay with these newer people, turn yourself inside out and upside down to become what they need, to be the "good news to the poor," but do not leave and remove to some comfortable area and congregations and pretend that you are still being faithful to that de Lubac vision.

The other part of my anger is my naive expectation of any institution. So unreal. We all brought that hope to Vatican II. The truth might be right there between the lines of the Gospels. The religious institution in which Jesus lived seems to have been incapable of the renewal and honesty which he required. He finds more faith in outsiders than in the authorities. He tells parables like the Good Samaritan, where ritual prevents real religion. He finally does what needs doing without worrying very much about whether his healing someone violates the Sabbath.

No doubt my anger is connected with unreal expectations of mother – Holy Mother Church. One thing the anger tells me is to keep my distance, do without the expectations or official support. Wait for better days which might never come if the Gospels are any indication.

One further thing the anger reveals: at 61 I am still a most unfinished man. Perhaps that is also acceptable. Either Catherine of Siena or Catherine of Genoa said that she had more faults than a cat has hairs.

Letting Go

Saturday evening and friends from the far suburbs arriving to treat me to dinner. As we are leaving the house, Jean Baptiste arriving to prepare for three different Haitian meetings here tonight: choir practice for the Haitian Mass tomorrow evening, a prayer group gathering, and a more political group forming to assist President Aristide with reconstruction back in Haiti.

This morning our own parish prayer group met for two hours here in the house. Tomorrow after the two Sunday Masses, each followed by a coffee hour, a Catholic peace and social justice group will meet in the house as well. Before that, dining room and office and meeting room are classrooms for the 30 children who are preparing for First Communion in the springtime or even Baptism at the Easter Vigil. Tomorrow night after the Haitian Mass, a social in the school hall where the Haitian political group is meeting tonight.

Seeing all this activity, my visitors comment how wonderful that this church and school and house are here in these desolate streets and available to the neighborhood and whomever. Last autumn a newspaper reporter was here for the Haitian celebration for the return of Aristide to Haiti. The reporter also remarked how wonderful the goings-on in the 103-year-old no-frills school hall, and that he and others downtown just presume that nothing is going on up here but the mayhem that makes the newspapers.

Living in the midst of these demands takes work. The effort to surrender privacy and time and even good order. Especially on Sunday morning the children are all over. Looking for a parent or a bathroom or smaller sister or brother who seems to have disappeared.

The effort is not unlike that "letting go" of Thomas Keating and his centering prayer. And the cost of letting go is considerable: all those neglected books which people give me or I cannot resist buying. A new novel of Shusaku Endo or a study of the literary deconstructionism that interests me or some new theology or the autobiography of Nelson Mandela that came as a Christmas gift. The poems of the Welsh priest R.W. Thomas are sitting unread for more than a year now, along with that new biography of Gerard Manley Hopkins. And there is my own wanting to shape a poem out of the death of Father Terrence Doyle or that visit to the

Florentine Illuminations Exhibit at the Metropolitan Museum in New York.

I begin to realize at 61 that most of those books will remain unread and the poems will remain unwritten unless I am given some later years in a kind of retirement.

Yet even retirement is a luxury that does not quite fit the neighborhood. People here have nowhere else to go, and I should try to be here without imagining some escape. Learn simply to be here with the press of the meetings and the worry in deep winter whether the school boilers will hold up and the school will be warm for the children arriving on Monday.

Just be here. Allow the "letting go" that is required for prayer to become a habit, a way of life so that all the hours are prayer, the overflow of the solitude of church or of bedroom.

I will read when possible and give myself the space and distance of a day away or even a week away on occasion. Yet the main reality will be just being here and becoming more and more generous in responding to the needs of the place and the people who pass through. And in the process of becoming more generous to the demands of the place, I become what we are all supposed to become. "Let this mind be in you that was in Christ Jesus who, though he was God, emptied himself, taking the form of a servant. . . ." The servant image. The edge that makes all the difference. Rather than showing by body language that I am overextended, ask whether still more visitors want coffee . . . "You are to be like servants waiting the Master's return. . . ." Like servants. Come Holy Thursday, I will be washing feet at the Evening Mass of the Lord's Supper. Cannot let that sign be empty gesture. The ritual should say accurately what is going on around here day in and day out. When that daily task seems exhausting or extreme, I shall recall the visit to my Brooklyn priest friend and his effort to prepare dinner for the 40 refugees who inhabit his rectory with him. Or I shall remember the Gospel advice to push ourselves: "If someone wants your coat, give your shirt as well."

Social Justice

Today that small Catholic Peace Fellowship meeting and tomorrow the 50th anniversary of the World War II bombing of Dresden in Germany. The newspapers tell the memorials going on there. A

Catholic group outside the Cathedral in Dresden protests: "... too much attention . . . to German civilians killed half a century ago – and too little to people dying in Chechnya today."

Almost 800 British bombers followed by 300 United States B-17s. Thirty-five thousand dead and some estimates double that. These statistics challenge the significance of a dozen people in the dining room here trying to continue the tradition of Catholic Peace Fellowship or Pax Christi or whatever we call ourselves.

Just one more meeting here on a crowded weekend, but a meeting that should happen just as well as the others. No hope for these cities or Haiti unless the peace teaching of our tradition and other traditions can come to bear on world affairs and the militarism that cripples everything else.

Our main man at the meeting keeps up on these matters and says that the new mood in government is to put the military budget over with social security as something intact, something that does not suffer the reductions of other government spending.

Not much time in this place to give these matters the attention they deserve. Not even the time to read the newspapers so that my information comes from this meeting in which I am in and out because of the traffic of after-Mass Sunday morning.

I am glad these few keep CPF/Pax Christi going, and I am complimented that they choose to meet here and that I am part of them. Important that we keep that hope and concern alive, even if the only vital sign is the discussion of this meeting, which has absolutely no effect on war or peace or the military budget. After Vietnam and civil rights I am constantly dismayed and confused at how little interest exists in a humane Catholic social vision so shaped in Europe by the horrors of Dresden and two World Wars and so legitimated by Vatican II. I wonder how priests and people can go about parish life and how Catholic colleges can house ROTC and how a Sunday newspaper can be full of the Dresden story and none of this enters the Catholic consciousness. The United States bombs Baghdad or threatens a Nicaragua and a few more people show up for these humble, almost pathetic meetings. And if these few people did not meet month in and month out to plan a mailing or a talk, social justice concerns would disappear from the local Church. I guess what happens here is an occasional blowing on the ashes, lest the tradition die altogether to the notice of no one.

Priority Confusion

A newspaper has a photograph of a 21-year-old man being led into a courtroom to receive a death sentence. The accompanying article says he came here from Haiti when he was 15 to visit his uncle and never returned because of the political turmoil back in Haiti.

The condemned man was convicted of killing one policeman and wounding another when they stopped the unlicensed cab the Haitian was driving. The weapon was a service revolver wrested from one of the officers.

Haitian. More or less unofficial chaplain to the Haitian community, I wonder whether I should try to visit him on death row or wherever. He has been in the United States long enough so that my inept French or nonexistent Creole will not be a problem. He probably is Catholic, and the new law coming down in this Commonwealth is that executions should happen within 90 days of sentencing.

I have no idea what pastoral care is going on at the local prisons. Just the Haitian connections and wondering whether I might pull the Haitian people here into some concern. Not political concern. The Haitians have no political clout. Just that the faith of his people might help this fellow in the dark months ahead. Or, perhaps after six years here the man has little sense of being Haitian.

In any case these musings and questions strike me as madness: do I really have the time or energy to take this on? A prison visit is an all-day ordeal, and if he is on death row at the state institution in a far suburb, that day is even longer. And one visit would not be enough. The ordeal ahead for him needs someone up close and often. And who says that he will not be adequately tended at the prison? Who says that I have anything to bring to a Haitian on death row? Who has anything to say or bring to someone on death row?

Just yesterday that passage from an old standby: *The Intellectual Life* by A.D. Sertillanges: "to proportion one's task to one's powers, to undertake to speak only when one knows, not to force oneself to think what one does not think, or to understand what one does not understand."

The hint here of an old piety that said: better not to act rather than to act from flawed motives. The opposite advice from Chesterton: the enemy of the good is the best.

No insight here about visiting that fellow. The sense that I cannot take one more thing on. The sense that I should take on one more thing.

Weaving Human and Divine

Camden is by statistics the poorest city in the United States, and Chester is second. Curious how both cities are urban sprawl of Philadelphia, the green utopia of William Penn spawning the two poorest cities in the country. In the six weeks of this new year Camden with fewer than 70,000 people registers 14 murders.

Here on this side of the Delaware River the Catholic Church has almost vanished from Chester with the recent closings. The Catholic high school and Catholic hospital are gone, and most of the parishes are going. I have a Catholic friend, a businessman, who continues to volunteer with the newer evangelical street ministries. Those folks do not know that he is a Catholic, and he hears them speak of "the Catholics, the Church which just left."

This Saint Valentine's Day I am off to Camden, only ten minutes across the Benjamin Franklin Bridge which, when new, was the longest suspension bridge in the world. A clue to the vanished glory of this area when Philadelphia was a world center.

Off to Camden because Saint Valentine Day was chosen to mark the 10th anniversary of the Heart of Camden, that remarkable housing effort of my friend Michael Doyle and Sisters Marge Sullivan and Peg Hynes. Only Irishman Michael Doyle could pull off Heart Day as anniversary for the Heart of Camden, an overflow of his Sacred Heart Parish.

The banquet with red and white balloons at each table anchored by a brick from the housing rehabilitation was wonderful. And the almost spontaneous talk of Michael Doyle was more than wonderful, better than anything he might have written out by way of preparation. "Out of the abundance of the heart the mouth speaks."

Michael takes the slant of an Irishman who has been here 35 years observing us Americans. He acknowledges the generosity of our people, and then he goes on to tell the blindness in our midst. The tragedy of Camden sitting impoverished on the Delaware River, once one of the great trade routes of the world. He spoke of those 14 murders, of Campbell Soup and RCA and the historic metropolis of Philadelphia across the water and the closing of 40 sewage plants in Camden County and bringing all that sewage into Camden City. He told of the three new prisons Camden had to accept to keep other needed welfare services. All this is an apartheid, says Michael, a fear of the poor in our midst. Fear to touch the leper as did Jesus and Francis of Assisi. He told the businessmen at that banquet to consider the kind of beauty and surroundings they want for their own family and want that for poor children as well. Peter Maurin was mentioned: his wanting "a society in which it is easier for people to be good." And Dostoyevski as well: "It is beauty that will save us." Indeed "out of the abundance of the heart the mouth speaks."

The religion of Michael Doyle is healthy, a weave of the human and divine as attractive as an Aran sweater. No mention of observance or what Dan Berrigan called the churchy thing which has been proposed as the real thing. Yet faith is there, and Church is there as warp and loom on which the fabric is knit. Eucharist there not as ritual but as sign of a deeper truth of human unity violated by our apartheid, even as we are celebrating the Mass. Michael weaves the full human fabric out of those holy signs. The Heart of Camden is a weaving of the sacramental life of Sacred Heart Church. Another Irishman, George Bernard Shaw, said something about Christ having to die in every age because of those who lack imagination. I can only marvel at Michael Doyle from rural county Longford in Ireland, now here in the ruins of Camden. Ninety-nine out of a hundred are paralysed by the task at hand or distracted by a more churchy view of the task. Michael sees the sewage flowing into the new disposal plants, and his concern and, yes, even soft Irish indignation, rises to the occasion: I will see what lilies I can grow in the compost heap.

Colorless Tasks

Another snowstorm. Well, hardly a storm. Just some large flakes starting in the late morning and the promise is that all will be rain before nightfall, and tomorrow will be much warmer than it has been for a week.

In the great park that wanders all over this city of William Penn the bare trees are like pencil lines on the white parchment of fields. The beauty of the world. Life seems to become colorless, a monochrome of keeping warm and making certain the furnace works and the paths around church and school are clear of snow and ice. The children are only in the school yard when passing from one building to another.

And with snow banks preventing parking and the cold discouraging a walk, I neglect the home visits I should be making or the hospital trips downtown. People use the telephone more, and I could pass the day going from one call to another.

Yet the severe lines and black and white of snow on street frame clearly an important part of life: the round of colorless incidental tasks. I need to write notes of thanks to the many who were generous to us at Christmas. At meetings with others I need to plan Lent and even Easter, still two months off. I need to meet with contractors to plan repairs that require doing when the weather changes.

I so dislike those bulk mailings that advertise Lenten literature and programs. Anything that gives religion the smell of observance or even business is so unattractive. I almost like the Quaker tone that resists feasts and seasons for the truth that every day is like every other day. And yet I know the wisdom and joy of a Christmas or an Easter.

I dream that someday we will finish this round of repair and paving, and these old buildings will look clean and bright and attractive and be so shining that the whole neighborhood will lift itself out of the grime and winter by sympathetic response.

For now I must be content with the slow pace of everything. A call from the convent about plumbing problems on the third floor. One rain spout from the church roof is such a huge icicle that we must discover whether the problem is roof drainage or sewer backup.

The discipline of these tasks. I know I am better with all that. Saint Benedict wanted his monks to work with their hands as well as to pray or to study. I have hardly read anything for weeks, but I am more patient and accepting of these endless tasks. And yet I do not want to become so lost in them that I forget the old man confined to his bed whom I have not visited for weeks. He depends on our concern and visits as sign that we do not forget him now that he cannot be with us for Sunday Mass or with us on Thursdays to sweep the church in preparation for Sunday.

Searching for Nourishment

A graduation ceremony today in the dining room. I often bring visitors into the grand place and, with a sweep of the hand. I describe the place: the glory that was Rome. I once read somewhere that a departure party was given here for Bishop, later Cardinal, Dougherty when he went off to the Philippines after the Spanish-American War. The sendoff included a purse of $10,000, a huge sum of money in 1903. Just a story to tell the elegant origins of this old place and the pretense of the dining room.

Several years ago I mentioned to parish social worker, Sister Catherine, that we should not sit here closeby one of the poorest public housing projects in the country, doing little more than giving food to neighbors who drift in from those concrete courtyards for food or baby formula. How often I have gone to the door and met a young emaciated woman with a shopping cart no less, asking: Got any formula? Some need here for nutrition classes.

The graduation ceremony was for 20 women from the nearby projects. The women graduating are hardly emaciated. Here and there along the streets of the project are food vendor trucks permanently parked. Chinese food and pizza, Philadelphia cheese steaks and barbecued spareribs, all foods that put the weight on. Years ago one project had 15 minutes of national fame when a HUD secretary toured the site, followed by network television cameras. The local fellows so blasé that the secretary noticed how neither his presence nor television cameras slowed down the drug deals happening at the dumpster areas.

The graduation of 20 women was ironically for an "Eating Right is Basic II" course which Sister Catherine brought into the biweekly meetings of these women, who also hear lawyers and social workers and psychologists at these gatherings.

Food is always part of the meeting, and the hope is that some small part of these classes on nutrition will stay with the women to help them control diabetes and high blood pressure and stay alive and around for the children who so need them.

The chairs in the dining room are turned sideways, and another row of folding chairs front and back. The nutritionist from the county has certificates for each woman, and each graduate is invited to comment on the course now completed.

How easily these besieged women smile and even laugh. Through their smile I notice how many need a dental overhaul.

Living so close to them these many years, I am by race and privilege so distant that I have no idea how dental care works for the very poor. Is the care just not available, or is the neglect part of the larger picture of disorganization that has them running to the corner trucks for Chinese food?

As the talks and diplomas are progressing, I notice one woman with a baby. I ask Sister Catherine beside me how old the young mother is. "Fifteen," says Sister Catherine, "and not in school anywhere."

I have my doubts about this nutrition course prevailing over the food trucks at the project corners. With the sister I have no idea concerning the long-term meaning of this effort. We are here. We do what we can. By the remarks of the women these biweekly meetings make a difference in their lives. Friendships are strengthened; they enjoy coming. They are proud of this perhaps first graduation beyond elementary school.

And the big old house and dining room here are better for the visits of these women who often cook up a storm of their "Eating Right is Basic II" menus in our kitchen. We are more connected, more human for their visits.

Personal Responsibility

Early morning convent Mass. The reading is the tower of Babel. These last weeks I notice how tentatively the Bible regards the human enterprise: the flood story telling how the Creator wonders whether the creation was a good idea, the Fall suggesting that something must have gone wrong from the very beginning.

And the tower of Babel. Curious how the Scriptures consider the many languages as confusion rather than human richness. And the Divine concern over the tower construction: "This is only the beginning of what they will do." Not unlike the Greek story of Prometheus stealing a flame from the gods on Mount Olympus and giving fire to humankind, who proceeded to build their own cities in defiance of the abode of the gods.

Yesterday the newspaper has a guest article by a former CIA director, no less, expressing his dismay at the ongoing nuclear buildup of submarines and star wars without another superpower in sight since the fall of the Soviet Union. And this in a liberal democratic administration because recent electoral defeats require a shift to the right. So much for the human enterprise of politics, which in our secular times is considered the work of salvation by left and right. Religious people want to be saved from abortion by legislation or save their schools by tax vouchers.

Years ago Dorothy Day noticed the worship of law. Somewhere she tells how building codes intended to protect the poor are legislated or enforced, and all that happens is the inadequate or unsafe buildings close, and the poor have nowhere to go at all.

Commonweal magazine reprinted a 1949 Dorothy Day article in a recent anniversary issue. Her words echoed the "Easy Essay" of her friend, Peter Maurin, about "passing the buck" in turning the care of the poor over to the state by way of welfare and even social security: "We no longer practice personal responsibility for our brother but are repeating the words of the first murderer, 'Am I my brother's keeper?'"

Dorothy Day was aware of the criticism of her stand as letting the state off too easily, that she and Maurin were "lining up with Wall Street and private enterprise and the rich opponents of state control and taxation." Yet she is consistent: "Anarchists that we are. . . ." She wants people to give of themselves, of their own resources and practice personally the works of mercy. So the transformation is not just the poor from need but also the transformation of those who practice voluntary poverty. This transformation might be the more necessary change toward a just society.

Her vision would seem appropriate everywhere. Besides insisting that state and church do what needs doing with their resources, people should go and be with the poor themselves: staff the soup kitchens and work Saturdays rehabilitating houses in Camden, tutor after school in our parish school.

That seldom happens. We think that money or politics or Church renewal can do this for us, and all we need is the money. If all that happens is that money is passed along, no transformation occurs when building codes close the only shelters the homeless have.

Human Error

The morning newspaper has me searching for an obituary in a back issue of *The Tablet* from London. Of course, I cannot find the issue or article.

The search because of a newspaper article about a choir in a small prestigious local college which is preparing for Lent or Holy Week with *The Passion According to Saint John* by Johann Sebastian Bach.

Some choir members, Jewish and others as well, are offended by the seeming anti-Semitism of Bach and the Fourth Gospel as well. A college meeting will determine whether the performance should happen at all.

I have to deal with this and so the search for the old issue of *The Tablet* talking about the death of a philosopher and a believer in England who, together with his Christian faith, had such a keen sense of the flawed condition of human nature that even in the salvific event of the crucifixion he found the seeds of anti-Semitism. Inherent those possibilities in the historic nature of the act. And this despite the prayer: "Father, forgive them, for they do not know what they are doing," Romans or Jewish leaders or both.

Of course, the fierce tension between Jew and Gentile so real in the early Church will come through in the Gospels. If the Gospel is Jewish in origins, the Jewish law will be upheld: "Not one iota will be done away with"; if Gentile, the awful: "His blood be upon us and upon our children," to remind the Jews of their past. I have a priest friend who has a hard time with Good Friday because of the Passion according to John read at that liturgy. In other ways, the Fourth Gospel is the most wonderful and mystical of all.

I was always taught that the inspiration of the Scriptures meant that the books were works of the Holy Spirit and the human author as well. Inevitable then that the limitations or culture or world view of the human author come through. Inevitable that the Gospels and Acts of the Apostles and Epistles reveal those struggles of the early Christian Church: stories about Greek-speaking widows being neglected in the daily soup line, stories about Paul ignoring the other apostles in their desire to impose the Jewish law on Gentile converts.

Or that curious story about a Syro-Phoenician woman asking Jesus for a cure and Jesus saying that he cannot give the bread of the children to the dogs!

I have seen explanations saying that Jesus spoke thus to test the woman. I cannot believe that. Jesus did not go around testing people, or at least I hope not.

An Epistle says that he became like us in everything but sin. I want to believe that the seeming rebuff of Jesus to the Gentile woman is his struggle with the limitations and prejudices that small-town life would impose on him. In Nazareth they probably called Gentiles "dogs," and Jesus, like the rest of us, meets the hemorrhaging woman with all those prejudices. Sin is not sin until conscious and deliberate. Jesus confronts those cultural prejudices in himself and overcomes them: he heals the woman.

Religion is as flawed and crazy as the rest of the human enterprise. The Jewish tradition has those awful stories of Adonai telling the Jewish people to go into a city and kill everybody, taking no survivors, not women or children. They are even to kill the cattle. These stories were a strong reason why Simone Weil kept some distance from Judaism and Christianity as well. She said that no true God ever gave such orders. I have no idea whether the anti-Jewish sentiment of Bach or the Fourth Gospel should prevent a choir performance. I do believe that we cannot allow the flawed human origins of our religious tradition to paralyze us. At best those sources call us to a grace and holiness that is sublime, and we must make our way through the dross and mud to those heights. Simply.

When after Lent we come to Good Friday, and I hear that strong blame of the Jewish people in the reading of the Passion, I will note that this is an historic circumstance of no importance, and the lesson for me here is the words of Jesus concerning Roman legionaries and Jewish leaders alike: "Father forgive them, for they do not know what they are doing."

And if the Gospel words would harm others less tuned into these nuances, then by my homily I have the responsibility to tell them. I am aware of the historical tragedies these readings have spawned. They do give me the opportunity to say to others: never again.

Vespers

What a luxury this winter Sunday! Nowhere to go after the morning run of Masses and a coffee session after each and a Baptism after the later Mass followed by another coffee hour.

After a stretch in bed in my darkened room, I awoke to the awareness that the Church would still be warm from the Sunday heating and that I could take that audio cassette of the Solesmes monks singing Sunday Vespers, and with a warm shawl over me, I can do Vespers myself: sit quietly in the darkening church fragrant with the incense from morning Mass. I can gaze at the Agony in the Garden window and watch the sun fall left to right across the southern sky and in the glorious windows. At the far end in a window of the Saint Malachy story, the red robe of an Irish king flames out when the sun reaches there.

The Vesper psalms sung by the Solesmes monks bring such nostalgia. Every blessed Sunday in seminary years we sang those psalms in the same psalm tones so that I need no book. In my memory I know what psalm verse is coming next. And the incense odor enhances the nostalgia. Graham Greene said that smell is the sense most connected to memory.

After the psalms, the *capitulum* or short lesson. The "Brief Responsory": *quam magnificata sunt opera tua Domine,* "How wonderful your works, O Lord," repeated either side of a *Gloria Patri.*

Sitting here in midwinter, when everything seems frozen or futile or just dead and I go through the motions, *quam magnificata sunt opera tua Domine,* "How wonderful your works, O Lord."

Here I am looking at the Agony in the Garden window, a literal image of Jesus praying and apostles sleeping and Jesus on the verge of catastrophe, *quam magnificata sunt opera tua Domine.* I cannot make much sense out of life on a winter Sunday afternoon, a respite in the endlessness that will begin again tomorrow after these brief and rare hours of a winter Sunday afternoon. What sense did Jesus make out of his ordeal . . . ?

Yet my heart is into the chant of the monks, *quam magnificata sunt opera tua Domine.* Beyond mind and reason and my bleak sensibility, my heart is singing with the monks that all is wonderful and magnificent. The work at work in Jesus, even unto betrayal and ordeal and death, is at work in us, in our world of earthquakes and starvation and the disaster of these cities and the freeze of winter.

All this must be coming from my heart. I cannot make sense of it in my head. I pull the shawl more closely around me for the increasing chill of the old church. Part of the shudder is perhaps the distance between mind and heart which I feel.

Restored, Connected

A break in winter this Monday holiday of Presidents' weekend. Early afternoon and ideal for another walk home from down town.

In the midst of the projects, a team of housing authority police on bicycles eye me with suspicion. I am the only white man in sight. Closer up, one officer recognizes me as the priest to whom his wife dragged him last spring. I recall that he was angry with her and went storming out of our meeting. Things are better now, he says. He will have to get down to church on Sunday . . . .

A spring-like day and everybody is out, though weather reports claim that winter will return later in the week.

Farther on I meet Antonio. He was a school child when I came here 13 years ago, and his mother had the whole family at Sunday Mass every week. I guess she grew tired of holding it all together and years ago disappeared back into the projects.

Of course, Antonio is not working. I asked about his mother, and together Antonio and I climbed the project steps to their apartment.

There in the tidy and colorful rooms with windows already decorated for Saint Patrick's Day is his mother, Beata, in colorful yellow sweat suit. Beside her on the sofa, an aunt who made her way out of these projects and has a city job. This aunt is in a blue sweat suit, and I say something about "Charlie's Angels."

Up the stairs and into the overheated apartment comes oldest brother, Jorge. With these Latino names, one might think they are Latino. After all these years I ask. Aunt who is city worker says that her father was from Puerto Rico and mother an African American, and growing up in this project was rough because of this mixed identity.

Jorge is leaving, and I leave with him, promising to return with coconut candy Irish potatoes, which Beata says she always has for St. Patrick's Day. As the only Irishman in sight and with the middle name of Patrick, the least I can do.

Jorge tells his friends out in the seamy courtyard that he will be back in a moment and is walking me to the edge of the project and still another block. His courtesy and concern are for my safety.

Unlike his younger brother, Antonio, Jorge is working as a steamfitter in the far suburbs, and today is a holiday. Every work day he takes a commuter train and then two buses to get to work and rises at 3:30 in the morning to get started.

I ask whether he has any children, and, of course, he does: one daughter who lives some blocks away with her mother. He pays $25 dollars a week support. What with that big piece out of his pay and the commuting costs, he cannot have an easy time of it. I do not ask whether he is alone or with another woman in his apartment in the projects near his mother. Jorge is the only family member who still appears occasionally at Sunday Mass. Why he appears, I do not know.

So a walk which seemed at first the luxury and leisure of a holiday turns out to be a pastoral visit, as we once said in the trade. Sometimes I wonder whether the pastoral life ended when priests acquired automobiles. I remember that when I entered the seminary only pastors had cars, and most priests were not pastors, but assistant pastors in huge parishes of four or five priests.

The two more blocks home I notice in myself the refreshment of reality: being where I should be, doing what I should be doing, visiting the people. When I am home, I go looking for those quotations from E.M. Forster and W.H. Auden at the end of *The Fate of the Earth* by Jonathan Schell: "E.M. Forster told us 'only connect!' Let us connect. Auden told us, 'We must love one another or die.' Let us love one another – in the present and across the divides of death and birth. Christ said, 'I come not to judge the world but to save the world.' Let us, also, not judge the world but save the world. By restoring our severed links with life, we will restore our lives."

Restored. Connected. I am home with more life than I had when I started home. The tonic of reality, the reality of those projects, those impossible, chaotic, heroic lives. I know that most priests are in the suburbs these days. I know that in those suburbs one needs a car to go anywhere. But I also know that the automobile disconnects. All the way back to seminary days I remember a classmate complaining that the priest in his home parish would leave the car motor running when he ran into the house to bring Communion to the invalid brother of my classmate.

"Only Connect"

Surfing the net. A television journalist confesses knowing little about the information highway and asks his guest about all the new high-tech. I hardly know how to turn on the computers around here, and I excuse myself because of age.

We were eager to install computers and a computer room in our school. It would be unjust not to prepare these children for their brave new world.

I hear all the awes and claims for the information explosion much as I remember Kenneth Clark standing beside a Gutenberg press in his *Civilisation* series years ago. He said something about the invention of moveable type as probably a good idea, although he was not certain. With a hint of humor he wondered whether that information explosion had done more harm than good.

Or my priest friend who is a Bible scholar, musing on so much crazy religion and suggesting also with humor that the best thing the Catholic Church did was to keep the Book away from the people!

I know my need is not more information. I do not need to be surfing the net. Interesting how California the image is. I have books and books I will never read for want of time. I suppose the resource is precious to scholars doing research or graduate students writing dissertations or people just needing more information on something or other.

Yet most of my education has come from browsing in library stacks more or less looking for something and then coming upon some other book which made me forget my original search. Of course, I am not often in libraries any more. No time. The Greek word for learning, *schole,* means leisure. Learning was a luxury of the leisure class. Now education is a commodity one buys to increase earning power. Money is the bottom line everywhere, so powerful that money can generate research that can work wonders: medical cures, space travel, the information highway.

Five years ago with 15 local clergy I went to California for a 10-day training course in community organizing using the Saul Alinsky method. My comment on the training was that it provided method rather than more social vision. I did not sense that I needed more social vision or information about what problems our society or world suffered. Always I am almost bursting with that awareness.

We do need method: how to take the slow, painful steps toward transformation, both personal and social. Building relationships, taking time for reflection.

More information can even be an evasion of the transformation or change. Someone remarked that futurist films and books almost presume that man and woman down the years will be more impersonal, mechanical, situated at control centers and monitors rather than connected. A problem is the difficulty of connecting. "Only connect," says E.M. Forster. Janet Malcolm in her study of psychoanalysis, *The Impossible Profession,* says that the concept of transference in Freud denies that possibility: " . . . we cannot know each other. We must grope around for each other through a dense thicket of absent others. We cannot see each other plain. A horrible kind of predestination hovers over each new attachment we form. 'Only connect,' E.M. Forster proposed. 'Only we can't,' the psychoanalyst knows."

No wonder the sitting at a console trying to connect with information. Often a distraction from the real task.

No wonder my friend Ivan Illich wants to "deschool" society. No wonder his classes at the Graduate School of Architecture at the University of Pennsylvania. He lectures on the need for *sapientia,* wisdom, rather than knowledge. Seeing with the heart or inner eye. The monastic *lectio divina.*

Futility

A friend passes on to me a brief study of St. Vincent de Paul. With all my unread books I hope that during these weeks into Lent and Easter I can read at least this one.

Somehow I have the idea that Monsieur Vincent suffered a chronic sense that he was spiritually lost, a sense that would have come easily in that century of Jansenism. A quick turn of the pages reveals no such burden in the saint. Only a brief mention that once in a generous moment Vincent asked God to give him the doubts and scruples which were paralyzing a theologian whom Vincent was trying to help. The book says that the scholar was healed "but Vincent now became burdened, worried and consumed by doubts. His spirit tumbled into darkness. It was an interior night for him." But the book does not say how long the ordeal lasted. Vincent seems to have wandered much before finding himself and his phenomenal work. Besides founding his congregations and taking on the poor of Paris and all of France, the estimate is that he wrote 30,000 letters in his lifetime.

So whatever his troubles or doubts they did not paralyze him. At 72 years of age at the Church of Saint-Lazare in Paris he provided soup twice each day "for thousands of poor people." One can only imagine the state of the poor in a city like Paris in such a century as the 17th. From his fancy carriage, the aristocrat Blaise Pascal saw them wading through the mud streets and began something which became mass transit to help them. Pascal and de Paul were contemporaries in Paris. I wonder whether they ever met.

Perhaps my interest to discover whether Vincent de Paul suffered some sense of spiritual doom rises out of a recognition in myself of a deep sense of futility.

Who knows where these afflictions begin. I guess we all have them. No wonder I so respond to the plays of Irishman Brian Friel. Friel draws large-life pictures of joy and sorrow, hope and duty, failure and courage. At the end of his plays all that has gone before disappears like mist off the fields. One is left with the question: what did all the living and hoping and wanting mean?

And these streets are a hard place for someone afflicted with a sense of futility. Everything around enhances that sense and can paralyze me.

Yesterday I was in such a different world: an academic convocation in a grand university – professors in gowns and academic hoods and speeches about preparing for the next century. Success begets success and vigorous planning for more success.

Well, I shall just have to shape my soul for being here because this is where I want to be. And if the surroundings enhance or enlarge that chronic sense of futility, I shall recognize the demon for what it is and not allow that futility to envelop me. What a precious location I have to be with and for people who need friends and someone with a clerical collar who has resources and connections unavailable to them. Besides the debilitating sense of futility which comes from wherever, I also have the refreshing tonic of reality. This is a real world: real people with real needs. I need travel no farther than the school next door at lunch time: first the kindergarten and first-graders having a fast-food, mean-looking government lunch, which might be their best meal today. And they are so happy for the carton of fruit juice and sandwich that they fill the place with loud happy banter.

Mysticism

I read the mystics and contemplatives to sustain the effort at prayer. For years the experience is great emptiness, and the hope is that this is the prayer of quiet or something. The experience is so ephemeral that I hesitate to encourage people on a journey that often seems to be going nowhere. Herbert McCabe, English Dominican and theologian, has a wonderful reflection on prayer in his book *Faith Matters*. He says that the satisfaction of prayer is not the immediate satisfaction of an Irish whiskey. More the long-time advantage of a well-furnished room. Over the long haul you notice the difference in your life. Similar to Thomas Keating saying not to measure the success of your centering prayer except by the long-term difference effected in your relationships with others – how you treat people.

McCabe would agree that words like experience or satisfaction are not adequate concerning prayer. Prayer is an act of faith, and John of the Cross talks about that Dark Night:

No sign for me to mark.
No other light.
No guide except for my heart. The fire, the fire inside!

For John of the Cross the more he is empty, the darker "the experience," so much the more does he proceed by faith and the purer is his prayer. Tough stuff. The image that comes to mind is that of rare tropical orchids hanging from trees, with roots feeding on empty air.

Right now I ponder some words from the Dijon Carmelite mystic, Elizabeth of the Trinity (1880-1906): "Should I fall every moment in spite of my faith and trust; I will let Him raise me up. I am certain of His forgiveness, certain that He will strip me of self, divest me of all my misery."

So mysterious that more deeply than her own reality or person, she was by faith aware of the Divine Reality sustaining her.

But what is that awareness? Gerard Manley Hopkins in his Dublin dark night did not seem to have it: "My taste was me," he says in one of the terrible sonnets. And he gave up his meditative prayer for fear of madness.

I am sure that he was not giving up prayer. He probably knew that for an interval his prayer would be what the Scriptures call a "patient endurance," with the hope that someday something more might return. Teresa of Avila says that we should never abandon prayer, "whatever may come."

Physician Sheila Cassidy calls prayer a "waiting game," an echo of Simone Weil, who, at the Solesmes monastery during Holy

Week 1938, described her prayer during her terrible migraine head-aches: " . . . by an extreme effort of concentration I was able to rise above this wretched flesh, to leave it to suffer by itself and to find a pure and perfect joy in the unimaginable beauty of the chanting and the words."

"God Will Provide"

Dinner last night with Dave Hagan and a friend who teaches in a public high school. Sometimes I think the catastrophic sense in me paints too grim a picture of these neighborhoods.

So the next morning I test with another friend the conversation of the previous night. His truancy work measures public high school attendance.

The figures are that on any given day attendance is 50% and in some areas as poor as 38%. The teacher described having a college counselor into a special class to discuss ways to enroll in college without the usual entrance requirements.

Six students show rather than 30, and several of the six attend with head sideways flat on the desk or coat pulled up over head hoodlike. The talk of the visiting counselor is pure gesture.

Teachers working in such a situation either stop noticing how many come, or say: if only we can help one or two. Not enough comfort for my teacher-friend, who softens her discouragement with her easy and even light-hearted manner. What else can she do?

Both conversations encourage me in the maintenance of our poor parish school, where only 20 of the 220 are Catholic. Our situation is smaller and more manageable and not high school. And if the new Contract with America politics removes the funded lunch program, well then, in the spirit of Dorothy Day and Peter Maurin, we shall continue the lunch program at our own expense. The noise level and shouts of the children at lunch are a delight. When Dorothy Day asked Peter Maurin where they would get the funds for a newspaper, he replied: "Read the lives of the saints. God will provide."

Nourished by Beauty

A quiet Saturday evening and I am drawn away from the setting sun firing the broken factory windows eastward by figure skating pairs on television.

A pair is skating to a Strauss waltz, and I cannot but watch them. So wonderful the beauty of human bodies graceful and tuned to one another. A beauty of the world as much as the light of the setting sun here in late February.

The music brings me back to Vienna those years ago when I attended the Vienna Dialogue as a guest of the Soviet Union (no less). My friend, Father Richard McSorley, was invited to this peace conference and was able to bring me along.

Besides the peace conference, the fancy Vienna hotel was housing a high-school prom, and after dinner we found ourselves looking down into a ballroom of handsome couples dancing all in unison to the Blue Danube Waltz there on the banks of the Danube.

What is this world of beauty and courtesy and elegance so distant from these ruinous streets? What am I doing when I watch the ice dancing, so transported from late winter and the monochrome here and the quiet or loneliness of this huge old rectory?

I hope I am nourishing my spirit, my need of beauty. The task might be to bring the whole world here. Not that the Strauss waltzes should be given to Africa or Latin America or inner-city Philadelphia to the neglect of the natural beauty of these other peoples and places.

Yet the kind of grace and pleasure which so enthralled me looking down from that balcony on a Viennese waltz is something I want to share with others by way of faith and social gospel. I do not want to bypass that human fulfillment so that an affluent Vienna is rare elegance in a world which is mostly people looking for food or warmth or survival. The vision is to shape these good things, make them available to everyone. The transformation of the world does not bypass this very human fullness.

In Vienna the tense, hard, political talk happened alongside the school prom without any relation to it. Perhaps even the sense that these distractions of the idle rich are decadent.

All I know is that I am as drawn to those skaters and their Viennese waltzes as I am to the beauty of a sunset. I want both beauties for those who walk these dull streets, burdened by life.

They have neither the thought to look up, nor the house space, nor quiet to take in the ice skating.

Personal Tragedy

Sunday morning and perhaps 30 people from the far suburbs are visiting for Sunday Mass. They arrive despite the beginnings of snow and ice that can make their return home a perilous drive. They are an old Catholic society, and a member has persuaded them to benefit our school by their annual dinner dance.

While celebrating Mass with them, I am aware of our songs and singing and prayers for Haiti, our exuberance at the exchange of peace. We are probably quite animated at Mass compared to what these visitors know back in their home parishes.

After Communion, our choir leads us into the Black National Anthem which is in the *Lead Me, Guide Me* Catholic hymnal prepared for use in Catholic churches with an African American congregation.

It is the end of Black History Month, and this hymn as Communion meditation is acknowledgement of that finish.

All those in the congregation, including our visitors, have hymnal and words in front of them. As I sing along, I am looking more at our white visitors than I am at the page. Never have the words come home to me so. A people long downtrodden, giving voice and soul to words that give their ordeal, yes, their tragedy, faith and hope. My pencil hesitates on the word tragedy. That fear I have of melodrama, sentimentality.

Yet I know that just outside the church door, just beyond the hearing of this hymn, that tragedy is still very real: these streets and projects, the drugs and violence, the unemployment and abandonment and neglect. I hope our visitors can hear and sing the words in front of them with the awareness that I bring to that hymn today.

Sunday Morning

I have an Irish greeting card which was one of six in a package. I notice that over the year I have used all but one: a picture of some old folks seen from behind. They are walking alone or as couples along a rural Irish road toward a church down the road. A milder version of *The Angelus* by Millet, I guess. The dress and quiet manner of the walk suggests Sunday morning; these folks are on their way to Sunday Mass.

I suspect that I have held onto the card because the scene reminds me of everything soft and green and quiet that I like about Ireland. That fantasy of mine of being somewhere other than here.

Another attraction of the picture is the deep sense of peace and normalcy that comes out of the picture. More than normalcy, an image of sanity, the wish that I had made more normal, sane choices than this fierce life in this huge old house that is such a thoroughfare always but especially on Sunday morning, when visitors and Sunday-school children and Mass-goers needing something or other are in kitchen and on the phones and blocking passage as they converse with one another in the doorways.

Sunday morning because Sunday morning seems in my mind a most normal and sane time for people: leisurely rising, a cup of coffee and off to Mass and back home to the Sunday newspapers with family members in other chairs of the living room or den, reading other parts of the same Sunday paper. A late breakfast that is more brunch than breakfast, either at a restaurant on the way home from Mass or breakfast at home with pastries purchased at some very special bakery.

Interesting how affluent my dreams are: a "den," no less and restaurant and expensive pastry. Apparently, I want to live well, which is what I already do compared to the other realities of my neighborhood. Not many family rooms around here, not much restaurant-going.

But the pace here is frantic and the stress real and the escape wish real and even understandable.

In early seminary years, we were introduced to Saint Jean Marie Vianney, the Curé d'Ars, a French peasant parish priest who is the patron saint of parish priests. Apparently, he was not very bright and had a difficult time learning the essential Latin. He was ordained only because anti-clerical laws in France at the time created a priest shortage.

Much later on, I learned the most attractive quality of the Curé d'Ars: he was, more or less, a conscientious objector to military service. He went off to the army but simply wandered home again, and his frightened family had to avail themselves of the practice that his brother could go off and fill up the ranks instead.

That was not the Curé d'Ars story proposed to us aspiring parish priests. Instead we read or were told about his pastoral zeal, his personal holiness, his 16 hours a day hearing confessions, his boiling a pot of potatoes weekly and grabbing one or two potatoes a day on his return to the church confessional from a bed where he slept poorly because his pastoral work was so fruitful that evil spirits tortured his sleep to prevent that work.

Well, later more scholarly authors tried to make more sense out of those bad nights, and I recall the diagnosis: a kind of hysteria. His stable, peasant sensibility breaking down from the inhuman demands he was making on himself: sleep deprivation, loneliness, poor nutrition.

And flight. Not unlike my own dreams of Sunday morning. At least twice the Curé d'Ars tried to run away from his impossible life by thinking that he should be in a Trappist monastery because here in the parish his inept work, as he imagined it, was ruining people. Imagine wanting a Trappist monastery as unconscious relief from 16-hour work days in a cramped confessional listening to all the woes of the world.

There is still a Curé d'Ars here and there. The 80-year-old Dutch priest in Port-au-Prince, Haiti who, with colon and prostate cancer and cataracts, stays on in that "open sewer," as the press calls it, because "you have to be crazy to do this," and few want to take his place. That "necessity" of Simone Weil. We are where we are. We do what we do almost by fate.

Necessity enters into all lives, and my dream of Sunday morning normalcy is the idealized image that an unmarried person might have, forgetting that husband and father reading the Sunday morning paper in "the family room" is often enough completely distracted by a child on drugs or pregnant or involved in a relationship going nowhere, and that mother cooking up the Sunday morning eggs might want a life completely more open to city and neighborhoods and intellectual or social interests than her spouse can sustain.

So maturity comes by dealing with all this. Blossoming where you are planted. *Mutatis mutandis,* changing what requires change. Not taking so much on or living so intensely that you go over the edge, as did the Curé d'Ars several times, before he came back to his hard life. As poet Thomas Kinsella says: "get on with it."

One More Thing

Mardi Gras. Not my favorite time of year. And this year a worse season with waiting and worry about some medical tests. With the years I discover another sense besides my chronic sense of futility: a sense of catastrophe. Whence and how that comes, who knows? Neither do I know whether many have it or whether others cope better. Many say that I cope well: this place, this work, these abandoned neighborhoods . . . who knows?

What I do know is that my outward calm accompanies an inner sense of falling apart. And what provokes that sense of falling apart can be something very minor.

The fear is that bad medical news means the end: that I must leave off being here, doing the work, fearing that days ahead will mean simply coping with illness, reduced to wondering how I will feel today or tomorrow.

The truth is that we must cope, and more than cope with most illness; life must go on. People continue to work, to enjoy, to believe, and to pray.

And if the medical report is bad, I shall have to do just that: one more thing. Become the wounded healer, to borrow a phrase from Henri Nouwen. How many people I know who have serious illness, heart disease and malignancies, organ transplants and chronic impairment. I encourage them to believe that God is with them in all this, that the Word took our flesh, our vulnerable human condition so that we might make our way through these hazards with faith and patience and hope. Again, the 80-year-old European priest who continues his work in Haiti with colon and prostate cancer and eye cataracts is still there, and the work needs doing.

"Physician, heal thyself," scriptural words. I need to embrace the advice I give to others. I see how suffering and worry cripple the afflicted, how difficult the task of coping or continuing on can be. I have no idea what those words of Saint Paul mean, words about making up in our own bodies "what is wanting" in the sufferings of Christ. Perhaps the closest to that meaning are the words of Leon Bloy on the wonderful greeting or sympathy card from the Carmelite Sisters of Reno, Nevada: "There are spaces in the heart which do not yet exist and suffering enters into them so that they may have existence."

A long time since I read Leon Bloy. Perhaps it will be a hard Lent for me. Or on the other hand, an easy one.

5.

Ash Wednesday Should Be Omitted Here/Ash Enough

Ash Wednesday should be omitted here
ash enough   the soiled streets
the limp limbs of this old woman
whom I tend with sacraments and such . . .
                      –"Hospital"

Last Ash Wednesday
burying Jack Beatty in winter cold
we huddled so close around his grave that
wet sod wedged off our shoes onto his casket
making our earlier Lenten rite almost trivial . . .
                      –"The Burial"

This week of Lent has
more than ashes as reminder:
Johnny   twenty-six   twice a father

                 Church full
family elders children
(The Brothers do not face the final truth)

                 For Word
morality at the expense of comfort:
"get your house in order . . . "

                 A singer tries:
"There is Balm in Gilead"

                 Something from Paul:
"We are afflicted . . . weary . . . "

Before night
this weeklong shroud will be
as torn as spinnaker in hurricane

The squalls here
too   frequent   fierce
for lasting tears

Before dark
wine joins these waters
to form a Lethe

Weeks hence
when some few come here
in praise of other Wounds
Faith
be earth enough
to take all this
to Friday
to Easter even

—"April 1979"

Observances

Ash Wednesday. Difficult to say what the observance means when the substance of fasting is gone. In the Gospel stories the Lord seems less than patient with observance for its own sake: the objections to his Sabbath Day miracles or the disciples plucking a handful of grain while walking through a field on the Sabbath.

The usual explanation is that some minimal reminder is even more necessary in our world. A world where Lent and Good Friday and Easter can be eclipsed or lost in basketball playoffs going on when Catholics should be at the Easter Vigil. Instead they stay home to view on television even Catholic colleges observing Holy Week with basketball. In such a world, the explanation goes, some reminder is important. Some observance.

This morning on network television an anchorman said that later this morning, he would be going across the street to St. Patrick Cathedral for his ashes. I guess that is some reminder.

Years ago the Christmas Eve fast was being modified to allow abstinence from meat either on Christmas Eve or the previous day because of the modern reality of travel and such. One could choose which day. I recall a December 23rd standing in an Italian shop in South Philadelphia with my first pastor, who was purchasing victuals for *la vigilia* dinner, an important custom which he saw threatened by the changes.

A woman, hair up in curlers in preparation for Christmas, came into the store and seeing his clerical collar, asked what happens to her abstinence intended for today since she forgot and ate breakfast meat already. Need she abstain tomorrow since she had already broken abstinence today?

My pastor gave her an eloquent Italian shrug of indifference. As I say, he was quite unhappy about these changes, the confusion and loss of traditions. The woman responded with a shrug of her own: "Ah, so I make a sin!"

Lenten Mindfulness

Some years ago I was making regular visits to an Irishman who was dying. He came some distance to the earlier Sunday Mass here often enough, and when he became sick, he sent word asking for a visit.

Once when he was very low and in considerable pain, I said for want of anything else to say: "Well, Harry, it's Lent." His answer was: "Yes, Father, and your Lent this year is going to be longer than mine." He was dead in another week. I recall that this quiet Irishman from Derry died close to the Feast of Saint Patrick and fellow Derryman, Eugene O'Donnell, played the fiddle at the funeral Mass. His sounds on that instrument, more eloquent and touching than any words of mine by way of homily. I guess if Lent can remind us of our frailty and mortality, then Lent is worth doing. Again with Chesterton: if something is worth doing, it is worth doing poorly, and doing Lent poorly might be the best we can manage in a world where basketball tournaments on television eclipse the Easter Vigil.

A friend says she likes Ash Wednesday because for some unwelcome reason she thinks of death every day, and she is glad for a day when the others who succeed in putting death out of mind join her in this meditation.

Our Suffering World

Books by or about Simone Weil spread around my rooms because last evening I was looking for something.

What I was searching for was the connection she makes between the suffering Christ and our suffering world. I did not find her passage about devotion to the Passion of Christ, the honorable tradition exalted by the great saints. She says they gave Christ compassion precisely because when Christ was on earth and suffering in his flesh, He received so little comfort. A variation on the theme of Pascal: "Christ is in agony until the end of time; wherever men (and women) suffer. We must not sleep."

I was searching the books because I wanted to question myself by way of Ash Wednesday homily last evening. To question the connection of my childhood devotions during Lent: Stations of the Cross and Holy Hours and Good Friday Three Hours Agony. What is the connection between these perhaps sentimental devotions and the concern of more recent years: the suffering Christ and the crucifixion of our world of wars and ghettos and capital punishment and cancer?

Have I grown up and left sentiment behind? Perhaps by asking these questions out loud by way of homily, I can speak to this Catholic world of collapsed devotion, of no more Friday night Stations of the Cross, no more Holy Hours of reparation. I recall the prayers of the Stations of the Cross: "O my dying Jesus . . . pity your Savior thus cruelly treated."

I searched Simone Weil, because I sense she brings it together: the *coincidentia oppositorum* which the mystics grasp. Her devotion to the suffering Christ was immense. Her own Holy Week experience at Solesmes in the midst of a migraine headache. She knew "the possibility of loving divine love in the midst of affliction." She grasped how Christ, abandoned by his Father was able to continue His love of that Father, much as we must continue to grasp and return the love that sustains the heavens and the stars in a world seemingly abandoned by that love.

I am probably losing expression here. Difficult to do justice to Simone. We can only try as I tried by Ash Wednesday homily to connect my earlier pieties with my later concerns.

Concerning the terrible pity that Simone Weil felt for the crucifixion that is our world, I cannot find that passage either. I do know that she says somewhere that the suffering of the world annihilated her senses. She says as well: "Wherever there is affliction, in any age or any country, the cross of Christ is the truth of it."

Conscious Transformation

The feast of a saint whom I have been hearing about most of my life: Blessed Katharine Drexel, who was baptized at the neighboring parish of the Assumption in 1858. One of two neighborhood saints: Fourth Bishop of Philadelphia John Neupomecene Neumann died on the street down by the Assumption and is buried in the crypt of another neighborhood church. I guess the neighborhood has possibilities. Leon Bloy says at the end of one of his books that the only real tragedy is that we are not saints.

Katherine Drexel gave her immense inheritance to Catholic works among Native and African Americans and founded a religious order for those works, including a university in New Orleans. We have parishioners who attended her convent schools and actually knew her. Interstate 95 passes close by her burial place and mother house just north of the city.

When I try to discern what would possess a woman of her time and place for such generous service, I need look no further than her memoirs. It was her parents. She tells how her mother "employed someone to go around and visit the poor . . . I often think my mother had no human respect. She never seemed to wonder what the neighbors would think or say when they saw the crowd gathered day after day during the winter months." She meant the neighbors around their fancy downtown home, with the sidewalks filling up daily with the poor whom the neighbors would consider a nuisance, much as people now consider a nuisance the beggars and homeless all over downtown. It looks like the hard times are back, and most people seem as indifferent to this social chaos as were the neighbors of Emma Drexel in the 1870s. For all the celebration of Blessed Katharine Drexel one could make a case that the local Church which celebrates her spirit either never acquired that spirit or gradually lost it. One could make that case.

In the Gospel of Matthew Jesus makes that complaint about his church and city: building monuments to the prophets; yet, ignoring their message.

Katharine Drexel was able to see the impoverishment of Black and Native Americans at a time when they were still the *Invisible Man* of Ralph Ellison and before *The Other America* of Michael Harrington helped others to see. She was able to see, much as Thomas Merton from his cloister saw the racial injustice of Harlem or smelled the burning flesh of Vietnam and napalm before others did. Black militant Eldridge Cleaver would read a 1940s Merton description of Harlem. That description of Merton so stirred Cleaver that in *Soul On Ice* he describes his own response to that reading: " . . . whenever I felt myself softening, relaxing," Cleaver says, "I had only to read that passage to become once more a rigid flame of indignation."

Of course, the Katharine Drexel story fits into the tradition of philanthropy with which the Church is more comfortable than protest or social struggle. But it also fits the Catholic Worker vision of Dorothy Day and Peter Maurin, who do not want us to let ourselves off easily by saying that government has the task. They emphasize the Works of Mercy, not trusting government to do the task, not making social transformation merely a matter of money.

Understanding Reality

A wedding in a storefront church. A friend of 20 years from the streets, trying long and hard for some normalcy. His bride and he have children together, and both have older children from earlier relationships. His grown son is there, and I admire the understanding this tall, lean, handsome and somewhat stylish young man has for this occasion. The acceptance he has for this father who has been in and out of the life of the son. I marvel at the whole tone of the service in this impoverished church. The wedding prayers and words stress how hard life is, how we mess up, how patient and merciful we need to be with one another and, over all this, how much our lives and loves need the mercy of God.

This older son seems pleased at this try of his father for normalcy and even happiness. I watch him applaud and smile and respond gently to the much younger children who share the same father.

I sense some understanding in this older son concerning how young and unable his father was to take on a family, to move in with or love or sustain some relationship with his young mother.

Once 25 years ago, I was an assistant pastor at a parish which had weekly bingo. Among the devoted workers one African American was at table with the other workers for a beer or two after the bingo players went home. A conversation came up about that 1960s word, "soul." One white worker finally asked the black man what soul means. "It means you understand," said the African American. "Understand what?" insisted the questioner. "It just means you understand!"

That memory catches the tone of this wedding, the genuine manner of the older son of the groom. When I entered the makeshift church, I was with a white couple who had befriended the bride and groom through me. My first sight was familiar faces from the streets of that neighborhood of 15 years ago. I had on my Sunday priest suit and was looking more proper than any memory they had of me. Our mutual smiles became more than smiles: outright laughing because I was looking more proper and they more settled than in the days when their behavior was so outrageous. Once I was out on the street and so angry with them for something or other that the rectory housekeeper had to feign a phone call to call me off.

Our seeing one another brought those memories back. Now their friend is getting married, and they are all, well almost all, anchored by some relationship or other.

After the ceremony we proceed upstairs to the parish hall for a buffet dinner. No drink or dancing or loud music because this is a strict church. Perhaps a drink or a dance later back at the house of the newlyweds.

What I like about the afternoon is that everything is real. The prayers and vows are real. No pretense, no effort of anybody to impress anyone else. No lofty theology or rhetoric about marital bliss. Just the lean hope that these two who have already been together for years can stay together, despite the stress that has torn them apart more than once in years and even months past.

And that older son: so real in his taking in and accepting all that his father has had to manage. That acceptance probably comes in part from the son having to deal with some of those impossible problems himself. I do remember several times the father taking son in when the son was down and out. I think he took the son in even when that meant the father having to sleep on a sofa in his one-room apartment. It is all so real, and the wedding anything but boring. Despite the limousine and gown and flowers and tuxedos which the couple can hardly afford, the afternoon was real. That reality a relief. I was glad to be there.

Quick Fixes

By way of homily for the First Sunday of Lent I do what I often do: I wonder out loud, hoping my questions are the questions of some listeners and that I am not just crazy.

I wonder about capital punishment executions planned next month. A new governor plans the first executions in this state since

1962. No word from the local Church yet. I wonder about that conversation last week with a public high school teacher concerning attendance under 50% in local public schools. I wonder about this society having more people per capita in jail than any society in the history of civilization.

I wonder out loud about the quick-fix solutions of capital punishment and discontinuing lunch programs and whether the temptations of Jesus in the desert are those kinds of temptations. This familiar First Sunday of Lent Gospel has Jesus tempted to throw himself down from the pinnacle of the Jewish temple to impress a crowd, a "quick fix" for the impossible work still before him.

I mention another recent conversation with a physician friend working to have medical students become involved in these drug-ridden, poorly-attended schools by way of substance abuse education.

The physician is reading William Lynch, S.J., and reminded me how Lynch thought the "quick fix" was really an expression of despair, not knowing what to do. The politicians do something dramatic, even theatrical: execute somebody or cut out a program which, for all the waste, is the only daily meal these children have.

Despair because nothing comes from the empty gesture: no healing, no restoration of "family" meals, no lessening of crime. The theatrical gesture is either ignorant or worse – playing the crowd for future votes.

The Human Condition

A stark gray Monday morning, and during the long drive to the dentist I observe Lent by playing a tape of the Good Friday offices at the monastery of Solesmes.

So wonderful the chant. The antiphons tell the tragedy and brokenness of our world and ourselves: betrayal and abandonment by His friends, mercy from the cross for those who execute Him: "Father, forgive them for they do not know what they are doing." Mercy for the thief beside Him: "Today you are with me in paradise."

Despite the New Testament showing the tensions between Jew and Gentile in the early Church, I do not believe the Gospels want to blame the Jewish people for the death of Christ. The Good Friday antiphons and psalms seem to take up older Jewish

Scriptures and new Christian texts into one embrace which tells the tragedy of the human condition. The tragedy we call original sin.

This Good Friday chant seems to say that the only appropriate regard for human pathos is profound pity and patience and mercy. No capital punishment. The look of the young son at that wedding recently, the acceptance of the foolishness of his father in younger years. Jesus says that he came not to judge the world but to save the world.

Driving home from the dentist and again hearing the chants of Good Friday, I am almost moved to tears by some of the words. Jesus cries out: "My God, why have you forsaken me?" Or that trust in spite of everything: "Father, into your hands I commend my spirit." Which is not to say that terrible treatment of the Jews did not happen around and out of that New Testament story. Again, the human condition.

I have a scholarly friend who surprised me sometime back. After an initial attraction to a creation theology which would say that creation is the significant event, he returned to a more traditional theology of redemption: "I feel the need for saving our world and myself."

The reading for this Lenten Sunday suggests that the new creation is much greater than the old. By the Easter Vigil we shall be calling the human condition or original sin a "happy fault" to require such a saving.

"Father, forgive them for they do not know what they are doing." How should I read these daily newspaper articles about a hearing in local federal courts concerning some old Eastern European who came into this country concealing his dark Holocaust past? The hearings are for withdrawal of citizenship and deportation.

Such a tragedy, all that history. The Eastern Europeans probably regarded the Germans as protecting them from the encroaching Soviets and the Jewish people in Eastern Europe looked to the Soviets to protect them from the Nazis. So out of the tragedies and exigencies of coping and surviving, peoples become enemies to one another.

No doubt, more to the Jewish tragedy than that. European anti-Semitism goes back very far. And how do you even imagine a day of putting thousands of Jewish people to death? Easier for

me to spell the sorrow out in the dynamics of European history
than for the Jewish people to do so.

Mystic Sensibility

Twenty years reading Simone Weil and just now a breakthrough.
Mystics have that X-ray vision not available to us lesser mortals.
They leave us behind: Ignatius Loyola talking about the Holy Trinity
in the language of music. Besides everything else, Simone Weil
was also a mystic.

Ash Wednesday evening, looking for her explanation
concerning why the saints had such devotion to the Passion of
Christ, I was unsuccessful. So many books to search. Neither
could I find her exact words concerning how the suffering of the
world annihilated her sensibility.

The pages I did read, however, brought the breakthrough: in
the end Simone Weil is able to love the world and herself and even
the Mystery that is God because Christ, who experienced self and
world and even His Father by way of abandonment and desolation,
continued to trust and to love in spite of this seeming absence.

Her sensibility exacerbated by intelligence and seriousness
and being Jewish in Nazi Europe, Simone Weil might have shaken
a fist at heaven in outrage or denial. Instead what happened to her
at Solesmes monastery in Holy Week 1938 enabled her "by analogy
to get a better understanding of the possibility of loving divine love
in the midst of affliction." She describes her experience in Assisi
in 1937: "something stronger than I compelled me, for the first
time in my life, to go down on my knees."

I do know that for Simone Weil another passage through the
opaque world is beauty. She remarks how the book of Job, in
posing the problem of suffering, is eloquent about the beauty of
the world. Yet I suspect that for Simone even the beauty of the
world revealing divine love is because of Christ. I have framed in
my room some words from her to help me meet the morning sun:
"the beauty of the world is Christ's tender smile for us coming
through matter."

Personalism

I wonder whether wisdom comes with aging. Besides the new
understanding of Simone Weil from looking through her writings,

I also read an article of Dorothy Day as though I were reading her for the first time.

The article is from 1947 and was published again by *Commonweal* magazine in an anniversary issue. Dorothy Day talks about religious people turning over responsibility for the poor to "Holy Mother the State," who gathers them to her generous "bosom studded with the jewels of taxation."

She laments putting the responsibility for our brothers and sisters off to government or social institutions. Every parish should have a house of hospitality, which means that the parishioners would have to care for the poor themselves.

She even uses that scary Catholic Worker word: "anarchists that we are, we want to decentralize everything and delegate to smaller bodies and groups what can be done far more humanly and responsibly through mutual aid."

Ivan Illich talks the same way. Thirty years ago he said that given the reality of the American or even worldwide Catholic Church, the renewal of Vatican II would proceed according to the images of the American Management Association, which means the proliferation of bureaucracy. Over the years I wonder what wave-length or intuition of Day or Illich made such sense to me without my realizing the wisdom of what they were saying. Catholic Worker is a marginal movement; Illich, a utopian. The final faith of many people is in institutions. People believe in government or the organized Church.

Again the attitude of Christ seems to be a practical acceptance of his Jewish tradition. He goes to synagogue and temple and keeps the Jewish law – more or less. Yet he takes on the halt, the lame, and the blind himself – on the street and out in the fields where the lepers wander. He does not expect much, only trouble and obstruction from the authorities: "Do everything they tell you, but do not do as they do."

When friends wander in wringing their hands over the indifference of the local Church to the poor or peace or social justice, I should tell them to cease trying to jump-start the Church into doing what we all should be doing anyhow. I should tell them to leave their unreal expectations or their anguish and go to work themselves in that soup kitchen where the local Church at least allows the kitchen. "Only connect," E.M. Forster says. The wisdom of Dorothy Day is those daily corporal and spiritual works of mercy. She insisted that newspaper and protest and social vision of the Catholic Worker all came second or third or fourth. Personal involvement in the work comes first. Personalism is another Catholic Worker word. The personalism of French Catholic writer Emmanuel Mounier.

My friend, Martha, catches that vision. Almost alone of all her fancy friends she is daily at that tiny community center in the depths of the city, not content to raise funds or have intellectual discussions about the role of Church or government.

Divine Care

Just in the door from some medical tests with downtown stops here and there, including the purchase of a book by a Catholic theologian who is trying to bring his faith and words to bear on his struggle with bone cancer. I have two or three ailing friends who can use the book, so I bought several copies. My own ailments are nothing to concern me – at least for now.

I am just in the door when I have in hand a letter newly arrived from a friend whom I hardly see except by rare visits to the suburban "sister parish," so good to us. I see her, her fine husband and children in the pews, and we promise a dinner or an evening that never happens for their busy lives and my own.

Her note, enclosing a check to help our school, has a devastating close: please pray for me; I have been diagnosed with bone cancer.

I fold the note and enclose it within the small date book which I carry in a shirt pocket close to my heart. I do not want her or her family far from me.

I sit down and write a brief note to accompany the book of the theologian about his bone cancer. "It seems that I should send you this," I say, adding that I do not mean to dismiss this news and worry by a book. Across the distance of our lives we must be there for one another, for those whom fate or Providence have us meet. My note was written on the back of a flyer I have been using to write notes thanking people for Christmas care. The flyer credits the Irish for saying: "It is in the shelter of each other that the people live."

No end to this stuff. A close friend dead at Christmas, a young mother with a brain tumor, a religious sister-friend with serious medical problems, an old Quaker friend in hospice care whom I must visit in Virginia . . . .

I think of the priest in that theater piece of Bernstein's "Mass." Bernstein has the priest celebrant throw down the sacred vessels along the way of faith. The priest is weary, exhausted from the burden of faith, not only his own but his calling to help others carry theirs.

Not that the others ask or expect. We are all very alone with such tragedy, yet the Communion of Saints means that we should find shelter or comfort in one another. And the request, "please pray for me," surely that is an invitation into the ordeal and troubles of another. The problem is that we feel so helpless, so powerless.

The Lenten Mass reading yesterday was the Lord encouraging us to pray and not lose heart: "If your children ask for bread, do you give a stone? If you, evil as you are, know how to give good things to your children . . . ." With our powerlessness we can at least pray and not lose heart.

Two sisters who are physicians visited me with their brother-in-law, who is not Catholic or religious. As they were leaving, the brother-in-law heard the two sisters ask me to pray for someone or something. He asked how important something need be to deserve prayer. "We must pray for everything and everybody," was their answer.

So we pray. Sitting at my eastward window this morning, I notice there is a moment of dawn when the birds fly out from wherever they pass the night. One moment no birds, the next moment a bird flashes past the window off into the dawn sky over the abandoned factories that scar this neighborhood all the way to the river. All the signs are that we are alone. The gutted factories are a metaphor for how I experience my own insides even while praying: we are alone. The world is unto itself, abandoned.

Then a bird lights on a tree or bush growing on the old factory roof, no less, and I remember the promise: not a sparrow falls without your Father's notice. We are not alone. Everything is in Divine care. So we pray and do not lose heart.

Waiting for Death

My search over a lifetime to find a spiritual director has been unsuccessful. I suspect that is the story of many people who have made that search.

From the Desert Fathers down through the early Jesuits to our own time the warning has been that whoever has only himself for a guide has a fool both for guide and for the one guided. The old Latin saying is *nemo judex in causa sui.*

One such effort years ago was with a Quaker gentleman who had a lifelong interest in the Mystics. Earlier in his life he had been an Episcopal priest, and during his seminary years he studied under the Quaker, Rufus Jones. Quakers and Catholics can connect through the great Catholic mystics, such as Meister Eckhart and John of the Cross and Teresa of Avila. For the Catholic, Teresa is eminently a daughter of the Church. For a Quaker, she is someone who was very much in touch with her "inner light," so dear to Quakers. That of God in every woman or man.

What drew me to the Episcopal priest-turned-Quaker as possible spiritual director was a lecture series he gave years ago at a local Quaker center where he was indeed spiritual director, the closest the Society of Friends around the Quaker city comes to priest or minister.

The lecture series was titled the *Apostolic Succession of the Mystics:* 1) the God-centered mysticism of the Fourth Gospel: Jesus, the Jewish Mystic, 2) the Christ-centered mysticism of Paul of Tarsus, 3) the aesthetic mysticism of Augustine of Hippo, 4) the philosophical mysticism of Meister Eckhart, 5) the material mysticism of Teilhard de Chardin.

Not much came of the effort to find spiritual direction in this friendship. We did indeed become friends who could talk "on the way" but even that was limited by his move several hundred miles away.

Well, now that friend much older than myself is dying, and I know he wants a visit. A few months ago his cancer required the removal of his leg up to the groin. He said then that he would choose surgery as faithful to the biblical advice to "choose life." The cancer now is back, and he has little choice but to prepare for the big journey, a journey he will probably make before my return from the Holy Land.

So. The same week as my departure for Jerusalem, another journey for me to say farewell to an old friend.

His sickroom is clean and has such wonderful light coming through the drapes, with none of the odors we encounter in sickrooms. He is weak and hardly able to speak, yet his eyes are clear and bright, and he is propped up in bed.

Those wonderful eyes tell me how grateful he is for my long journey to visit him. His wife is better able to understand his slurred speech and responds to his words by fetching from another room a book he wants to give me. A new study of the poems of George Herbert. I wonder whether he recalls my affection for Simone Weil and her affection for Herbert. Probably so.

My friend directs his wife to inscribe the book to me "with love."

I am also hoping that the book means that he is moving closer to the mystery of Christ so prominent in the poems of Herbert. Years ago this Quaker friend mentioned to me that he had wandered beyond traditional Christian faith and even his dear Teilhard. The wandering brought him to the idea that the Christian Church, in those early councils defining her Christology, should never have "broken the metaphor," should not have tried to define literally "who the Son of Man is," should have been content with metaphor.

Now that he is dying, I want him to have the full Christ, the Christ who is Word made flesh, walked this way of suffering and death before us. The Christ who gave us such promises: "I am going to prepare a place for you."

I want my friend to have this promise. I am taking this gift of George Herbert as sign that he is open to that mystery and promise. Of course, in the end I shall accept wherever he is. We are in good hands. Catholic theologian John Carmody, who has a fatal illness, has a fine new book: *Psalms for Times of Trouble.* I notice he is faithful to the Jewish nature of the psalms so that they address the Mystery that we call God in a way that can embrace Christ, yet not so as to exclude Jewish people or others like my friend here. Whenever people wanted to gaze on Christ in some exclusive way, Christ seems to have directed them further on to His Father.

Anyhow. I shall go home to send my friend those psalms of Carmody. Perhaps his wife can read aloud to him in these long days and nights of terrifying waiting.

Not Impossible

A gift of coconut candy, called Irish potatoes, came for Saint Patrick's Day. I remembered that Beata down in the projects had her windows decorated for the feast a week beforehand. She mentioned also that in honor of the Irish Day, she treats herself to a box of Irish potatoes. I had told her that I would treat her this year. She did not expect me to come through. The candy gift to me was a reminder of my promise.

This visit Beata was home alone. Daughter Teresa was outside in the concrete courtyard and saw me coming. She ran over to embrace me, which dispelled any suspicion her friends might have had of this white fellow entering their space.

The daughter of Teresa and a granddaughter of Beata followed me up the steps and into the apartment. Beata tried to chase her out again and turned somewhat away from any kiss I wanted to give her.

What unfolds is that since my last visit, Beata has had radiation for some throat growth and was sent home to this four-room apartment with the warning to avoid her family until the radiation is gone.

She takes all this in stride: the malignancy, the radiation, the difficulty of keeping the granddaughter who followed me upstairs away from her lap. As we talk, the television reads "mute." Cartoons. She says that she prefers cartoons to the afternoon soap operas. I wonder where she gets her strength. The only answer surfacing in me is that concept of necessity in Simone Weil. Beata has no choice but to stay strong and to accept this worry and illness as one more thing in her impossible life. Impossible is my term. For her the throat trouble, trying to keep some distance from her family in four rooms, coping with still another pregnant daughter, all this is simply life, not impossible life. Not impossible because she does it, does what she must do every day without any expectations that things will become easier or better.

Again I wonder what brought Beata to church so faithfully those Sundays when I first came here 13 years ago. Of course, her children were younger then, and she had them with her. I wonder also why she stopped coming: what died in her or was worn down by life in the projects? Her friendship with me seems unchanged. Almost as though she knows that I understand, that she need not explain anything.

The Mystery of the Church

Off again. I notice that occasionally I need some space, a retreat from my crowded life. Where this need takes me does not seem to matter. The idea is just being away for a week or two weeks or even a month.

This year Jerusalem. Jerusalem, because I am reading *The Life of Jesus* by Shusaku Endo, who goes on about Galilee in the springtime. Jerusalem, because friends were recently there and enjoyed the visit. Jerusalem, rather than a French monastery with Gregorian Chant. Jerusalem, because I am travelling with frequent flyer miles that are a gift of my brother, and Jerusalem was an option.

In any case, the vacation is an exotic luxury unavailable to my North Philadelphia neighbors, who suffer the daily crowding more than I do and never get away. These thoughts press upon me as departure approaches and I can do little but be off and hope the time away refreshes me for Holy Week and summer in the city.

I suspect that I am going to Jerusalem for still another reason: to discover whether Catholic faith has other dimensions than the European culture so firmly within me from childhood and seminary. I recall a poem years ago by a priest who walked away from the Church and what he called "his morbid Gothic God." Certainly an image of God connected with those French monasteries I want to visit someday: dark chapels and the drone of the chant.

In Israel I want to visit Melkite Catholic priest Elias Chacour whose books I have read. Somewhere he mentions a Roman official asking whether Father Chacour is "in union with Rome." Elias answered with a question: "Are you in union with Jerusalem?"

In a recent synod in Rome concerning the Church in Africa, much talk about adaptation. I noticed cautions from Roman officials: the warning that Catholic faith took shape around European culture, so that this form is now the model or paradigm which must be respected by any variations on the theme.

I do not know how that understanding connects with an idea of Albert Loisy and his theory that the story of the Church is like the story of a tree: no predetermined shape, rather a form determined by random weather and soil, rain and wind and sun one year to the next.

In this understanding, the Church is shaped by history. The intense icon devotion of the Eastern Church was a reaction to an iconoclasm that did not happen in the West. And in the West, a strong devotion to the Real Presence of Christ in the Eucharist because the Protestant reformers questioned that doctrine.

Doctrine intrudes here, which is why Loisy was excommunicated. Catholics must believe, for example, that bishop, priest, and deacon exist in the Church by divine institution. Yet I know now what I did not know in the seminary years: that the primitive local churches did not have one model of organization. The Jerusalem church might have been administered by a collegium of elders and Antioch by a single strong personality.

Impossible to sort all this out. I can only turn the pages of the story, like John Henry Newman turning the pages of the early Church Fathers to discover a way "commending itself," as Newman discovering the papacy despite himself.

A secular model of this *fides quaerens intellectum* or *intellectus quaerens fidem* might be psychoanalysis. Freud believed that with attention and courage and therapy the thin thread of reason could be discovered and followed in the welter of human emotions.

So much to believe when we embrace the Church! More than many people can handle. The modern sensibility is overwhelmed with how little we can know and is not inclined to articulate the mysteries in the detail the Church requires.

Reflecting in the Holy Land

A bewildering experience, the Holy Land. Bending over to see out the shuttle van windows in the ride from Tel Aviv airport to Jerusalem, I find myself looking for fields where shepherds might have heard angelic choirs.

Instead there is Jerusalem with Israelis building a new society and Palestinians paying the price, as someone always must pay the price.

Such a terrible history, this city of peace. The Exodus people coming in and killing everybody, including women and children and even the cattle. Then the Babylonian and other captivities, Byzantine invasions, Ottoman Turks, Crusaders. Each wave so destroying all that went before that even the locations of basic holy places are uncertain for lack of intact remains. We do not know precisely where Jesus lived or died or was buried.

And yet, that lack of certainty is important. Whatever meaning these events of life and crucifixion have it cannot be tied to some shrine. It cannot be important to come here. Either the message is as available in my time and place as in old Jerusalem or else that message has no importance. Almost necessary that years and place disappear into the mists of history so that the mystery might belong to us all. Walking the *Via Dolorosa,* I am aware that perhaps Jesus was condemned here and perhaps he was not. The scourging probably happened across the Old City at the Citadel. So what? All of which suggests that the expensive effort of coming across the world to see these places is beside the point.

And yet and yet. Gabriel Marcel talks about the scandal of the particular. Years ago, Monsignor Ronald Knox went on about how our *credo* soars into the heavens. "I believe in God, the Father Almighty, Creator of heaven and earth, and in Jesus Christ, His only Son . . . who suffered under Pontius Pilate . . . " that sudden descent from the sky to this man, this place, this time. Our faith is in a historical event surrounded by all the particulars and scandals and concreteness of human history. The death of Christ, both the most important human event ever and something so unimportant that most of Jerusalem probably did not interrupt the business of Passover and visitors' weekend to notice the crucifixion of these three criminals by the Roman authorities.

These buildings and this "Holy City" are no different for these happenings. These buildings did not survive earthquake or war to mark more clearly these happenings. These buildings and their inhabitants over centuries suffered more destruction of their clear identity because of these holy origins. They inspired invasions and crusades. The scholar Jerome Murphy-O'Connor says of the 1099 massacre of all the Muslims in Jerusalem by European crusaders, "from such unthinking fanaticism was born the inflexibility of Islam. The memory of the massacre forever stood in the way of a permanent *modus vivendi.*"

Reason enough for many to walk away scandalized by such a history. Faith or inertia has me clinging to my childhood faith, that buried in this *haceldama* or blood field, is the pearl of great price for which someone is willing to give all.

So I walk through these streets filled with beggars and merchants look for still another Station of the Cross. Ah, there is the Fourth Station: Jesus Meets His Afflicted Mother. A Roman numeral and a carving over an unused door with the ooze and odor of urine signs the shrine. Standers-by here in the Armenian quarter look at me with curiosity. That kind of world, that kind of faith. The whole business so earthy that over the centuries a tragic anti-Semitism could result from something so holy.

A Second Christmas

Bethlehem is easier to handle than Jerusalem. Not because the story is happier but because a smaller town gives the mystery more a focus. A pilgrim must stoop to enter the large church because the doorway was made smaller by Crusaders and later Turks to prevent looters driving carts into the church.

Down in the cave with the crowds I bend over to kiss the glass circle on the floor where an inscription around the glass probably says in Latin that here Jesus Christ was born of Mary. Probably because the poor light and surge of the crowd prevent my clear reading of the words.

I kiss lips to hand and hand to glass not because I am certain that this is the place but because I believe – at least these years I seem to believe – the impossible truth that "the Word was made flesh and dwelt amongst us." Christmas is more important to me than Easter. Saint Paul gave the mystery his Jewish holocaustal understanding that Christ came to die for our sins. I am more in sympathy with Julian of Norwich and John Duns Scotus and Gerard Manley Hopkins. In the words of Dame Julian: "Wit it well, love was the meaning." Sin or no sin, He would have come among us to close the distance. This love union for which, in the mystics, human love is a metaphor. Here in Bethlehem I wanted some piece of that particularity. I went to one of those dreadful shops and bought crosses and rosaries made from the local olive wood. I wanted to connect with this physical place where the Divine Mystery physically connected with us. Here in Lent with Easter coming, I will not need Easter this year. I have a second Christmas.

Money Reigns

Bewildering indeed. Toward evening the scream of sirens and the throb of helicopters overhead. The Vice President of the United States is here in Jerusalem, and the never-quite-invisible military are everywhere.

I move downstairs to the chapel of this Catholic hostel for evening prayer and Mass. The antiphon for the second psalm of the evening prayer is: "The Lord has chosen Zion as his sanctuary." Zion is right across the street behind the walls in the Old City, where yesterday I tried to follow the Way of the Cross. Jesus did walk those streets sometime or other, even if his route to Calvary is not certain.

My bewilderment comes from antiphon drowned out by helicopter. The idea is that Zion is the Holy City, and divine protection means that by their own Scriptures the Israelis are neither to trust helicopters nor nuclear weapons. What does it mean that the military pushes all that aside?

The realities of our century seem to push faith and Scripture off the stage altogether. National security, foreign aid from the United States and expansionism into East Jerusalem are the realities.

Perhaps these are the realities of every century. Yet, St. Paul says somewhere that the things that are invisible are real, not those that are visible.

The opposite seems true. That visit today to the Hebrew University of Jerusalem. Such a presence of impressive architecture and law schools and school of social work and tunnels connecting these handsome buildings and good-looking young people speaking a Hebrew language brought back from oblivion by someone teaching it to his children in anticipation of the re-establishment of this state of Israel out of the desert. The "Miracle of the Mediterranean."

The Palestinians would insist that the miracle is possible because of money: United States foreign aid. A quarter of all United States foreign aid goes to Israel, to helicopters, and this grand university. Money is so real. Money makes things happen. What the psalm phrase "The Lord has chosen Zion for his dwelling," means in the midst of all this bewilders me.

By contrast the small Christian Brother school of Bethlehem University seems pathetic, few or no graduate schools. I suspect the students are more subdued, so many of them seeming to be right off the dreary streets of Bethlehem, more of them Muslim than Christian. The whole thing is so less able and energetic an enterprise than the Jerusalem school. Again, the difference is money.

Yet both my religious tradition and that of the Israelis insist that money cannot be the bottom line, the final reality. I know that Zionism is mostly a secular movement of people who, after the Holocaust, want a security that will promise no Holocaust "ever again." Yet their claim to this city has religious origins: "The Lord has chosen Zion for his dwelling." Perhaps the religious origins are just a source that became less religious and more practical over the decades: If not here, where? If not now, when?

And my own religious tradition deriving from theirs says: you cannot serve God and money. Yet the decision to withdraw the church from poor neighborhoods back in my city happens because of money. No one even suggests that other considerations can prevail. It seems that the modern world is a place in which the most precious of our traditions cannot survive because other things are more real. Helicopters and the security state a more real necessity than that vision of Israel carved across that elegant synagogue facade back home: "My house shall be a house of prayer for all peoples." That vision of Israel now lost in military realities.

And that wonderful saying of my tradition: "You cannot serve God and money." The footwashing of the poor lost in a world where money reigns.

Diversity in the United States

The language question. Amazing how the Israelis revive a language more or less unused for centuries. And Hebrew is revived and used, not the Yiddish of European Jews in the centuries of the Diaspora.

And the embarrassment for us North Americans that ordinary people, waiters and chambermaids and taxi drivers, can manage in English and French and Spanish and German and Italian.

Because English-speaking people are so unable in other languages, English is becoming the *lingua franca,* so to speak. I hope that does not happen. The French will be unhappy, and the world will be poorer with everyone wearing T-shirts and sweat shirts saying Malibu or Dallas Cowboys. Someone called it the "New Jerseying of the world."

The Bible story of the tower of Babel suggests that diverse tongues are a curse making life more difficult. One could make a case that the many languages are rather a richness and express the variety and diversity of culture and expression: a garden of many and different blossoms.

Why am I sad in anticipating the acceptance of English as the common tongue worldwide? Is my dislike for my own country and culture so fierce?

I hope not. I want to consider the United States good and bad, weak and strong, like any other culture and country. There are wonderful things about us, and we have a contribution to make toward that rich diversity.

Yet I recall those years when the pull of Maryknoll was strong. I wanted to go off to work in a simpler society, among poorer people, for my own sake, as well as their need. What stopped me in part were the Civil Rights struggle and the Vietnam War protest. Both seemed to say "stay here and do these important works." All this confirmed by reading somewhere that young Americans visited Che Guevara and wanted to help his revolutionary work in Latin America. The advice of Guevara to those young North Americans was to go home and fight the Great Beast in his own lair.

I hesitate to go through life thinking of my culture and homeland as the Great Beast. Yet difficult here in Israel not to regard the pervasive militarism as a United States export.

Yesterday at the Hebrew University of Jerusalem, so wonderful to meet a New York Jewish man, now an Israeli, researching Africa and trying to show how Africa, which is a disaster by any World Bank measure, is at least in some areas more than the AIDS-stricken economic catastrophe we see. He has worked there and sees how African villagers sustain one another by mutual cooperation, distant and different from the massive institutions of development we require, yet which serve us so poorly.

I mentioned to him my new understanding of Catholic Worker anarchism after so many years. Of course, he knew that vision. I have awe for this tradition of American Judaism so prominent in the struggles of the early labor movement and later in the Civil Rights movement.

With hesitation I mentioned Simone Weil to the Jewish scholar. I was afraid that he would dismiss her as a self-hating Jew. Finally, I did mention her hope that after World War II the peoples of Africa might surface according to some other model than the nation-state because the world already had too many nation-states.

He seemed agreeable enough for my comments and reached for a recent book which he found helpful, a title something like "The Black Man's Burden: The Nation-State."

Union of Birth

An American friend in church work in Jerusalem took me away from the shrine visits for an afternoon. Driving north and east of Jerusalem, we came to a Palestinian village about 40 minutes away. The road into the village was little more than a goat path. On the ridges along the way, the Israeli "settlements." I knew for years that that word is misleading. Nothing has more the appearance of permanence than the new Israeli "settlements" on the West Bank. The message is: we Israelis are here to stay. This land is our land, and by immigration from Russia and new construction we shall render any other future here a practical impossibility.

Still another small Italian religious community inhabits this Palestinian village that is again little more than a goat path through the stone hills. The community comes from Bologna, Italy and includes priests, brothers, sisters, and married lay people who share community. Brother Alessandro informs me that back in Italy a lay person can be director of a local community. He or she may be married and with spouse and children live near the sisters and brothers.

No lay members here, but a house of brothers across a vineyard from the sisters.

We arrive at noon, and they are at prayer in a plaster-and-tile church which is also the Latin Catholic parish church for the village. Today is the Feast of the Annunciation, a feast full of meaning in these hills close to Nazareth or Bethlehem or wherever Mary and Joseph lived.

Brothers and sisters on either side of the church wear a rough brown habit which I take for Franciscan. Later Alessandro tells me they are not Franciscan, and the robe is more desert gray than brown. He wears this habit to class at the Hebrew University of Jerusalem where he is a student of Semitic languages. The Jewish students must consider him some Muslim or other up there on Mount Scopus; his desert hue habit, some variation of Islam.

After noonday prayers with lengthy Gospel readings, so poignant in these hills where whatever words of Jesus we preserve were heard, a feast day meal with the brothers, one of whom is a priest.

All the sisters and brothers are from Italy and have come here to the hills of Palestine to insert themselves invisibly into the life of a village almost entirely Muslim. They want to share the life of the people. In church the prayer was in Italian and Arabic and, for our sake, also in English. The sisters and brothers are here in the hope that despite the human face of the Church – Italians have no illusions about the Church – that Christ and his inheritance are the reality which can bring our wounded world together. And nowhere are these wounds more obvious than on our ride home through burnt-out Ramallah, once the "Switzerland of Jordan," now a wasteland with Israeli checkpoints on the road to Jerusalem.

During dinner the community superior is called to the back door. He reappears after a half hour with an apology. Some Muslim neighbors know this is the feast day of these two Catholic households of sisters and brothers across the vineyard and bring food and gifts. The sisters and brothers take that visit as sign that their presence here is worthwhile. Some connection or union between Muslims and Christians in this pathetic village with no telephone service.

Sunday Mass

The Christian Brothers at Bethlehem University had mentioned Sunday Mass in a French Benedictine monastery at Abu Ghosh. Sunday was coming and that mention stayed with me. The only difference between a liturgist and a terrorist is that one can negotiate with a terrorist.

Abu Ghosh is one of three possible sites of the Emmaus story. Apparently the Byzantine tradition locating Emmaus elsewhere was unknown to the Crusaders, who measured 60 stadia (11.5 km) from Jerusalem and chose a village with a spring and reservoir as a likely site. The Gospel story, too important to neglect, describes "a village named Emmaus about seven miles from Jerusalem" as the place where the risen Christ joined two disciples walking home forlorn from the defeat of Good Friday.

Despite the uncertainty of the shrine, the attraction of Sunday Mass was enough to draw me. I was not disappointed.

The Crusader Church was dark as night. Darker still the crypt chapel where Mass would happen because the upper church is undergoing restoration of peeling frescos.

At the entrance to the monastery, an Arab beggar. Just inside a Benedictine from Zaire praying his beads and assuring us that Mass with "Gregorian Chant" would begin in half an hour. Upper and lower church, still so empty and dark that I had to leave the entrance door open to make my way at all.

A half hour. Time to look around. Dark because the Romanesque arches needed the support of thick walls with small window openings. A young woman arrives carrying a portable instrument, something like a harpsichord.

Others arrive: tourists with booklets in German. A white couple with two little daughters, a dark woman with two small sons, a French group, an Italian group.

The Mass is the Fourth Sunday of Lent, and the Solesmes *Graduale* which a monk hands me begins *"Laetare Jerusalem."* Laetare Sunday telling us: "Rejoice, Jerusalem." Easter is coming.

The entrance procession includes monks and nuns. White nuns who are probably Benedictine, two black nuns in some African habit eclipsed only by the prior or abbot-celebrant wearing a festive chasuble, so wonderful that it might be a Matisse. So slight the pink for the Laetare Sunday that I wonder whether pink might look white in such a dark crypt.

The Mass could not last long enough for me. Coming here to Jerusalem was a casual enough choice over going to Solesmes for a stay. And here a Solesmes morning on a Lenten Sunday when the Mass could not be more festive. And Latin and French. My ear for French more alert from the monthly Haitian Mass back home. So here we are. I am so happy. Latin Gradual in hand and invited to sing the Mass parts with the sisters who alternate in the *Asperges* and *Credo, Sanctus* and *Agnus Dei* with the monks. Lovely to hear in French the Gospel parable of the Prodigal Son, the Epistle of St. Paul saying that "God in Christ reconciles the world to Himself" and that our work is that of reconciliation.

And here we are at the table of the Lord in a dark crypt, reconciling ourselves through Christ. The man beside me is as attentive as myself, even with his two daughters moving between him and wife just below us on a cold stone shelf. He is so attentive and familiar with the chant that I wonder whether he is a priest, now married and still drawn to these places as am I.

Strange how we Catholics hold onto this hope and desire for the Church. The Epistle goes on: God "has entrusted the message of reconciliation to us. This makes us ambassadors for Christ, God, as it were, appealing through us." All this alongside the Gospel of a father welcoming back a wayward son.

Perhaps I should have some problems with our European taking of these stories and letters from these sunwashed hills into a somber crypt, so that the shadows need be lightened with a Matisse chasuble. Yet even the bright and comforting Emmaus story has the play of light and shadow. Jesus walking with the two disciples to an inn over the cistern beside me said to them: "Was it not necessary that the Christ should suffer these things and enter into His glory?"

The darkness is not a contrivance. A dark mystery this faith, this Church, this play of shadow and light, like the festive Matisse vestment in this crypt. I look around me. Somehow those bringing these expectations to the faith find these places, and one another. The beauty draws them. Here, they believe, is the reconciliation of Jew and Arab, black and white monks chant together the *Credo in unum Deum . . . et unam sanctam Catholicam ecclesiam.* The Church, Ambassador of Christ – they, we, are being reconciled to God and to one another by this Eucharist.

I did not catch all the French homily. I did understand our response to the intercessions. So lovely for this Sunday of the Parable of the Prodigal Son: *Soit beni, o notre Pere, avez pitie pour nous.*

House of Mercy

Bethesda. House of Mercy. What began as a search for what guidebooks call the loveliest church in Jerusalem becomes the discovery of ruins just beyond the church. The ruins are the pool of five porches, where Jesus healed a man waiting 38 years to enter the pool first after an angel stirred the water.

The whole story is that the pool was not a Jewish shrine at all, rather a pagan shrine to the god Asclepius, where the sick and disabled came because they were not welcome in the Jewish temple. Coming here was an act of desperation or hope beyond their Jewish world. Perhaps the pool was no more than a refuge, a place where beggars and disabled people could loiter without being chased away. Bethesda. House of Mercy.

So. Here is Jesus not rewarding faith in His Jewish tradition. Rather He is just opening up to some poor fellow hanging out at a pagan shrine because he has nowhere else to go and is passing the years with an eye on some legend saying that a ripple on the water is an omen of a passing angel and a cure for the first one in.

The story thus told makes Jesus even more generous by not requiring any kind of real faith. He helps out in a very unorthodox situation, simply. House of Mercy.

Jacob's Well

The driver stops in Nablus saying: "Tourists do not come here." Nablus or Shechem has been a tense city and a place to avoid.

A knock on the steel door under a sign, Greek Orthodox Convent, brought a porter soon enough. No need for words. I followed him through a littered yard to some steps leading down to a crypt of a Greek Orthodox chapel.

And there in the middle of the chapel, sure enough, a traditional looking well. The porter took a pewter mug from the edge of the well and poured water into the opening. Deep indeed. A long silence before I heard the splash.

Deep indeed because this is Jacob's Well. The well where a Samaritan woman asked Jesus how he was going to give her a drink since the well is so deep and he has no water jar or bucket.

The Samaritan woman, whom Jesus sent to call her husband, said she had no husband – Jesus told her about her five husbands and the man living with her now, who was not her husband.

So many of these shrines are approximations or conjecture. But not Jacob's Well. This place, this crossroad, the identity of this well in the Jewish world, before and since Jesus, makes this very real.

So much came in on me. That Gospel story of John so important to me. That Christ would have such a sublime conversation with such an unlikely pupil as this much-married matron. That He, like us, had to use such ordinary images as water to talk about the mysteries. Once He even made mud with His spit to give some expression to a healing. Often when I am baptizing, I am mindful of how impoverished and pathetic the ceremony can be with infant crying and parents distracted and family courteous but bewildered by what seems more distraction than substance.

Sometimes I then recall the strange story that happened in this forgotten place, in a littered yard guarded by two mangy dogs. I do not read the Gospel of the Woman at the Well because the story is very long, and the child might begin crying if he or she is not already crying. I do reassure myself that water and grace and a half-interested congregation are not an altogether impossible situation.

After splashing some of the well water on my face, saying some distracted but more fervent prayers than my usual, I lit a candle to remember ailing friends whom I brought with me in heart to the Holy Land. Leaving, I remembered still another lovely part of the story. Over the objection of His disciples Jesus took an unlikely route to Galilee. Jews did not venture through these unfriendly Samaritan territories. He was looking for this woman. Simone Weil says this is always the case: we do not look for God; rather, God searches out us. Samuel Johnson would weep every time he read or heard the old Latin sequence *Dies Irae.* The whole story of the Samaritan woman is evoked in nine words: *Quaerens me sedisti lassus tantus labor non sit cassus.* (Seeking me you sat down weary; may such an effort not be in vain.)

Incarnation of Nazareth

Nazareth. Even more bewildering than Bethlehem. Archeologist Murphy-O'Connor says, quite easily, that Luke was wrong about the home village of Mary and Joseph, so that the Annunciation or good tidings to Mary did not happen here but in Bethlehem, just as did the Nativity nine months later.

All of which does not stop a stone inscription in the grotto altar from reading: *Verbum caro hic factum est.* The particularity takes my breath, difficult to give it the best English: here the Word became flesh or the Word was made flesh here.

Well, the dubious site does not hinder my faith, at least for now. I am with Duns Scotus here. Any God looking down on such a world had to come down and "walk our walk," as they say these days. And the descent means that the Incarnation or enfleshment or whatever we can call it had to happen in some particular place. Nazareth or Bethlehem. It does not matter. That descent or walk had to happen in some century and not another. And across the centuries we must live off that story as handed onto us as any human story is handed on, full of variations and gaps. The tradition suffers all the limitations of the human condition because that is the only condition we have.

Sowing Hope and Joy

Nazareth is very close to the village of Ibillin and the work of a Melkite Catholic priest, whose two books I have read. I wanted to meet him because I need his strength for my own work.

Difficult in Ibillin to tell the field stones from the stones that are houses. Up and down unpaved streets I wonder whether the village has any center at all. Up close the houses have a woman in a doorway or children in a littered yard.

We find our way to the Prophet Elias Community College, the work of Abuna Chacour for his Palestinian people so neglected and humiliated in the development of the state of Israel.

Without help from state or local Church, Chacour now has a school for a thousand children. After Easter he is off to Philadelphia, no less, then California on the weary work of getting the word around, gathering the funds he needs to continue.

On the playing field just beside his house where we have a noonday meal, our conversation is over the shouts of students, children really. I try imagine how this forsaken village would look without these new buildings, so white in the brilliant sunshine. Impossible that thought. What comes to mind is the prayer of St. Francis: where there is despair, let me sow hope; where there is sadness, joy.

I think of my own work back in Philadelphia, so much smaller an enterprise than this; yet, so arduous the fund raising. Like this Palestinian village, my neighborhood would be so much more in decline without our parish presence on that corner – church and school. I recall trying to say that much during the planning sessions which closed so many parishes two years ago: these places are often the only stable institutions in an otherwise precarious and fragile neighborhood. Their closing will mean that conviviality or the quality of life or hope or joy will diminish on those corners, and no one might ever notice that this decline has happened.

Abuna Elias Chacour was as interested in my work among the African-American peoples of Philadelphia as I was in his work here in Ibillin. This long trip north was worth the considerable effort. We embraced as *compañeros* in the struggle and brother priests. I plan to have him meet with Catholics in our Pax Christi/Catholic Peace Fellowship group when he comes to Philadelphia after Easter. He is coming at the invitation of the local diocese of the Episcopal Church.

Calvary

So confusing my first visit to the Church of the Holy Sepulchre, that I felt an obligation to try again. This time to prepare by reading the archeological guidebook more carefully.

Just inside the door, a stone stairway to a second level with a Byzantine and Crusader Chapel side by side. I am glad that I did not miss this. The Greek Chapel is built over a large glass cabinet that encloses a rough rock ledge, that might well be Calvary where Christ died. And those stone steps, the ascent where Christ walked His last steps.

The hour was early morning, and the Greek Chapel still empty. An older man back in the shadows against a pillar looks by his prayer posture very like the Muslims I saw yesterday praying at the Dome of the Rock. He was sitting on his heels with his head touching the cold marble floor in front of him.

I withdrew to a bench and discovered from the guide book that beneath the Greek altar a hole in the glass cabinet enables the pilgrim to reach through and down to touch the rock that is Calvary. I looked up to see a couple who had entered the chapel doing that.

I was embarrassed either by the primitive faith that had me want to touch the rock or the lack of faith that I brought to the gesture. As John Carmody says in his *Psalms* written as faith expression for his own terminal illness: "Our faith is too weak to keep you real." I thought of the woman in the Gospel who had been hemorrhaging for years and touched the cloak of Christ. Her faith must have been as vague as mine. I decided to go all the way with it. Rising from the stoop necessary for the touch, I left an American dollar in the bronze dish guarded by an almost invisible Greek nun just beside the altar.

She did not even look up as I took a slender candle and placed it in the candle stand. The words coming to me were names from home: Barbara and two Johns, Loretta and two Marys who are struggling with cancer. All that I could ask in faith was that somehow the grace of this Calvary might be with them in their own. Other names came: the friends who lost a young daughter to anorexia. Their suffering, so like that of the mother up there in the Byzantine mural or mosaic. I found a kneeler farther back in the shadows. The need I had to drink more deeply of this place. This mystery important, incomprehensible to me. Words came from my childhood in church: "We adore you, O Christ, and we bless you, because by your Holy Cross you have redeemed the world."

Surrendering to the Commonweal

The newspaper here, so inflammatory. Israeli politicians calling the other party traitors and cowards and Arabs in disguise.

And the Queen of the Netherlands visits, and a comment is that she should have been even more apologetic for the failure of the Dutch to save Jewish people in Holland from the Holocaust. Another mentions how few European Christians showed any courage in the Nazi years.

A bizarre and tragic nerve gas incident in a Tokyo subway this week is translated into still another attack that Arabs might try here. An Israeli defense expert comments: "I don't have to tell you how sensitive Jews are to the word 'gas.' "

Impossible to speak lightly of the Jewish Holocaust and the movement of Zionism toward a restored sovereignty, a homeland where they need never again trust their destiny to others. "Never again." And the part played by religion in all this. Religion had a large part in the tragic history of the Jewish people over the centuries of the Christian era.

And before Christianity, religion already created bitterness here. Those brief phrases from the Fourth Gospel about Jesus in his journey through Samaria: "How is it that you, a Jew, talk to me who am a Samaritan, for Jews do not speak to Samaritans?"

Now Israelis and Palestinian Muslims and Christians. You do not ask a Jew for directions to Christian holy places, nor does a Christian stay in Jewish hostels.

And new injustice waters this religious desert, bringing new bitterness and violence and the invective of politicians and newspapers.

I leave what Muslims and Christians call the Holy Land and Jewish people call Israel with further dismay at the pathos of the human condition. As though North Philadelphia were not dismay enough.

Again, I do not know what to make of all this. That even in the effort to reach beyond ourselves to the Mystery we call God, we corrupt that work with hatred and violence.

We must begin to surrender more than we imagine possible. Returning from a place where three peoples side-by-side celebrate separate Holy Days every weekend, I wonder whether the Christian Church might make the conciliatory gesture of returning to the Jewish Sabbath observance. The Jewish people would not feel free to make such an accommodation of their sacred tradition. Of course, the Muslims might not be open to any accommodation either. Sad how little I know about Islam.

The newspapers did report some conciliatory gestures: a picture of the King of Jordan visiting a Holocaust memorial in Los Angeles, collaboration between Israel and Jordan on water problems. So far to journey in all this and each group fearing that conciliatory gestures might be received as weakness and exploited.

So much must change. I recall the friend speaking to our peace group about the dangers of the Bible with that often paranoid, genocidal image of God. With much humor he suggested that the best thing the Catholic Church ever did was to keep the Bible away from the people.

The season was Lent, and immediately the speaker added how beautiful the generosity required of the older son in the parable of the Good Samaritan, which was the Sunday Lenten reading that week. He meant the sublime love to which we are called by these same Scriptures: the older son is not allowed even a pout about the celebration for his returning brother. He must join the party even if he has no stomach for the fuss.

So. Simone Weil says that creation is God throwing part of God out into infinite distance. Our task, to make our way back across that thick infinity. I must add that Simone Weil did not believe we might do that very well. She claimed that human progress was a secular religion and an illusion deriving from the Bible, no less. The Greek view was more to her liking. Like a Greek tragedy, humanity plays out the same stories generation upon generation. Our task is ourselves, each bringing whatever good that return journey to God can contribute to the commonweal.

Distance from Beauty

Back with a vengeance, as they say. I hear the phone going as I lean against the door, suitcases in hand. Just inside I learn that we have two funerals, one tomorrow and another after the weekend.

Both funerals mean having the extended family back to the rectory for "repast" after cemetery and burial. During the week the school hall is not available because of the school lunch program, and the general student traffic through that lunch room and foyer and auditorium and detention and tutoring space is endless.

The rectory connects with the altar end of the church by way of a sacristy, which is also a daily Mass chapel. The rectory is a wonderful space, and I am glad that we have such elegant rooms to welcome our neighbors. These gatherings are often difficult with their intrusion into personal space. Just back from the luxury and privacy and distance of a vacation, I feel more than ever the crowding and confusion of people in the dining room and kitchen and restrooms and parlor and office. And still others arriving or looking for coffee or where to put their coats.

What I do is think about my Brooklyn friend, the priest with all those refugees living with him day and night. I think about the Lord wandering Galilee and Samaria and Jerusalem, which I just left. The Gospel says that with the demanding crowds, He and the disciples had neither space nor time "to eat their bread."

So. Just do it. Hitch my belt and just do it. Absorb the crowds, the questions. So distant the Church and all that theology seems from the lives of the people here. Even the Mass of Christian Burial seems an obscure sign, fraught with mystery about something other than the remembering of the deceased person just buried.

Unless I can make the connection, tell them by homily that what we are doing is taking up their departed loved one into the suffering and death of Christ by this Eucharist. St. Paul says: "When we eat this bread and drink this cup, we proclaim the death of the Lord until He comes." So our dying goes to the throne of mercy through His dying. Christ our brother takes us along the path he walked. The cantor sings the shepherd psalm with the verse: "Though I walk through the valley of the shadow of death, no evil shall I fear. . . ."

Short of their taking in all this in church when they are confused about standing and sitting, I must be content with their understanding this simpler gesture: that they are welcome here, that we want to do everything possible to soften their grief.

Holy Week is coming, and the brisk ease with which work and television and daily life wash out the awesome symbols of this week of washing feet and kissing the cross and waving palm causes me anguish. The distance of everyday life from all this fragile beauty saddens me. Simone Weil noted the beauty of Catholic liturgy and ceremonies; but, she adds: "They are unrelated to the rest of life."

I shall content myself with the far humbler sign of making room for these funeral-goers in this spacious old house. I shall hope that the welcome can connect with where they are in mind and life rather than where I want them to be.

6.

'April is the Cruelest Month'
Indeed

"April is the cruelest month" indeed
melting winter into soiled sluices
like the bleeding veins of a city
lying wounded in the glare of surgery . . .
                    –"After April"

. . . the full moon had Easter late in April
a warm night sent shoppers everywhere
street sounds poured through open windows
drowning the sound of water running
ewer to basin over bare feet . . .
                    –"Holy Thursday 1973"

. . . last the addict daily at the door
here tonight because the lights are on
and this line must go somewhere
halfway up he sees me and
his new devotion will intend
the two dollars he will later want

no matter
together we stumble to Easter
the *carpe diem* of the good thief
was, it seems, acceptable:
today you are with me in paradise
                    –"Good Friday: Adoration
                        of the Cross"

. . . Making the most of my distraction
I note we are a week from Good Friday
and the wound
that opening will be my access
                    –"Oratory: Easter Friday"

Victory Over Death

Palm Sunday. The reading of the Passion, so lengthy that I must speak very briefly. I tell the people at the earlier Mass about getting lost in Jerusalem while leaving the western wall and looking for the Temple Mount. I found myself in a Muslim cemetery looking up at the Jerusalem walls from another side.

I could not read a single letter of the Arabic inscriptions on the tombstones; but, I could understand the symbol of a palm branch wedged into holes dug into a tombstone.

These people of the Book share our story, even though they have a further story of their own. Beyond the barrier of foreign script and words, I could understand the palm. The Muslims share my faith in the biblical promises of victory over death.

Our waving palm today is doing what ancient peoples did welcoming conquering heroes. In our case Christ coming to reign on a cross and wear a royal crown of thorns and rule by washing feet. Such a strange vision.

In Holy Week, so rich the Catholic imagery. The signs, like washing feet and kissing a cross, take us far beyond words. They take me into an even deeper silence than the silence of, say, Quaker meetings which sometimes seem so attractive. Relief from many words, much homiletic nonsense, my own as well as that of others.

This Holy Week I am grateful for the Catholic richness of these signs. They seem to take me more deeply than words into these ineffable mysteries.

I am still reading *A Life of Jesus* by Shusaku Endo. He says that even for a writer like himself, the Passion story of Holy Week tells a mystery deeper than the words: "No other tragic drama introduces to the stage a sacred aureole to match the halo which radiates from the Holy One."

Serving God, Needing Money

More and more I notice how removed or distant I am from mainstream Catholic life.

I was required to attend a meeting where the matter of school vouchers surfaced. The local Church sees an opportunity to obtain public funding for Church schools. Opinion concerning the disarray of public schools is creating a climate where helping private schools

44

seems attractive. Even the editor of the daily newspaper, so often critical of the Catholic Church, is supportive of tax vouchers.

I find myself not wanting the Church to become aggressive in the pursuit of money. The biblical phrase comes to mind: "You cannot serve God and money." Whatever that means.

The Catholic Worker tradition comes to mind. Dorothy Day and Peter Maurin did not want tax exemption privilege or tax resources to perform the corporal or spiritual works of mercy. The idea is to do these things on your own like the Gospel woman at the temple box "who gave from her need." The twist that Dorothy gave to "give to Caesar the things of Caesar and to God the things of God" means have nothing to do with Caesar and do not let Caesar finance the works of mercy. Do them on your own. Personal responsibility. Do from your need, at your own expense, like the Good Samaritan taking the wounded man to the inn and asking the innkeeper to tend him, with the promise of the Samaritan to absorb the expense upon his return.

The Palm Sunday call from California comes to mind. A friend out there 15 years calling to tell me about the new book and admission of Robert McNamara that the Vietnam War was a terrible mistake and more or less his doing.

I do not want to see my Church, which was not aggressive or assertive about the evil of that war, be aggressive or assertive about money now. That sounds too much like giving money a priority or importance money cannot have in the Gospel.

I believe that if I can, more or less, manage this parish and school for poor children by begging, then the larger Church can do the same with even greater success. Everybody from the Lord to St. Francis of Assisi to Leon Bloy says that begging is an appropriate posture. A good posture for the Church. A humble posture, better than lining up with government. Word is that the Church tax in Germany is bitterly resented. And here in the United States, the Church is belatedly looking for these same privileges.

The Catholic Worker perspective is not going to win this one. In the next months I am going to feel more and more isolated. I know that my beloved Simone Weil thought the secular state, the total separation of religion from public life, was a great evil. I would want her around for this discussion. I am not sure that the state she would want helping religion is the nation state of our time.

I know all this sounds naive and sectlike. I know that Catholic colleges and universities prosper and compete better with secular schools because of government assistance. I know that the government assistance means ROTC and other inappropriate military presence on campus, and the diminishing of any strong religious identity in the pursuit of that funding. Most welcome that growth, possibilities of intellectual and academic prowess. I wonder what gets lost. I wonder what it means to say that you cannot serve God and money.

Grace Upon Grace

Holy Saturday: while parishioners dress the church for Easter, I slip upstairs and find myself at the desk, pencil in hand. A need to put words onto some Holy Week impressions.

Word comes from Dave Hagan that a fellow Oblate of Saint Francis de Sales has finally died. A letter arrives from the wife of my elderly Quaker friend who is dying. His wife says his big question is: "Is there any personal survival after death?" Word also comes that a friend from the 60s has an article in the morning newspaper about her inability to celebrate Easter with any religious faith. Nevertheless, she plans to attend Easter Mass at a church where her friend, who is a priest, tends the poor over many years. All reports are that she means me and this place.

Just now the phone rings against the Holy Saturday quiet. A young sister telling me about the death of the Oblate priest. Her idiom is faith: here at Easter, God wanted to raise up this son to Himself as with the raising of Christ.

This Holy Week I realize more than ever how much I want or need to inhabit a world most people are content to visit. If the visit becomes too lengthy or quiet, they are impatient, eager for the distraction of the holiday that Easter weekend is, besides the Holy Days of Maundy Thursday, Good Friday, and the Easter Vigil. Some friends are off to the seashore this sunny April Saturday. My hands and head are full of the mysteries and the preparations for the Easter Vigil which I briefly escape by this retreat to my room.

I love the words of Saint Paul that are an Easter reading: "You are dead now. Your life is hidden with Christ in God."

Years and years ago a cousin would take me to the Cathedral in Holy Week for *Tenebrae,* the solemn singing of the Holy Week Office. I remember the dark cathedral, the gradual extinguishing of the unbleached orange altar candles, the old Cardinal Archbishop nodding at his throne chair . . . .

That need or desire to inhabit some other world continued into my seminary years. The seminary near my home was a place free of distraction. It was a place of books and silence, a place away. During summer vacations, I would search out monasteries for even greater seclusion.

Is all this in me, then and now, a fear of the world, the tempestuous terrain just outside the door here in the desolation of North Philadelphia? Is that withdrawal a fear of life, or women, or sexuality?

I hope not. I think of Simone Weil insisting that her father take her to Solesmes for Holy Week in 1938. She stayed for hours in the chapel where, during the chant and her migraine headaches, the thought of the Passion of Christ entered her "once and for all."

Simone Weil was hardly afraid of the world. Farm workers and Renault factories and Spanish civil war, she threw herself madly into human suffering. One could make a case that she feared friendship and human love. She said things to that effect.

Then, of course, there is the Gospel story of Martha and Mary, with Mary leaving housework and hospitality to her sister while she attends "the better part, the one thing necessary." Christ does not dismiss that withdrawal as cowardice or evasion. He says that her choice will not be denied her.

So here I am in Holy Week, overwhelmed with the awe of these holy signs of palm and foot-washing and raising the cross and Eucharist and Baptism.

They overwhelm me, these signs. The mysteries they tell, beyond words. The joy, that as pastor I can tend their celebration with the care and reverence they deserve.

And sadness too. Sadness that I cannot persuade or beguile more friends and neighbors into this hidden world which the busy world quickly passes by. There are parishioners eager that their children and grandchildren have whatever Catholic grace graces our old school. Yet parents and grandparents were not here Thursday to have feet washed, were not here Friday to kiss the cross, will not be here tonight for the Great Vigil so precious to me even in my worn-out sensibility. And always the fear that this holy world which I inhabit this week is unreal or an anachronism. That people who are up and about catching the new spring sun to visit the seashore or downtown doing last-minute Easter shopping or even home filling an income tax return are more about reality. Well, I shall have to live with that doubt and ambivalence. I want to continue to choose that "life hidden with Christ in God." I do not mean that my choice is better or more real than the work of family or home which others make. All I know is that beneath the dark mystery of Holy Week, my attachment to these days is a great grace. I can only try to be faithful to such a gift. And I know that *The Life of Jesus* by Shushaku Endo, which I am finally finishing, and my recent Holy Land visit, have made Holy Week this year an even greater gift. Grace upon grace.

Enduring Wounds

A Washington, D.C. friend asks by phone what I think of "this Robert McNamara business." Holy Week I tend to skim the morning newspaper more than usual. The usual is a quiet read over morning coffee before the first phone call or visitor. Whatever is not read by then never gets read.

And Philadelphia does not have the "beltway fever" that comes on friends who move to the District, that fascination with political intrigue and personalities. The McNamara revelations are that he and others knew the Vietnam war was wrong and kept the war going anyhow and kept their secret from the rest of us. I am sure these revelations get more notice and study in the D.C. newspapers than here in Philadelphia.

Yet, another reason I am unaware of this McNamara business is that some fear or distress in me is wary of stirring the pot, that stew of memories from 20 years ago. So few were trying to stir the Church to some action, some protest against what surfaced more and more as something terrible. Hard to believe that "business as usual" mind of prelates and priests, as though the tasks of the Church were just the routines of churchgoing and school-tending and marriages and funerals.

I recall a parish assignment where I often appeared at dinner fresh from a draft card burning at City Hall which was covered on early evening television news. Priests at table with me had watched that news and were so angry at my presence at the draft protest that they could hardly speak to me across the table. The judgment was that down there with Black Panthers and marijuana users, I was compromising their priesthood as well as my own.

I recall once leafletting defense workers leaving their plant at the end of the workday. One motorist asked: "Is this the best you have to do with your time, Father?" I answered, "Yes."

That motorist gave words to the resentment of many then-older priests. I was still young, and Communion calls and parish chores were the extent of ministry. Time away from those works was for play – golf or seashore. Larger concerns, such as civil rights or the Vietnam war, were for the bishops to discern. Very Irish, this mentality. Many a person of Irish origins has experienced that pervasive repression of childhood: expressing an opinion at table and the reaction of the older folk is to ask: who do you think you are – the Prince of Wales?

The seminary enhanced all of that. The tasks of the parish priest were the daily routines. Comment on larger issues was for the Bishop. The whole sense was that even an accurate comment on some issue like Vietnam was out of line or stepping beyond one's competence. The clerical system enhanced that servile sense.

Meanwhile, with Vietnam and civil rights, the bishops were silent. Perhaps they too suffered the sense that someone farther up the line, such as Cardinal or Pope, should speak. Or perhaps they were of the mind of the fellows across the table on my return from the protest: the Church is about routine religious observance and little else.

The excuses for silence were many: well, McNamara and the rest must know what we do not know, and our protest would be presumptuous. Or the clerics advising Martin Luther King, Jr., in Birmingham jail: "You are upsetting people, doing more harm than good." A comment not far from the objections to the ministry that had Christ tried and crucified.A long time since Vietnam. Amazing how the wounds endure. Vietnam as much as civil rights has shaped my life, my regard for government, my confidence in the Church, friendships lost and found.

Lifting Up

No chance to disappear to the seashore this Easter week. Too much coming up, including a funeral this morning back in my childhood neighborhood. I do need the rest and space of a day or two away, but that luxury must wait another week at least.

The only answer is to try for space within. Leaving the funeral, I saw a lifelong friend coming into church for a second funeral. Easter Monday can be like that in the Catholic Church. No Mass of Christian Burial permitted during the last days of Holy Week, so that the deaths back up into Easter week.

Alb and stole in arm, making my way to the car, I was told by the friend that I should really stay for the second funeral Mass, if possible. For a week I had thought or read little else than what needed doing for the services of Holy Week, and I did not know about this other death.

I decided that the "letting go" of my agenda, my tired rush to be anywhere but church after a week in church, was connected with the discipline of prayer. I would go back into church, "let go" of my vague Easter Monday intentions and simply be there. I would watch the priest lift the Cup and Bread of Life at Mass, and even if my tired body was earthbound, I would lift deeper self or spirit as Christ was lifted on cross or from grave. This lifting up or letting go was the heart of prayer, even if on Easter Monday the experience was great fatigue.

At the Easter Vigil I wanted by way of homily to communicate the image of the "lifting up" of Jesus described by Herbert McCabe in two separate passages of his collection of essays called *God Matters.*

McCabe says that the Fourth Gospel does not want to make clear whether that "lifting up" means Crucifixion or Resurrection because both are the "hour" of Jesus, the fulfillment of his life and work.

Later on, speaking on prayer, McCabe says that the "lifting up" is the whole loving exchange revealing who and what Jesus is. He is "sheer prayer," utter obedience to the Father expressed by allowing himself to be lifted up on the cross: "The world must be shown that I love the Father and do exactly as He commands."

And the lifting up that is the Resurrection is the Father accepting that sacrifice. The other thread of this wondrous weaving.

So. All this is too much to say at an Easter Vigil where 25 baptisms require a very brief homily. I must be content to tell them about the Saint Patrick Day greeting from the German priest and teacher of theology who lived with us here during a sabbatical at the nearby university.

With the Latin phrases so rich and meaningful to priests his age and my own, Günter called this place in these neighborhoods:

sacramentum (levatum) visibile gratiae invisibilis in successione Domini nostri Jesu Christi. "A visible sign (lifted up) of invisible grace, in the tradition of Our Lord Jesus Christ."

What a wonderful compliment: "lifted up" – so expressive of the baptismal Passover mystery that the Easter Vigil proclaims.

Christ said: "If I be lifted up, I will draw all to Myself." Yet this lifting up was full of the fragile weakness of suffering and death. Saint Malachy can be that kind of sign: weak and poor and shaky here in these neighborhoods so needing some sign. We can at least be that. Even when people come filling the church for the Easter Vigil, they find a weak sign indeed and none weaker than their celebrant.

The mystery of the lifting up that is Calvary and Easter is a mystery of weakness. Both Hebrews and the letters of Paul to the Corinthians proclaim that.

Wonderful, that Holy Week letter from the wife of my dying Quaker friend who uses the phrase, "we must lift that up," referring to the uncertainty of whether he will survive until his 82nd birthday at the end of the month. Dear patient old man, unsure whether he will survive death at all. Perhaps his surrendering any clear hope shares the abandonment and surrender Christ knew – that awful and mysterious cry from the cross, "My God, my God, why have you forsaken me?" Christ, continuing to trust the love in which we live, yet sharing the plight of those around the world who, then and now, die in seeming despair from famine or torture or whatever. The mystery of weakness.

Carlos

Sometimes I lose touch with the street. Holy Week can do that. Or meetings, or getting into building maintenance and repair.

Today I came down for the five o'clock daily Mass to hear that a Latino fellow had come to the door to ask about "baptizing his baby." I was tired enough from Holy Week to respond to the volunteer generous enough to be here answering doors: "What are you talking about? What baby?"

We started Mass. A lean day, only two of us for Mass to hear these wonderful Easter readings about the appearances of the Risen Christ: "Mary Magdalen went and said to the disciples, 'I have seen the Lord.'"

Suddenly, fierce pounding on the front door only a few yards away. It was Carlos, the fellow who had reappeared recently in the crowd after Sunday Mass looking for a dollar or whatever. I suspected he was the one with the baby story. The woman had sent him away, and he was not going to be put off that easily. All during Mass he kept pounding on the door and shouting, "Father," as loudly as he could. Perhaps he had appeared in the vestibule Holy Saturday night during the baptisms at the Easter Vigil. Baptism then seems a way to reach the "Father."

Carlos is a regular at the Catholic Worker House. The dementia or whatever probably comes from his AIDS condition. Sometimes he appears here at the door with one shoe looking for another shoe.

Carlos quiets down with a dollar or two. All during Mass I wondered how I would deal with this after Mass. The woman, kind enough to cook dinner here, answered his doorbell rings while I was at Mass. When I finished, I could not just "take over," presume that my gesture to quiet and dismiss Carlos with a dollar is a better judgment than her more ignoring response. If Carlos discovers that this door and this hour every evening is a two-dollar resource, he will return and return and that shouting presence at the door will be her problem more than mine.

After Mass I could hear Carlos from various places around the property shouting, "Father." A voice and shout reminding me that beyond meetings and maintenance, the main fact of this place is the street, the projects down the street, all the people appearing now from the tomb-like apartments and row houses, like Jesus out from His tomb.

Tumultuous Reality

Last night, an assembly at a local high school and this morning with clouds hiding dawn, I sit at my eastward bedroom window listening to a recording of the Solesmes chant of the Easter Mass: "I am risen and still with you . . . ." During these weeks of Easter I fill myself with these alleluias and Easter readings by way of chant. An effort to sustain myself, keep going against the realities of the city and world and neighborhood that press me down, send me under.

Press me down as that public high school gathering did. The evening was a social and athletic and memorial gathering. About a thousand students streamed into their large auditorium for an assembly that never quite happened. There were speakers and singers and a drill team on stage, but the evening had no real beginning or center or finish. Students with small children kept coming and going, talking and changing their seats. The children took a cue from the drill team and imitated the marching in the aisles. The on-stage speakers kept talking into microphones, either oblivious or indifferent to whether anyone was listening. Teenagers looked around from their seats and quickly moved off to other seats where friends had newly arrived. With them went the beverages and potato chips they were eating.

I seemed to be the only one around even noticing the confusion. Afterwards Dave Hagan told me that these assemblies were the hardest part of his year teaching in public high school. He recalls with humor and dismay and awe his own high-school days 40 years ago at a Catholic high school not too distant from here. The enrollment was 4,000, twice that of this public high school, and he remembers with terror and admiration the priest "Dean of Discipline" of that school. "When he walked through a crowded auditorium toward the stage, there was complete silence. We were in mortal fear of him," says Dave Hagan.

People criticize that rigor of the old Catholic school, but Hagan, who has little patience with excessive discipline, remembered that scene against this modern reality.

After the assembly, we all proceeded to a gymnasium for basketball. A brief ceremony at the gym entrance had the crowd backed up and squeezed into the hallway in a manner that seemed dangerous. As though a push here or a stepped-on-foot there could bring bedlam. There was the real fear that we were in a dangerous situation. The whole affair so perfunctory. No preparations for seeing or hearing the brief ceremony. All we knew was that we were in a volatile crowd.

I do not fault the teachers or administrators. I wonder how they can manage day and week and month in such tempestuous disorder. Their going through the motions must express some despair of being able to make a difference or even a fear of being too demanding. A case might be made that physicians flitting from examination room to examination room, patient to patient, are just as perfunctory in a much more manageable situation. Or sitting in the back of church for Sunday morning Masses in a large Catholic parish could create the same impression of us priests at the altar: going through the motions.

And here I am, the morning after that high-school scene, sitting at my dawn window listening to a recording of Benedictine monks. The music summons up a scene of Gothic order and symmetry. The silent procession of monks to and from their services and offices. Such a contrast to the tempestuous world of that high-school gathering last evening.

And what is real? Obviously, the tempest is the overwhelming reality of the world. My world. That other world exists as far away as Solesmes in France or as close as the Quaker Retreat House where I spent a month last summer. No doubt that order and reflective quiet exists as close as the seminars high up in the towers of the nearby university, which look out on the high school of last night.

What is real? William James said that modern life needs some disciplinary form to provide what is now given only by the military. I suppose the monastic life is an alternative, but that regime is mostly gone now, even in the Catholic Church. Of course, most people, especially those young poor inner-city people of last night, are far from that influence.

And what am I looking for, sitting by my window in pre-dawn quiet, listening to Gregorian Chant? Some other world than this tumultuous world that is mine and soon begins with dawn and the life of the streets?

The memory of the Jerusalem visit remains. I can imagine Jesus squeezed in those dirty and crowded alleys, pushed along to Calvary. The life squeezed out of Him quite literally. The *Via Dolorosa,* the Way of the Cross: "Jesus falls the first . . . the third time . . . ."

But then that other Jesus, up before dawn, up all night praying, away from the disciples, alone, gathering strength from the prayer and solitude for the press of the Jerusalem streets.

"Things Fall Apart"

Saturday morning and remote preparation for First Communion next month has me sitting in the old church fragrant with Easter lilies. We shall keep the flowers and alleluias going for the 50 days of Easter.

Will the image of the bombed and devastated Federal Building in Oklahoma overwhelm any effort to lift up the Cross, now dressed in blossoms and festive vestments for Easter? What can we do in our world except to hold up the Cross against such horror? By all traditional theology, the death of Christ was the tragedy to measure all tragedy.

One could make a case that the racial hatred and neglect of the poor that spawns a high-school scene I experienced the other night has all the tragic fallout of the Oklahoma City disaster. My sense at the high school was that nothing worthwhile is coming of this mess. These children, by neglect and permissiveness, are being harmed beyond measure. Only this social disaster is less visible than Oklahoma City, not less destructive.

I am sitting in the church to hear the confessions of the 10 or 12 children who will make First Communion on a Sunday in May. During Holy Week I sat in church for confessions for an hour on Holy Thursday and again for an hour before the Easter Vigil on Saturday evening. No one came either Thursday or Saturday.

So what am I doing here but helping the children with a First Confession which will be their last confession?

Even as I sit here with the children, I notice that the disciplines of my own childhood are gone. Despite the heroic efforts of Sister Catherine and her catechists, the handy outline and prayer texts she has each child holding, nothing is forthcoming. The children cannot read. Or television has destroyed any capacity for memorization. Any minimal understanding of this human encounter of child and priest as sign of encounter with Church as sacrament or sign is not there. When I was a child, we came into a dark confessional more intimidating than this congenial setting. The sense was that the initiative must be mine; I had to tell my little story of disobedience or whatever. I was the penitent; the burden was on me to confess and ask forgiveness.

Catholic liturgists among others would say that television has wrought this passivity, such that I, the confessor, must do all the work: ask the questions and lead the prayers. No wonder that after the hour I am exhausted, even a little strung out. Sister notices my exasperation and gives a knowing nod: you know this is all we can manage these days.

Yet while listening and helping the young penitents, I cannot but notice the basic good sense of this discipline of the sacrament against the reality of that high-school assembly the other evening. I will not justify all the worry and fear that happened over the years in confessionals, but to bring children into the examined life early on is worth the effort. Years ago I was at a Benedictine priory. At chapter the Rule of Saint Benedict went on about the need for the monks to go around mindful of the psalm verse: "I am a worm and not a man." The elderly prior said the meaning beneath all the hyperbole was that the monks were to carry themselves as "men whose lives were lived out under judgment."

I continue the confessions one by one with that sense of futility: going through the motions of a discipline that has more or less collapsed. What are we to do, go through the motions in the hope that some older, calmer order will restore itself? The little worries of the children seem insignificant against the week of disaster in Oklahoma City. Yet what can we do to push back the darkness except for me to sit here with patience for each of these little ones and help them one by one to notice and face unafraid the darkness that is in each of us? I do not mean that we cannot extend our embrace, create a society, a climate that is life-giving and nurturing. Yet sometimes it comes down to this. Like a physician seeing patients one by one, a teacher tutoring an individual student having difficulty, the Lord saying to the apostles who wanted to chase the children away as unimportant: "Let the children come to me and do not hinder them."

As I say this, I know that a failing of the Church and priests is often a preoccupation with the individual, to the neglect of making what Peter Maurin called "a society in which it is easier for people to be good." For now, here I am, and here comes the next child, and everything comes down to this.

My sense even as I try to engage the child with gentleness is that this is too late or too little against such a world where the discipline of the sacrament is disappearing faster than I can minister the sign. A poem of Yeats' comes to mind:

The falcon cannot hear the falconer;
Things fall apart; the centre cannot hold;
Mere anarchy is loosed upon the world,
The blood-dimmed tide is loosed, and everywhere
The ceremony of innocence is drowned;

The best lack all conviction, while the worst
Are full of passionate intensity.

Kenneth Clark quotes those lines at the end of his *Civilisation*. He cannot manage any optimism in the face of what he calls the heroic materialism that is upon us. I know that my friend, Ivan Illich, believes that in such a dark time, I must do what I am doing: stay here and do the little in hope of better days. Or stay here and do this small "lifting up" that is Saint Malachy, with or without the hope of better days.

A Healing Season

Years ago Father John McKenzie wrote a book or an article on "Taking the Old Testament Seriously." Just the title tells the problem: Christians reading the Jewish Scriptures without seeing them as a full testament in themselves, always reading them as some backdrop to the fullness that is Christ. The truth is that these writings have their own fullness. The sacred authors were presenting a revelation and law which brought people to God. Such a miracle in the ancient world, that Jewish monotheism.

And yet and yet. These mornings as I watch spring arrive outside my bedroom window, I listen by tape and disc to the Easter liturgies at Solesmes. Wonderful, the way the psalms are sung as though phrases actually meant the Resurrection. For example, the Entrance Antiphon or Introit for Easter Sunday Mass from Psalm 139: "Lord, you have probed me and know me. You know my going down and rising up." And, of course, Psalm 118(117): "The stone rejected by the builders has become the cornerstone . . . This is the day the Lord has made. Let us rejoice and be glad."

The Chant and Mass texts go on and on about how good God is, how immense and eternal the Divine Mercy, as though the Resurrection were the crown of creation, the centerpiece of the spring renewal and miracle going on now just outside this window and presumably adorning that Passover which was the first Easter.

And yet and yet. A morning newspaper has a headline: "Rabbi in Israel snubs prelate, a Jewish convert."

Jean-Marie Cardinal Lustiger, Archbishop of Paris, is Jewish by birth. His mother died at Auschwitz, and the now Cardinal Archbishop became a Catholic in 1940 at the age of 14.

Lustiger was in Israel because Tel Aviv University invited him to give a Christian look on the Holocaust on this 50th anniversary memorial.

The Chief Rabbi of Israel, who is an Auschwitz survivor, denounced the visit and the Cardinal as a bad example, "a man who at the most difficult hour turned his back on his people and beliefs." The Rabbi suggested that the Cardinal represents a spiritual destruction not unlike the physical destruction of the Holocaust.

So. A tart chaser in this Easter season to my reading of Jewish Scripture in the light of Easter. How can that awful wound ever heal? Easter is a healing season: the spring healing of our winter world. The healed and risen Christ, inviting His disciples in off the lake for a cooked breakfast – those who had abandoned Him. He takes Peter aside and invites a threefold profession of love to heal the threefold denial. All this, the Gospel of this Third Easter Sunday. The First Reading of the same Mass tells the Acts of the Apostles story of the Jewish High Priest accusing the apostles of being "determined to make us responsible for the blood of that man."

The Eucharist which Christ left us means to be a sign which brings healing. Paul says: "We, though many, are one who eat the one bread and drink the one cup." The same Paul so deeply felt the wound of separation that he said: "I would gladly be anathema, cut off from Christ myself, if that would help my Israelite brothers, my own flesh and blood" (Romans 9:3).

I am glad that wound gave Paul such anguish, even though the poor man did not need more trouble. Imagine his driven sense of mission to travel those wild Greco-Roman cities of the Mediterranean with such an incomprehensible message: "Christ has died; Christ is risen; Christ will come again." Often people do not like St. Paul. They are wary of this man of one idea. I find his understanding of Christ in the imagery of Jewish holocaustal sacrifice less attractive, say, than the Johannine idea that the Incarnation or Christmas is the central mystery. "Wit it well," says Juliana of Norwich, "love was His meaning." I hear this referring to the Incarnation more than Calvary.

Anyhow. I do believe that the work of Easter is the healing of the world. I do believe that someday we will get the Eucharist right, and the whole world will be faithful to the sign that we are one "who eat the one bread and drink the one cup."

For now, all we can do is the healing within our reach. I hope this little parish school is a healing presence here. I hope our emergency food and the meetings of project women here and home visits and jail visits are extensions of the Eucharist celebrated here every Sunday, every day.

Sometimes we have to stretch our reach. A capital punishment execution scheduled here in this Commonwealth. This week the condemned man wants to die to end the torture of 12 years on death row. What about the wound between us and people in the terrible prisons of ours?

About the big wounds, the offense and even hatred between Jew and Christian exists from our very origins: "You . . . are determined to make us responsible for the blood of that man." Or the hatred between Jew and Arab whom Palestinian Catholic priest, Elias Chacour, calls "Blood Brothers." Again in the spirit of the Easter Gospel today, we are like the apostles on the lake before the breakfast invitation. We have fished all night and caught nothing. We shall have to keep at the work of healing until the healing happens. St. Paul himself was the embodiment of offense; yet, described his and our work as "this service of reconciliation."

7.

I Grasp That Illusive Life

Again after dinner
I am saved by a shaft of light
The climb has the difficulty of vertical ascent
Then I see the sun burning the stairwell wall
Those sad swirls of imitation grain transformed
Lifting me these last steps
Preparing me for empty rooms
Unread books   parts of the morning paper
I grasp that illusive light
Somehow pull it inside
Nourishment enough for this one awful hour
                              –"Untitled"

. . . sun   sky
green overgrowth wild enough
to repossess the road

the beads beside me a kind of
flute   horn   string   anything
to join the flourish . . .
                    –"Christmas 1991"

. . . Again *deep down freshness* to renew with
You I manage some sense *that we are wound*
With mercy round and round.
                    –"In Memoriam
                    Gerard Manley Hopkins"

Laity: *"Measure of the Catholic Spirit"*

When I am around and available on Monday evenings, I attend the weekly Legion of Mary meeting in our sparse rectory parlor where a huge safe holds the parish archives. Good for me to say the rosary with our legionaries. I pray the beads too seldom. In seminary years and long afterwards, the rosary was a daily devotion. The parish presidium is called *Virgo fidelis,* Virgin most faithful. An appropriate title, since the minutes announce this the 1,755th meeting.

Like much in Catholic life, the Legion has come upon hard times. I was never comfortable with all the terms borrowed from the militarism of ancient Rome: *senatus* and *praesidia* and *acies.* The Catholic Church already burdened enough with the heritage of Imperial Rome without making up more. I suspect that the Holy Orders, in which I received the laying on of hands, have their name from the *ordines* of the Roman legions, which were such a scourge on the ancient world. A few years ago the Church quietly put aside the entry to Holy Orders called tonsure – a symbolic haircut in the image of the shaven heads of Roman slaves. Indeed my obligation or relation to my bishop is in the tradition of Roman slavery or indentured service, which scarcely has a better history. Simone Weil thought that the inheritance of Imperial Rome was a great misfortune for the Catholic Church. She hated Imperial Rome and thought it to be the only ancient civilization without real religion. The civic religion of Empire and Caesar was the only faith. Rome borrowed from Greece and in the borrowing debased everything.

What I do like about the *Legio Mariae* is that the few aging women do something. They do not study the social problems or read Thomas Merton or worry about the gender language of the Handbook. Each week they accept the two-hour assignment of visiting the poor or sick or lapsed. The discipline is that they are to work in pairs so that they are responsible to one another.

This discipline is so unlike the world of study and analysis and research grants and dissertations where we think that because we have talked about something, we have actually done something.

I suspect that Dorothy Day would be as comfortable with the concept of symbolic action in the Legion Handbook as she would be uncomfortable with the military images. The liberal impulse is to spend time and energy getting government to do what needs doing with our taxes. Dorothy Day would doubt that government will ever quite get around to the Works of Mercy, and she would have us go out and do them ourselves. We are our brothers' and sisters' keepers.

Over the weekend I was with some old time Social Gospel activists and intellectuals at a conference on urban ministry. Amazing, their enduring faith in the power of the Scriptures to transform "the structures of injustice." Our speaker was 75 and on a hunger strike over an issue quite alive back in his New York City. He spoke the way I have been hearing these fellows speak since the 60s, and I marvel at his spirit. Everything seems so much worse. The morning paper today talks about the Daniel Patrick Moynihan report of 30 years ago. How, even then, Moynihan thought the problem was beyond repair by means of social programs.

Still these Social Gospel activists talk on about how more funding can transform things. I always find myself brought up short by how easily they include abortion as a solution, a form of human liberation. Simply.

This sensibility seems to reverse what ought to be: Catholicism as a tradition having more confidence in the possibility of a Christian or religious culture. Reformation people more distrustful of government because of a theology that distrusts human institutions and relies more on biblical prophecy.

The Legion Handbook reading this evening quotes John Henry Newman: "In all times the laity have been the measure of the Catholic spirit."

How true. Besides the few Legion of Mary women, that same rectory parlor hosted earlier today another group of women. Latino women from the parish beside us suppressed just last month. They have lists of 50 or 75 families, mostly Latino, who need to be contacted and reconnected to the Church.

Not that these families have been active or even aware that their geographical parish has been closed. More that these women have the sense that faith and hope depend on the Church. The Church where they will come to have their children baptized or their spouses and parents buried. These poor women from the projects do not expect or ask the Church authorities to prevent the fish of the Gospel parable from falling through the net. Like the Legion of Mary women, they will do the task themselves. They have more faith in this diminishing local Church than I do. They know the sacraments are here and help is here against all the hazards of these impossible neighborhoods. Everything from emergency food and clothes to prayer groups. They will connect themselves and try to make that connection for the others. They might require Spanish from my aging self still struggling with Haitian French and completely unable with Creole. Well, their faith will even require faith from me, whether I have it or feel it or not. The Communion of Saints. We keep one another going.

Just today a generous check from "Group Divine Misericorde," a prayer group of Haitian people who meet here weekly and who, completely on their own, ask a second Sunday Mass each month in Creole and French. Again my sense is that their concern is both for their own faith and, even more, for the other Haitians who might slip through the net here in Babylon.

A Heavy Mood

Sometimes a mood haunts me. It can be quite heavy and last for weeks or a whole season and be quite at odds with a season like Easter, when the weather is turning lovely and trees are blossoming and the prayer of the Church is so full of alleluias.

Surroundings can deepen this heavy mood. Surroundings, like this emergency room just beyond our neighborhood and well into what police and local press call the "Badlands." The day is not what we expect from May. A gray sky is giving us a heavy downpour. Three days of this, but we need the rain badly.

The waiting area of this emergency room is overlighted, and the television is too loud. These late morning programs are just terrible. Talk shows about a young woman getting involved with the husband of her best friend, and someone has persuaded or bribed both young women to appear on stage and call one another names. The episode ends with live audience applause and after the commercials and a station break, more of the same.

Meanwhile this emergency room empties and fills, Latino people mostly. Some have babies in tow and the mothers so small themselves that I wonder how they can hold the baby on shoulder and hip all day.

I am with my Haitian friend waiting to hear whether his wife has appendicitis or not. A doctor referred us here, and the wife has disappeared into the mysteries of triage, and we are, well, waiting like all the others here. I have no idea whether we shall be here another hour or three hours.

Noontime newsbreak. The news is that still another judge has refused to halt "the first execution in 33 years" in this state.

Outside the window of this emergency room or up there in living color television, such a seamy world. I turn to ask my Haitian friend what he thinks of the death penalty. He says that it is not right. I know that in his years in Haiti and years here in jail as an undocumented alien, he has seen a great deal. His opinion has more meaning for me than the prosecutors giving off up there on television.

An old woman sitting nearby has only one shoe. She gets my Haitian companion involved in searching for her lost shoe. No avail. The shoe is either out in the entrance foyer or she arrived without it. Both entrance foyer and waiting room have glass-enclosed interview booths to protect workers from the berserk behavior of psychotic patients or people just tearing up this space with the frustration of the waiting. I suspect nothing is happening to our patient back in triage. She is just waiting somewhere else as she was waiting here with us for the first half-hour.

The old woman with one shoe has a consumptive-like cough, so deep, that at first I thought someone was rolling a drum in another room. A vague fear surfaces: what airborne disease might I contract here with my fragile respiratory system. That heavy mood weighing down on me since Easter looking for some reason, *affectus quaerens rationem*. Mood looking for a reason.

Starting the Procession

In the morning I am downstairs not too early, about seven-thirty or eight o'clock. The idea is to have orange juice and coffee and bread before the traffic starts. I have taken on the habit of squeezing fresh orange juice. An electric squeezer makes the task easy, and the juice transports me for the moment to a luxury hotel. Sometimes there is orange marmalade for the bread, and I can imagine that I am in Ireland for a soft morning that I associate with Ireland, if only that I am a man of leisure when I am there.

Often enough, newspaper and coffee are interrupted by the doorbell. As early as 8:00 people are at the door for food. The easy thing is to throw a few cans from our emergency food cupboard into a bag and pass the food on to the caller and get back to the morning paper, wondering whether I should do more to discourage the early callers. Once someone goes down the path away from here, that bag of groceries is sign to the many others out there that we are open for business. All day the procession is endless. I have no idea what the food means. Some women want baby formula, which to my surprise we often have. Other callers look like derelicts who would not even have the can opener or stove for their can of soup. I suspect the cans of food are an underground currency for wine or drugs. To track that would need more than Sister Catherine and her gracious volunteers who arrive by 9:00 and do the door all day with great courtesy and patience. Of course, sometimes the cupboard is empty, and a week passes before provisions arrive from wherever – Archdiocese or sister-parish or social agency.

Hearing that first ring this morning, I thought: well, I will just tell this caller that we do not open shop for another hour.

At the door I buzzed a tall fellow into the small foyer. He greeted my hand gestures and words with words of his own: "Hey, man, I know all that, but I'm here now and, man. . . ."

What could I do but nod and head for the pantry and choose a variety of soup, tuna, beans, knowing that I was starting the procession. One of the things that priests do, start processions. On Saturday, we will have a fancy wedding here, and my appearance at the altar signals bridesmaids to begin their walk down the aisle.

Sharing Prayer

A letter from a missioner in the Philippines. A priest younger than myself. He spent some years in development work here in Philadelphia before his overseas assignment. Because of him and because I know vaguely the troubles of the Philippines, I mention those Islands at Mass every day. At Easter, I sent the priest a card telling him little more than that he and his adopted country are with us every day in heart and at the altar, together with Bosnia and Chechnya and Haiti and Ireland. My Irish friend, Michael Doyle, taught me this practice of naming peoples at prayer, lifting them up to God by name, keeping them in the heart of God and my own heart as well. Somewhere I read that John Henry Newman went about with lengthy lists of people who asked or needed his prayers.

This letter from the Philippines told of an attack by Muslims on a town near this young priest from Brooklyn: " . . . indiscriminately killed about 50 people, very innocent people, mostly girls working in shops, two church workers in a barber shop, etc. They burned the whole market down, robbed and burned four banks. Then they took hostages and killed them . . . now about three weeks later people are still afraid."

The killing, an expression of Muslim-Christian hatred in the Philippines. More wounds for me to ponder in my Easter world of alleluias and the delicate, beautiful, pink blossoms of trees out my window healing our winter world.

I think of that Brooklyn fellow off there alone in the rural Philippines so far from his beloved Brooklyn. Everyone from Brooklyn seems to love and miss Brooklyn . . . .

I wonder if the real wonder and beauty is not that missioner and his lonely life in a remote and now scary place: "A blessing on the person who puts trust in God . . . like a tree by the river." My missioner friend from Brooklyn, his life – there is that fragile, beautiful tree, a healing presence in still another winter world. This generous, wondrous depth of Catholic faith has this priest out there alone.

His letter finishes: "Otherwise, I am still organizing, slowly, the new parish here. People are encouraging, then fall back a bit. But the Resurrection is the central feast for Christians, no matter what; the Lord is always with His people. Hope all is well with you. I also pray for the people at Saint Malachy."

The Aesthetic Image of Faith

A call from our bookstore venture to say that my order has arrived. An expensive volume, and my excuse for the extravagance is that I am not buying this study of Hans Urs Von Balthasar for myself. I know a cloistered sister in the city who is a fan of the great Swiss theologian, who died in 1988 just two days before he was to become a Cardinal. My intention is to pass the book on to her. Balthasar will be kindling for the incandescent flame of faith and love which she fans within herself in that enclosure.

The review which had me purchase the book mentioned that the great man probably wrote more books than most others read in a lifetime. I peruse these pages with the awareness and sadness that lack of time and frequent mental exhaustion will prevent me from really tasting the vision of Balthasar. One of those early choices: like Robert Frost choosing one path in the woods by which the possibilities of another path remain unexplored. Here I am doing the street scene in North Philadelphia. Balthasar and so many others remain quite unknown to me. So be it. I can at least catch snatches of him in this scholarly study before handing it over to the sister.

In the middle of the book a section called "The Aesthetics," with a chapter entitled "The Archaeology of Alienated Beauty." Formidable. Perhaps the parochial choice was the wise one for me!

Aesthetics is apparently the theological model of Balthasar. His higher studies were in German literature, not theology. His image of Catholicism is that of a great symphony in which the whole wonder is a coming together of Scripture and worship, Church Fathers and philosophy and art. The ultimate Catholic theologian, I guess, allowing these other human realities to build up the faith edifice. Something different from the Reformation *Sola Scriptura.*

Balthasar is called a conservative, and I note my prejudice: I am wary of anyone with an agenda. I may be conservative myself, but I am never certain that such a sensibility in me is anything more than a fear of modernity, fear of a world more disorganized and tumultuous than anything for which my mental and moral shaping has prepared me. I would be wary of Sigmund Freud also, with his revealing comment that man and woman find themselves alone in a hostile universe. Who says the universe is hostile?

The awesome theological construction of Balthasar seems too wonderful, too beautiful to be true. How can someone who lived through the failure of the Church during the Nazi years in his beloved Europe maintain such a glorious image of the Church as Bride of Christ? How can Balthasar want to be known as a "kneeling theologian" and still say that the world has become a place where prayer "seems an impossible demand to make on a larger number of people?"

A footnote quotes Jacques Barzun fleshing out Balthasar: the loss of a sense of God affects aesthetics. The ironic imagination loses one anchor: "The negative perpetuates itself as a habit of thought – it becomes the highest form of self-consciousness – and it destroys everything. . . ."

I know that modern darkness. It fills me with terror. Often I cannot get beyond it. It is the sadness I felt on my visit to Chartres: however beautiful, this construct and faith have been cast aside as having no meaning or value for our place and time. British historian Father Philip Sheldrake describes Chartres as such an elitist and aristocratic expression that, however beautiful, the image had to fail us eventually.

Yet these failures leave us in such dark times. I do not know whether the darkness can be so thick as Balthasar suggests in his rejection of the modern city: "Concrete and glass do not speak of God." Sometimes in an ugly church I imagine what new church I would design if I had that task. A glass wall looking out on trees or even city sky seems attractive.

The same Balthasar who witnessed the failure of the Church in Nazi Germany can go on and on about the Church with an ecstasy that suggests he is describing the Church of the Easter Vigil still fresh my mind and heart. That Church seems so idealized, so unreal. Too bad I will never have the time or intellectual energy to discover what fuels this vision. Perhaps I can steal a second week from this book before I deliver it to the cloistered sister.

The Influence of War

A beautiful May Day looking out on a small green patch full of blossoms. I listen to the Gregorian Chant. The hymn *Salve Festa Dies* has a second stanza: "Behold how the beauty of a world reborn proclaims that the gifts of the Lord have all returned with Him," as though the spring flowers are trumpets proclaiming the Resurrection.

Moments later I turn on morning television to see if this weather will hold. I discover that this Monday between the 36th anniversary of my ordination and my 62nd birthday tomorrow is the 50th anniversary of V-E day, the end of World War II in Europe.

So. I was 12 years old when that war ended, and my memory of war and ending is vague. Yet I am very much a child of that war. I do remember food and gasoline rationing and hotels in Atlantic City filled with wounded soldiers, whom nurses would push at night in wheelchairs on the Boardwalk. I remember too the Boardwalk lamps blackened on the side looking out on the ocean for fear of German U-Boats.

The next war was Korea, and I was spared any personal involvement or decision because I was heading off to the seminary and thus draft exempt. I wonder if that exemption retards the moral development of us priests concerning war. I notice the senior bishops of Argentina offered an apology to their people for their silence during the "dirty war" in that country.

Vietnam was a different story for me. I can trace my involvement in the antiwar movement to the seemingly harmless habit of reading poetry. Early on, I discovered the poetry of Dan Berrigan and looked for each new collection of poems. The poems developed from earlier poems from what he once called his "woodsy period," or comments on life in rural Jesuit novitiates, to later trips to Hanoi and even prison. I was along for the ride, and my own development, assisted by such reading, soon meant civil rights and antiwar protests. My whole sensibility and relationship to the Church as much shaped by those frantic years as by anything else. I might even be here in these neighborhoods because of the Poor Peoples' March through Philadelphia to Washington, D.C. Whenever I pass that playground only blocks from here, I remember the Poor Peoples' encampment there. I was so busy at a parish with many hospitals and many duties, any opportunity to join the March to Washington seemed impossible. I could at least walk through the city with them on my day off.

So the walk and walks that have me here. Who knows what has us where we are, doing what we do? My presence and work here and any civil rights or antiwar protests might go back further than I measure. All that might go back to the seminary reading room and those columns of *The Catholic Worker* about French worker-priests or non-violence.

Anyhow. The wars of my lifetime have shaped me.

Debt's Frustration

Whenever I try to be sublime about the work here, I shall remember two calls this week about tuition.

Two mothers called me, quite annoyed that their children were out of our parish school all week because their tuition payments were delinquent. They accused us of penalizing their children for parental default, or using children to punish adults, and so on.

For years we have tried to be reasonable about this matter of tuition. I would prefer no tuition at all, just take in whoever wants to attend our school and find the money elsewhere rather than from the pockets of these parents, most of whom are poor.

I knew a physician years ago who said he taught medicine at the sacrifice of a greater income than would come from practice. He said he did so because he could not suffer the collection of fees.

All that is now blurred by medical insurance and third-party payment.

We try to keep tuition under a thousand dollars because of the realities of this neighborhood, where we are surrounded by public housing projects. Anything more than the thousand would be a real hardship for the people. We try to fund the considerable deficit by outside fund-raising. So far a modest success because Catholic people and others believe in these Catholic schools and want to help. Most of the help is $25 here and $100 there with an occasional larger gift. I work very hard at this task and am pleased that we can maintain our school without asking assistance from the Archdiocese.

We have tried to have regular tuition dates and parish collectors other than the principal, who already has enough to occupy her. Yet the poor need to pay when they have the funds and not wait until the money is needed elsewhere. Often they have already spent the funds on other expenses and need our indulgence until they again have funds.

So it goes. The principal and her secretary become the collectors, and occasionally they must establish a deadline. My sense is that the poor can walk away from debts easier than others because often they must.

With the phone calls I notice my own annoyance that the parents are trying to get around the principal by calling me. Sometimes my annoyance provokes annoyance in return from a parent already on the edge that her child is at home and not in school. I wish that I had a better solution. I wish that we did not need any tuition, but that is not very sensible. We are nearing the end of the school year, and if we do not require the tuition, we shall never see it. The parents can walk away and next year find some other school, and we would go under if our tuition discipline breaks down.

As I say, next time I am feeling sublime about my work here or about some lofty theology I am reading, I shall remember the frustrated parent so angry with me on the telephone a few days ago.

Necessary Faith

A longtime friend is a professor at a local university. In recent conversation something surfaced which is hard to interpret. Or not at all hard to interpret.

Quite casually he mentions that the students have asked him to do the invocation and blessing at their graduation because they do not want clergy. He said priest, but I presume he meant any clergy. He continues by saying how he has students involved in a project at a neighborhood center run by an evangelical Black Christian Church. Again these graduate students balk at religion: the daily routine and even individual sessions at the Church center begin with prayer. The students do not like this requirement, feel uncomfortable and even resistant in such a religious environment.

One can wonder whether the resistance is that the students are often Jewish or Muslim or from Asian traditions and resent being pulled into a Christian devotion. I suspect other: the overall alienation of a younger generation from faith and Church. I do not mean to moralize this or blame. Dietrich Bonhoeffer had a phrase, "man come of age," to describe a new emerging sensibility of people not wanting or needing the traditional resources to deal with the dark side of life: death, illness, social upheaval. He thought that a religion which still tried to speak in ultimates to such a landscape was sure to fail. He was not praising his "new man" either. He saw him as someone who easily becomes a Nazi or whatever.

I do not know what meaning to give this situation in which students do not want a priest around nor want gatherings in which people pray. I shall try to hold onto the faith and prayer that seems to nourish me for the tasks at hand. I shall even grasp more fondly the priesthood, which enables me to bring here some sense of the Divine Love in which we live. Perhaps graduate students about to venture out with so much privilege do not feel the need for prayer or the faith community we call Church. I do, and apparently the African-American evangelicals farther up in these neighborhoods also feel that need and thus their gatherings begin with prayer. Well, I shall regard that need as gift and grace holding me close, not allowing me to be a "man come of age."

Wearing a Web

Two new books. I am like an alcoholic passing a bar or a package store. More books here than I could read in several lifetimes, but mood or need or desire takes over, and I decide: despite all those others I will read these first; then they disappear onto the shelf with those others.

Two books of Henri de Lubac, the venerable Jesuit theologian, silenced all those years before he was rehabilitated and became a Cardinal. One book, a recent reprint of his great study: *Catholicism, Christ and the Common Destiny of Man.* First French edition, 1947. This English edition, 1988 by Ignatius Press, a conservative Catholic press in California. Despite his avant-garde works, de Lubac was critical of some developments after Vatican II. The other volume, some reflections on those earlier works. What am I doing reading 1947 theology? Can anything from 50 years ago speak to our time and place? Even as I turn the pages, I am skeptical.

I know the reason I bought these books. I want to discover from de Lubac and Ives Congar and others how to survive in the Church. A recent practice in the Church is to rehabilitate these persecuted scholars by making one, then another, a Cardinal in extreme old age. That way the Church never has to express regret or apology for that persecution. Never apologize; someone once said that apology is a form of weakness.

Or perhaps the Cardinal-making is not unadmitted apology. More approval that a Congar or de Lubac or Balthasar came to his senses by criticizing the "excesses" of Church reform.

Anyhow. The most recent and only surviving of these to make Cardinal is Yves Congar, who is 90 and has been in a Paris hospital for more than a decade. Theologian Richard McBrien says that Congar is "perhaps the most distinguished ecclesiologist of all time." An American Dominican who stayed in the same Paris priory with Congar in 1974 tells how Congar once admitted being so angry that he urinated on the wall of the Holy Office in Rome.

I bought these de Lubac books because I think I share the attachment and – less learnedly – the vision which de Lubac had for the Church. As in the title of the book I just purchased: " . . . the common destiny of man (and woman)." Once I tried to tell that vision and attachment in a poem:

> de Lubac weaving that web
> where I am lifelong caught:the Church . . .
>   −"France: Inflight 1992"

So here I am quoting myself like a Pope. The withdrawal of the Church from these poor neighborhoods, the effort to obtain public funds, the appointment of an Archbishop associated with the military in El Salvador . . . all these things happening are making me more and more isolated in a Church going in an opposite direction from so much that the tradition means to me. How did Congar and de Lubac hold on; what kept them going when their writings and whole vision of ecumenism or grace or the interpretation of Scripture were condemned?

It seems their faith was elsewhere than in the Church as they then and there experienced it. They were onto something deeper which would surface again in better times. Or more: they believed a mystery deeper than their vision or that other vision which found theirs threatening and needing to be silenced. And if the better times did not come in their lifetime, they could die in peace knowing that better days would someday come, and they had helped that coming. Or even if the better days never came, the Church, however unrealized in her full truth, was worthy of their faith and obedient service.

Heavy stuff. We only have one lifetime, and de Lubac and Congar must have sensed that the Church without the courage or wisdom to respond to her times can do harm. The era of these men legitimated and even lauded a sacrificial obedience of mind and heart. A bloodless martyrdom. Now intellectual honesty and a self-assertion that accepts with courage the consequences seem installed. I guess what I want from the books, from Congar and de Lubac, is how to live in the Church I live in with something more than anguish and disaffection. A friend told me a story of being at the Jesuit novitiate where de Lubac was in exile. Strolling the grounds with a group, they met the great man on his lonely walk. Friendly at first, de Lubac courteously but quickly excused himself when he discovered they were only students, not yet ordained. Later, my friend learned that the restrictions were that de Lubac was not to have conversation with students lest he confuse their young minds.

Trust

A gray morning of drizzle unworthy of May the rarest, May the fairest. Quite early I am off to a hospital in those white working class neighborhoods east of here. Small row houses which lay within the shadow of now-abandoned factories. Immigrants once raised large families in these tiny homes and worked in the factories and died young of the respiratory diseases of factory work before this age of protection from occupational hazards.

The abandoned factories make the streets bleak, especially on such a bleak day. I pass a public school where a 10-year-old student waiting for me to pass is jumping up and down with joy or excitement. In her pink-going-purple sweat suit she is very like an azalea bush blowing in the wet wind. The closest color in this concrete neighborhood to the azaleas now afire in other neighborhoods.

The immigrant woman beside me in the car has an X-ray appointment at the hospital, and my spirit is as bleak as the day for the prospect of a long wait. Who knows why we are bleak on a particular morning? Bleak day or bleak task or what old Victorian spiritual writer Father William Faber called "the weariness of well-doing." Who knows?

The young woman in the azalea-colored sweat suit is joyful and jumping because she trusts life. She trusts the energy of her young body; she has a mother or grandmother out there who tells her good things about her young self. She likes the school which she is entering across the street, and she does not compare these mean forsaken streets where she lives against some other nicer streets because she does not know those nicer streets.

She is not bleak or downcast because she does not ponder her situation in the light of starving Rwanda or Haiti. *"Age quod agis,"* as Saint Ignatius of Loyola said. "Do what you are doing." To philosophize is to die.

And in this Easter season, that is the message of Christ: trust the beauty of the world, which is the backdrop of these mean streets as well as those affluent neighborhoods of azaleas. Trust that behind the sunrise, which was not much this morning but so wondrous other mornings, there is a wonder more wondrous than the sunrise: "See the lilies of the field." Faith might do just that: take us through all that presses us down or makes us bleak. Take us to a mystery deeper than the bleakness, just as a sunrise is somewhere beyond the gray morning.

Even on the cross in seeming abandonment, Christ continued with trust and confidence deeper than His experience of abandonment.

And I sense that the path to that deeper center is prayer. Here in Easter time I sit at the eastward window where I wait for dawn and listen to the Easter chant. This morning, no real dawn – only a steel, wet sky, and I notice I could connect with the Easter alleluias somewhere deeper than my bleak feeling. The chant does that. The joy of the Gregorian alleluia is so restrained that the joy comes from somewhere other than feeling, some place deeper. As though with Simone Weil at Solesmes in 1938 during Holy Week, when she said: "I was suffering from splitting headaches; each sound hurt me like a blow; by an extreme effort of concentration I was able to rise above this wretched flesh, to leave it suffer by itself, heaped up in a corner and to find a pure and perfect joy in the unimaginable beauty of the chanting and the words. This experience enabled me by analogy to get a better understanding of loving divine love in the midst of affliction."

When we arrived at the hospital, the immigrant woman and I entered the emergency room to see a fellow wildly tearing a bloody dressing from his open side and hurling the bandage against the inside door from waiting room to treatment area. He was cursing and swearing that he was being neglected and bleeding to death. Triage meant that his immediate wound had been treated, and he was sent back to await further treatment. Obviously, he was not content to wait. The nurse inside the assaulted door assured him that he was not bleeding to death. Security people arrived from various hospital stations to contain the situation. Rubber gloves went on everybody: with blood running down door and walls here in a high-risk drug neighborhood, the first thought is AIDS.

Well, despite the azaleas and sunrise behind the wet morning, not always easy to trust such a world. Not easy either to trust the Church as sign of God. A Baptist friend who loves the Catholic Church of Central America tells me about the change there with a new Archbishop from the feared military. A church chancery which was a gathering place of the poor, of refugees and human rights activists has become suddenly a security area with checkpoints and guards in full military uniform. Difficult to trust a Church so ready to dismantle a veritable Bethesda or place of healing. A Church so ready to restore an *ancien regime* which had been deposed with such blood and tears.

Yet this is the message from the cross: trust even in the midst of seeming abandonment, "loving divine love in the midst of affliction."

"Let Us Not Mock God with Metaphor"

Early morning convent Mass. The Gospel is that immense Easter promise from the Fourth Gospel: "Do not let your hearts be troubled . . . I am going to prepare a place for you." The sisters tell me that a priest my own age, a suburban pastor generous to me here every month, went down with a serious heart attack at graveside. This Gospel is something I often read at graveside.

I notice an Easter interview with an elderly hero of mine who is a priest and theologian. After a brief missionary career in China, interrupted by the Communist expulsion of foreigners, he set off on an intellectual journey far more concerned with comparative religion than traditional theology.

In the interview he seems reluctant to let his interviewer lock him into any clear vision of what Easter means for us: "The whole universe, in a certain sense, is played through in sequence, but it also exists outside this sequence."

Fair enough, I guess. Simone Weil says that we should not try to imagine life beyond the grave as some precise extension of our experience here. For her, far too much of ego or self in our earthly selves, too little of God, and life with God will correct that self-centeredness.

My artist friend, Robert McGovern, in trying to portray the risen Christ takes comfort in that Thomas Aquinas says somewhere that the Resurrection is not imaginable in any familiar human images.

And yet and yet. John Updike has a poem: "Seven Stanzas at Easter":

> Make no mistake: if He rose at all
> it was as His body;
> if the cells' dissolution did not reverse, the molecules
>   reknit, the amino acids rekindle,
> the Church will fall.
>
> . . . .
> Let us not mock God with metaphor,
> . . . .

I am sure that Aquinas believed in the literal Resurrection. He just thought that our imagination could not encompass it.

Several years ago I was on a Sunday morning television show with a liberal Protestant scholar, who suggested that eternal life was, perhaps, wishful thinking. I am not sure that we can presume moderns have that wish. The prospect might seem like more of the same painful thing we have here. Again that graffiti in the shambles of war-torn Catholic Belfast: "Is there life before death?"

Well, my own attachment to a traditional view of our sharing in the life of the risen Christ appears in those Gregorian antiphons I listen to these spring weeks: Thomas invited to put his hand into the Lord's wounded side, the risen Christ cooking a breakfast of fish and honeycomb for the apostles on the shore of Lake Tiberias, Mary Magdalene holding onto His risen body so fiercely that He says: "Let go of me for I have not ascended to my Father." Forty-four years since I entered the seminary. Immediately a retreat and I remember, as though yesterday, an old Jesuit explaining the *noli me tangere* – "do not touch me." In the Greek aorist text, the construction is an aorist imperative and means to stop an action already begun. Not so much "do not touch me" as "stop holding onto me." Of course, I know that we cannot be so literal about a Gospel text as to make something of an aorist imperative. Yet, the image of Mary Magdalene holding onto the risen Christ, so physical an image. So real.

Necessary Transformation

Graduation at the large urban university nearby. Over 6,000 graduating. One speaker spells out the ethnic mix. Not bad, all things considered. More minority people than most other social institutions, except the public schools around here, which are all minority.

Standing room only, unless I climb to the rafters of this huge civic auditorium. Instead I cluster in an aisle with others, and the coming and going and conversation makes any attention to the graduation speeches difficult.

One student quotes the university President as having said years ago that education is "the great equalizer." She is intent on telling how diverse the students are by race or nation or religion. Strange how religion, which means to unite us, becomes another barrier to human unity. We need not go to the Holy Land or the

North of Ireland to witness that division. I wonder what Christ meant when He said that He would cause division even within a household. His own great vision was to bring us together. That conversation of His with the Samaritan woman – He answers her question about whether true worship happened in Jewish Jerusalem or Samaritan Mount Gazarim by promising a day of neither Jerusalem nor Gazarim. True worshippers would worship in spirit and truth. I wonder what He meant. Again, Saint Paul in anguish over the division between Jews and Christians which he is causing, and yet, he is constrained to do it.

As I listen to the talks, I notice that the prayer by a preacher is more another graduation talk than a prayer. How refreshing it would be if instead of trying to instruct us further, we would be lifted up to the Mystery we call God, asking mercy and guidance for these graduates whose future is uncertain and depends on so much else besides their degrees. I guess the truth is we do not believe much in prayer except as some social ritual.

And I do not know what to think of education. The racial mix here is somewhat impressive, but not nearly enough. Ivan Illich says that First World education applied to developing countries will do more harm than good by further stratifying the society into privileged elites able to avail themselves of an expensive commodity requiring a mobility and sustaining resources which the poor do not have.

As I listen to speakers here, faculty and graduates, go on about the messianic role of education, I think of that nearby high school where daily attendance is only 38%. How does higher education as presently structured embrace them? And if it does not embrace them, are we not doing precisely what Illich predicts: creating two societies side by side?

My sense as I stand here listening to this graduation rhetoric is, of course, that we need the doctoral studies on the effects of certain drugs on depression; of course, we need studies of tolerance in Muslim countries or intolerance in Western cities. Yet, the study cannot be for the sake of the study or to enhance the income possibilities of the new Doctor of Pharmacy or of Political Science. Education as a cottage industry, an internal system, self-sustaining, degrees for the sake of degrees or the building up of a graduate system that justifies generous foundation grants here rather than the urban barrio school, where 63% of the students are daily absent.

Opaque all this. I suppose for prayer to mean anything or education to embrace the truants or religion to be more than a cause of division, we need a transformation. The transformation that Christ was trying to give the Samaritan woman. Hard enough to seek that transformation for myself without thinking that I can bring it about for others.

And who says my transformation is transformation? The papers are full of a Japan cult that sounds crazy and dangerous. A news photo of hundreds of police arriving at the hideout of the cult leader only to find him alone in meditation!

I was about to say that transformation comes from prayer and abiding in Christ, and here is a meditating cult leader claiming kinship with Christ as well as Buddha.

I guess there are no guarantees, just the daily prodding effort to be faithful to the connection within and society without. And do all this without succumbing to the Great Beast as Plato and Simone Weil call the social order. Balance. A high-wire act.

The "necessity" of Simone Weil can help here. In an imperious world we can be no more certain about the long-term meaning of our actions than I am about this graduation rhetoric. We should act only when necessary by moral constraint. The necessity of being in St. Malachy and keeping the place going because the presence is so crucial in a fragile neighborhood. The necessity of conscientious objection, say, for an unjust war or any war. The necessity of the corporal and spiritual works of mercy, as Simone says: "We should do only those righteous actions which we cannot stop ourselves from doing, which we are unable not to do, but, through well-directed attention, we should always keep on increasing the number of those which we are unable not to do."

And still we make mistakes. Simone Weil felt constrained to go off to the civil war in Spain. She was soon home, disillusioned by that crusade, claiming that revolution, and not religion, was the opium of the people.

Joy

After a week of rain, a May morning so radiant that I can see the dew glistening on the leaves of the three trees a hundred yards beyond my eastern window.

And I can sense that the heavy thoughts pondered during that graduation earlier this week are not all there is to me. My morning feast of Easter alleluias in chant reveals to me a joy deep within. I am not always in touch with that joy, but the chant connects me there.

It is as though Easter is such an event. The world is made in the image of the Word who, before any sunrise, was *in sino Patris* "in the bosom of the Father." Dawn then is the prefiguring of the Resurrection, and every sunrise, since is a daily celebration of that rising, greater still than the sunrise, which is already miracle enough: *Haec dies quam fecit Dominus* "This is the day the Lord has made." Every day is Easter. Every dawn the Resurrection.

I am not sure that creation theologians will like this talk, nor would I in another mood. They want to respect and honor the primal mystery of creation and not allow that wonder to be eclipsed by our redemption. Yet, the chant and prayers of Easter continue to sing how the new creation is more wondrous than the old. The *Exultet* at the Easter Vigil calls the human condition "a happy fault" since it needed such a saving.

The Offertory Antiphon of the Easter Mass: *Terra tremuit et quievit,* "The earth trembled and was still . . . ."

A psalm verse accommodated by the Church to Easter. As though the movements of nature from dawn to lightning and even to an earthquake were some symphonic playing out of Easter.

As I sit here watching the morning glisten on the new green of the trees, I let in the chant: "Give thanks to the Lord who is so good. . . ." The goodness sung here is the Resurrection of which the renewed trees are victory pennants, just as the palms of the children on Palm Sunday were pennants of that procession. Springtime proclaims Easter more than Easter proclaims spring. Blessed is He who comes, rises in the name of the Lord. Alleluia. On the surface, the weight of the day looms, heavy on me already. Deeper down I sense the joy that nothing can overtake.

Stretching

Waiting in an airport for a flight home from a wedding on the West Coast. Enough of this in the weeks before and after Easter to make me uncomfortable. As though I am removing myself from my home and streets which my neighbors hardly leave. I want to be there as they are there. Well, summer is coming, and enough will be happening to keep me grounded.

Here, plane-waiting, I stop people-watching long enough to pray the morning prayer of the Church. I am late with the Psalms. More a time for afternoon prayer. Psalm 87 proclaims:

> Babylon and Egypt I will count
> among those who know me . . .
> and Zion shall be called 'Mother'
> for all shall be her children.

I am reminded of the stone inscription over the doors of that elegant old synagogue back in my neighborhood: "My house shall be a house of prayer for all peoples."

Another Psalm verse. I wish I knew more about that expansive Jewish vision. All religions seem so narrow and tribal. Somehow we diminish the message or never sound the depths. My own tradition is full of stories of Jesus sounding the depths to be sure: reaching beyond His tribal tradition to commend the faith of a Roman centurion or bring faith to a Samaritan woman. I presume the closing of many inner-city churches and schools means that the local Church does not accept the same responsibility for others as for Catholics. Or perhaps the new realities of diminished funds and fewer personnel means that the authorities believe they must do less rather than more, even though the urban situation requires more.

The Church. I bring such hope to the Church. I have never outgrown that vision acquired in seminary days that the Catholic Church is the full realization of that vision of the Psalms: "for all shall be her children."

In flight I have been reading the Thomas Berry book which has been on my desk these many months. Berry would suggest that a biblical vision is not large enough for our present task: "Theology, in its fidelity to the past, has isolated itself from the larger community of life and existence in the present."

Perhaps my vision of the Catholic Church is obsolete. Perhaps the Church has a more modest role in gathering the world into a unity that would heal war and the poverty of my neighborhoods.

Yet today the feast of Saint Justin Martyr, the first of those Greek Fathers who expanded the biblical message to embrace the Graeco-Roman world of which Israel was only an unimportant outpost. Perhaps taking on the environment or really taking on these impoverished neighborhoods where I live would expand and stretch the Church into something more wonderful than Holy

Mother Church already is. A new acquaintance whom I met in San Francisco said that even as a lapsed Catholic he has begun reading Catholic peace and justice newspapers because they maintain awareness of the suffering need of the developing countries.

Stretching. My California friends send me off with a book by a Latin American woman narrating the illness and death of her daughter. Apparently the tragic story is told with no recourse to faith, to the Cross or Easter. I must stretch myself and read this journal of how secular people experience death and loss and suffering. I hope that I can learn from them how better to shape my faith, my expectations. I hope that I can learn how to communicate faith and Church so that we can have some common ground.

I feel the distance. That distance is an anguish to me, just as the inadequacy of Church and government is an anguish to Father Thomas Berry in his concern for earth and life and ecosystems. I do not have the confidence of Teilhard de Chardin, whom Tom Berry credits as a mentor. Teilhard was on a dig somewhere when a colleague died suddenly. Priest and Jesuit Teilhard was aware of the resigned and agnostic response of other friends and colleagues on the dig to this sudden sorrow and loss. He vowed on the body of the dead friend to give others that hope so precious to him as man of faith.

We are airborne. I decline the offer of a headset for the in-flight film. Instead I shall open the book, *Paula,* and venture into a secular world, foreign and threatening to me. A world where my faith and theology seem as inadequate as the Bible story seems for Thomas Berry in his concern to save the rain forests and prevent future catastrophe.

I must stretch myself. Christ stretched Himself for that unbelieving woman at the well. Justin Martyr stretched himself to understand his biblical faith by way of his Greek philosophical sensibility. Slowly I open.the book. . . .

Expectations

Difficult to abandon familiar expectations of the Church in hope of some less inflated expectations which might not be so disappointing. A gravity has me grasping quotes and prayer cards that firm up my familiar hopes.

I notice that here in this notebook I have marked my place with an ornate card with words from a Carmelite nun of this or the last century who is now a Blessed: "O love, consume my entire being for your glory that it may be poured out drop by drop for your Church."

And close to my heart in that month-at-a-glance calendar which I carry in my shirt pocket is a prayer of Pascal about not asking for health or sickness or life or death. Only that all this happen for the glory of God "and for the use of the Church."

Pascal was no fool, as they say. More than anyone of his time he had few illusions about the Church or the adequacy of the Church for the modern sensibility that he, more than anyone, was bringing to birth.

Another book I shall read was also sent home with me by my California friends: *Deep River* by Shusaku Endo, who also anguishes over his Catholic faith and Church so lost in the immensity of his Asia. When Japanese television interviewers ask Endo about his European faith, he responds by saying that Christianity is something he wears like his Western business suit. Something less comfortable than his kimono.

In a review of *Deep River* in the *New York Times*, Robert Coles quotes Catholic theologian Romano Guardini: "The Church is the cross on which Christ was crucified." Guardini, a German with an Italian name, must have experienced the failure of the Church to confront Nazi Germany, since he was part of that Catholic renaissance growing side by side with the Third Reich at the close of the 30s. Guardini was probably trying to deal with a Church ineffective with the Nazis, just as I must deal with a Church unable for this ravaged inner-city neighborhood.

Coping with Crises

A friend arrives from some distance for an "appointment" with me. Even the word tells how far I am from the normal routines of life. Here people do not make appointments. They just show up wanting to talk: are you busy?

Or they do not show up. Or when asked why, they respond with the enigmatic: I did not have carfare or I did not know you would be waiting. I guess if somebody does not have carfare he or she might not have a quarter for the telephone either.

This visitor did arrive, and we went to the rectory office where two huge safes contain not money but sacramental records of this parish and a neighboring parish closed 12 years ago. I hope no more parishes close, or copying baptismal and marriage records will become a full-time job.

Anyhow. I close the door halfway to drown out the noise of a food shipment arriving to hear that my visitor is having a spiritual crisis. In a moment I know indeed how far I am from ordinary pastoral chores. I hardly let my visitor finish: "Spiritual crisis, what spiritual crisis? Look out the door here. Life is crisis, bedlam is the rule. I am grateful to stay an hour ahead of the game!"

My visitor was not about to let me off easy or be intimidated by my manner. He told me how he could hardly go to Mass anymore or receive the sacraments. I was not intimidated either: "Well, then you just go through the motions. This too will pass. I have not been on easy street for years. Get used to it."

Weeks earlier I was with a friend who spent precious years in the antiwar movement. He has since married, and wife and infant child are requiring some effort toward a more secure career. "I am thinking about going back to school to become a counselor," he says.

I respond: "A counselor? You are too old to become a counselor. You are like me." I want to soften what comes next by including myself in the comment. "You are a talker. You lack the patience for listening." I go on about counseling being dependent now on managed medical care, which will soon exclude therapy from insurance coverage and so forth.

I guess my behavior with visitor and with friend says more about me than about them. The mayhem of these streets that seeps into me and has me always, well, excited and trying just to keep the wraps on. Fortunate for many and for myself, as well, there are good counselors around. My sense of myself is that over a lifetime I lean heavily on others. My sensibility seems so taut that I hardly trust my response or reaction. Before acting or choosing or speaking, I usually check out my plans with friends whose judgment I respect. Even in doing so, I notice that these same friends are often more inner-directed than myself. I have a theory about how the world can be divided into the inner-directed and the outer-directed. Some have a strong confidence all the way from childhood that their intuitions and responses are keen and accurate. Others, like myself, need constantly to test the waters, discover whether my perception has resonance or that I am as I fear: alone in the universe.

So here I am: a fellow who, more than most, needs a listening ear yet refuses my own ear to someone with, at least in his mind, a serious problem. What kind of priest blows a visitor out the door after hearing the phrase "spiritual crisis?" Over the years this landscape must shape me. A spiritual crisis seems such a luxury.

Recently, I was in a conversation with professional people discussing with concern the educational needs of their children. Almost rudely and without thought I began at great length to describe how any real education was unavailable to children in my neighborhood. I could not sustain talk about privilege anymore than I could be patient with somebody having a spiritual crisis. Well, I hope that when I am laid low by some spiritual crisis that will surely come, I find the help I always manage to find. Thank God not all listeners are like me.

Business Deals

In the morning newspaper a front-page story about how a small Catholic college became big-time government business by way of the wheeling and dealing of the priest-president.

The story is presented as an example of how politics is about politicians delivering funds to home districts, quite apart from whether the delivery represents responsible use of tax revenues.

Last month another front-page story about a local charitable foundation fraud in which many churches and clergy were involved. The fallout is ongoing, and Dave Hagan reminds me of the comment of Bible scholar John McKenzie that Jesus has little to say about money, and most of what he says is not very complimentary.

The business rationale is that the Bible children should be as enterprising as the children of this world: think of all the good we can do. Kenneth Rexroth says that was the temptation even a saint faced when Thomas More took the job as Chancellor of England after the fall of Cardinal Wolsey: I know the job is a bad one, but think of all the good I can do. Rexroth says that the next time around More made the better choice, even though it cost his head.

Friends in the Midwest asked me why religious communities participate in the managed health care industry now growing. Those friends are medical people and fear the new entrepreneurs will force physicians to treat a quota of patients each day or week and get rid of care-givers wanting to provide more generous care. Already in a neighboring state, a conflict in which a religious community was involved in a bitter labor dispute.

The arguments are the same as those of the small Catholic college: we are in financial trouble and do what we must do to survive, including throwing our lot in with the entrepreneurs. Or perhaps the logic is that which Rexroth attributes to Thomas More: overall this is a bad scene, but without us things would be worse; more abortions and such. I guess those arguments and that logic are not without some truth. The Church is not to exist in the world as a sect apart from the real action. Those Bible images about being the salt of the earth or the light on a hill.

Yet most religious congregations began by doing something that was not being done at all. The Christian Brothers educating the poor or the Rose Hawthorne Sisters and Little Sisters of the Poor taking in the destitute ill and doing it by begging, not asking government to finance the work.

A fine priest completely immersed in administration offered a generous compliment to parish work by dismissing himself as "a businessman." Certainly fundraising keeps this place going, but I hope we never do or speak with only money in mind. Another friend who works closely with a priest in a rural diocese says the Bishop there is removing his pastor and that everyone knows the main reason for the removal is that the pastor has sided with migrant workers in an area where wealthy Catholics own the farms and fields.

The Habit of Charity

A gray day for the schoolyard sale. Sister Catherine has a table for the bags and bags of old clothes that people bring here. I hope the weather holds.

Some of the women from the projects arrive to help carry the clothes out to the schoolyard, and among them, an older woman. I say older, but she may not be any older than myself. I know her better than the others: her daughter, her grandchildren by a deceased daughter are with her in those concrete courtyards. Her grown grandson is the man of the house, and he tells me that with nightfall they huddle in. Impossible to be out and around down there without the danger of cross fire or some trouble.

With the heroism and endurance, such living takes its toll. The older woman has the appearance of exhaustion. A terrible sadness and weariness marks her face. I am reminded of the phrase from physicist Freeman Dyson which Thomas Berry quotes in a cosmic context: "Tragedy is not our business."

Not enough for me to notice the patience of this older woman and admire her fortitude. I should wheel and deal so that I or somebody with more money might buy a house and get the grandmother and grandchildren and now great-grandchildren out of that project.

I had mentioned the possibility of a purchase to Sister Catherine, and she must have mentioned the matter to the woman who stopped while passing through the kitchen with plastic bag of old clothes in either hand. "Sister Catherine says you have a house for me," she says. The matter should be as simple for me as it is for her.

Simone Weil says the *habitus caritatis,* the habit of charity, should be thus. I would not go through some complicated thought process if the need were my own or that of my family. I should be spontaneous and immediate with this family's need as well.

Social Protest

Hot summer and Bastille Day as well. I begin early with Mass for a young woman from downtown who wants to remember the anniversary of her mother who died in Scotland four years ago.

Even in this fierce heat I put on alb and stole for Mass in our small sacristy become daily Mass chapel. The sacristy connects to both church and house, and, at this early hour, it is just the two of us. Even for that I don the Mass alb and stole. Something about priest at altar acting *in persona Christi* and needing more grace than my already sweaty sport shirt.

Just before we begin, one last knock at the door: workmen arriving to dig up our back street. New plumbing for our 104-year-old school. The children will finally have inside toilets. For the moment, my cotton alb is beside the cut-off jeans and bare chest and work shoes of a construction worker. The soft world of priest against the rough world of laborers. My mind fills with images of those French priest-workers now dying off. Something in me wants to live in that rough working world. Even bring faith and Mass there. The same thoughts as the other evening when I drove through the "badlands" neighborhood toward Children's Hospital to pray over the Latino child who was going to be disconnected from life support systems the next morning.

That sodden evening I passed through streets not far from here where everybody is out. The little row homes so furnace-like inside that the people are out on the front steps looking at one another across old Philadelphia streets no wider than my dining room. Fire hydrants are on, and children are screaming at the delight of being cool. Young women in halters and short-shorts are charming young men at corner stores. And I drive through asking myself the same question I ask at the back door here, robed as I am for Mass: who will bring faith and hope and Eucharist to this hard landscape?

No answers are forthcoming, so I proceed to sacristy and Mass. Perhaps all we can do is person by person. The wedding or funeral which brings the impoverished Latino or bare-chested construction worker in off the streets for some important moment in his or her life.

No, I do not believe that. I believe with Peter Maurin of *Catholic Worker* origins that we can "build a society in which it is easier for people to be good." I believe this Mass which I begin with one person in attendance has larger meaning. "We, though many, are one who eat the one bread and drink the one cup." That African American scheduled for execution next month in this Commonwealth is our brother and somehow, beyond my understanding, a potential sharer with us in this bread and cup. That awareness makes his execution as unacceptable to me as was the stoning of the adulterous woman to Christ with the leaders pushing the law in His face.

During Mass I am mindful that Bastille Day means a protest at the French Consulate downtown. France plans to resume nuclear testing in the South Pacific. "So outrageous of them," says friend, Tom O'Rourke, and I am aware that he will be there, the sole Catholic presence with Greenpeace and the Sierra Club and the Friends' Peace Committee people. A scorcher of a day, and the sun is hard on my aging Irish skin. Enough going on here to keep me home. Hard, that protest when I am knee-deep in these neighborhoods.

I should connect and carve out a noonday hour to run downtown for that protest. In the bustle of Center City business, the protest will seem as unreal and disconnected as this Mass in the company of one person. Somewhere Saint Paul says that the things that are invisible are more real than the visible. With everything else, I should storm the French establishment this Bastille Day. This lonely Eucharist requires such.